JAVA™ LOOK AND FEEL
DESIGN GUIDELINES

SECOND EDITION, REVISED AND EXPANDED

Please send your email feedback to us at jlfguide@sun.com

JAVA™ LOOK AND FEEL DESIGN GUIDELINES

SECOND EDITION, REVISED AND EXPANDED

Sun Microsystems, Inc.

Addison-Wesley

Boston • San Francisco • New York • Toronto • Montreal
London • Munich • Paris • Madrid
Capetown • Sydney • Tokyo • Singapore • Mexico City

The publisher offers discounts on this book when ordered in quantity for special sales. For more information, please contact:

Addison-Wesley Professional
75 Arlington Street, Suite 300
Boston, Massachusetts 02116
U.S.A.

Text printed on recycled and acid-free paper

Library of Congress Cataloging in Publication Data

Java look and feel design guidelines / Sun Microsystems, Inc. — 2nd ed.
    p. cm
  Includes bibliographical references and index.
  ISBN 0-201-72588-6
  1. Java (Computer program language) I. Sun Microsystems.
QA76.73.J38 J373 2001
005.13'3–dc21

                  00-049607

1 2 3 4 5 6 7 8 9-WCT-05 04 03 02 01
First Printing, February 2001

 Please Recycle

 Adobe PostScript™

CONTENTS

FOREWORD

User interfaces are hard. Both the original user interface toolkit, AWT, and its successor, the industrial-strength, all singing, all dancing Swing toolkit, sidestep the hard problem of defining a user interface by allowing it to be plugged in to the platform on which it's running. A Java application running on the Mac can have the Mac look and feel, the same one running on Microsoft Windows can use its look and feel, and that same program running on UNIX can use a UNIX look and feel.

Although this pluggable interface strategy has lots of appeal, the down side is that the same application running on different platforms has a different appearance and behavior on each one. Documentation is difficult to write. Users get confused trying the same application on different platforms. This situation created a demand for a common look and feel that is lucid, easy to use, and runs harmoniously on many platforms.

Coming up with the design for such a look and feel was quite a challenge. The real danger involved falling into a Tragedy of the Commons—giving in to everyone's wishes and ending up with a mess. The hardest task was striking a balance between all the conflicting concerns.

I had the great privilege of working a staircase away from the team that designed the Java look and feel and the associated design guidelines—hallways covered with design ideas; field trips to survey developers; prototyping; trading off; balancing; testing; testing; testing. Out of this effort came a design that is clean and elegant.

James A. Gosling
Vice President, Sun Labs Research

PREFACE

Java Look and Feel Design Guidelines, second edition, provides essential information for anyone involved in creating cross-platform GUI (graphical user interface) applications and applets in the Java™ programming language. In particular, this book offers design guidelines for software that uses the Swing classes together with the Java look and feel.

This revised and expanded edition contains a collection of toolbar graphics, lists of terms localized for European and Asian languages, and an appendix on look and feel switching. New and revised guidelines are provided throughout, and new sections discuss smooth interaction, the use of badges in button graphics, and revised standards for window titles. Also included with this edition is a companion CD-ROM that contains code samples for many figures in the book, and a repository of graphics.

Who Should Use This Book

Although an application's human interface designer and software developer might well be the same person, the two jobs involve different tasks and require different skills and tools. Primarily, this book addresses the **designer** who chooses the interface elements, lays them out in a set of components, and designs the user interaction model for an application. (Unless specified otherwise, this book uses "application" to refer to both applets and applications.) This book should also prove useful for developers, technical writers, graphic artists, production and marketing specialists, and testers who participate in the creation of Java applications and applets.

Java Look and Feel Design Guidelines focuses on design issues and human-computer interaction in the context of the Java look and feel. It also attempts to provide a common vocabulary for designers, developers, and other professionals. If you require more information about technical aspects of the Java Foundation Classes (JFC), visit the JFC and Swing Connection web sites at http://java.sun.com/products/jfc and http://java.sun.com/products/jfc/tsc.

The guidelines provided in this book are appropriate for GUI applications and applets that run on personal computers and network computers. They do not address the needs of software that runs on consumer electronic devices.

What Is in This Book

Java Look and Feel Design Guidelines includes the following chapters:

Part One, "Overview," includes two introductory chapters about the Java look and feel and the JFC.

- **Chapter 1, "The Java Look and Feel,"** introduces key design concepts and visual elements underlying the Java look and feel and offers a quick visual tour of an application and an applet designed with the JFC components and the Java look and feel.

- **Chapter 2, "The Java Foundation Classes,"** provides an overview of the Java™ 2 SDK (software development kit) and the JFC, introduces the JFC components, discusses the concept of pluggable look and feel designs, and describes the currently available look and feel options.

Part Two, "Fundamental Java Application Design," describes some of the general issues facing professionals using the JFC to create cross-platform applications, including visual design, the creation of application graphics, and behavior.

- **Chapter 3, "Design Considerations,"** discusses some of the fundamental challenges of designing Java look and feel applications and applets and of providing for accessibility, internationalization, and localization.

- **Chapter 4, "Visual Design,"** describes the Java look and feel theme mechanism, suggests ways to change colors and fonts, gives recommendations for layout and visual alignment of components, and provides standards for the capitalization of text in the interface.

- **Chapter 5, "Application Graphics,"** discusses the use of color for individually designed graphical elements (as opposed to components that rely on the theme mechanism), including cross-platform colors, the creation of graphics that suit the Java look and feel, the design of button graphics and icons, and the use of badges in the design of button graphics.

- **Chapter 6, "Behavior,"** tells how users of Java look and feel applications utilize the mouse and keyboard, provides guidelines regarding user input and human-computer interaction, and discusses drag-and-drop operations and text field navigation.

Part Three, "The Components of the Java Foundation Classes," contains a description of the components and accompanying guidelines for their use.

- **Chapter 7, "Windows and Panes,"** includes revised standards for window titles and makes recommendations for the use of primary, secondary, plain, and utility windows as well as panels, scroll panes, tabbed panes, split panes, and internal windows.

- **Chapter 8, "Dialog Boxes and Alert Boxes,"** describes dialog boxes and alert boxes, sets standards for dialog box design, and provides examples of typical dialog boxes and alert boxes in Java look and feel applications.

- **Chapter 9, "Menus and Toolbars,"** defines and gives guidelines for the use of drop-down menus, contextual menus, toolbars, and tool tips and provides examples of typical menus in Java look and feel applications.

- **Chapter 10, "Basic Controls,"** covers the use of controls such as command buttons, toggle buttons, checkboxes, radio buttons, combo boxes, list boxes, and sliders.

- **Chapter 11, "Text Components,"** explains and makes recommendations for the use of the JFC components that control the display and editing of text in the interface: labels, text fields, text areas, and editor panes.

- **Chapter 12, "Selectable Lists, Tables, and Tree Components,"** discusses and makes recommendations for the use of selectable lists, tables, and tree components.

The remainder of the book consists of the appendixes, glossary, and index.

- **Appendix A, "Keyboard Shortcuts, Mnemonics, and Other Keyboard Operations,"** contains tables that specify keyboard operations for the components of the JFC, including alphabetical listings of commonly used keyboard shortcuts and mnemonics.

- **Appendix B, "Graphics Repository,"** contains a collection of toolbar button graphics designed specifically for use with the recommendations set forth in this book.

- **Appendix C, "Localization Word Lists,"** contains terms and phrases that might appear in Java look and feel applications; English terms appear with their French, Spanish, German, Swedish, Japanese, Simplified Chinese, Traditional Chinese, and Korean equivalents.

- **Appendix D, "Switching Look and Feel Designs,"** presents some information about the pitfalls of changing the look and feel, along with guidelines on how to present this choice to users when you must.

- **Glossary** defines important words and phrases found in this book. Glossary terms appear in boldface throughout the book.

What Is Not in This Book
This book does not provide detailed discussions of human interface design principles or the design process, nor does it present much general information about usability studies.

For authoritative explications of human interface design principles and the design process, see Apple Computer's *Macintosh Human Interface Guidelines*.

For a classic book on usability studies, see Jakob Nielsen's *Usability Engineering*.

For details, see "Related Books and Web Sites" on page 7.

Graphic Conventions
The screen shots in this book illustrate the use of JFC components in applications with the Java look and feel. Because such applications typically run inside windows provided and managed by the native platform, the screen shots show assorted styles of windows and dialog boxes from the Microsoft Windows, Macintosh, and CDE (Common Desktop Environment) platforms.

Throughout the text, symbols are used to call your attention to design guidelines. Each type of guideline is identified by a unique symbol.

Java Look and Feel Standards
Requirements for the consistent appearance and compatible behavior of Java look and feel applications.

Java look and feel standards promote flexibility and ease of use in cross-platform applications. In addition, they support the creation of applications that are accessible to all users, including users with physical and cognitive limitations. These standards require you to take actions that go beyond the provided appearance and behavior of the JFC components.

Occasionally, you might need to violate these standards. In such situations, use your discretion to balance competing requirements. Be sure to engage in usability studies to validate your judgments.

Cross-Platform Delivery Guidelines
Recommendations for dealing with colors, fonts, keyboard operations, and other issues that arise when you want to deliver your application to a variety of computers running a range of operating systems.

Internationalization Guidelines
Advice for creating applications that can be adapted to the global marketplace.

Implementation Tips   Technical information and useful tips of particular interest to the programmers who are implementing your application design.

CD-ROM Resources   Code samples and graphics for Java look and feel applications, available on the companion CD-ROM.

Related Books and Web Sites   Many excellent references are
available on topics such as fundamental principles of human interface design, design issues for specific (or multiple) platforms, and issues relating to internationalization, accessibility, and applet design.

Design Principles   The resources in this section provide information on the fundamental concepts underlying human-computer interaction and interface design.

Baecker, Ronald M., William Buxton, and Jonathan Grudin, eds. *Readings in Human-Computer Interaction: Toward the Year 2000*, 2d ed. Morgan Kaufman, 1995. Based on research from graphic and industrial design and studies of cognition and group process, this volume addresses the efficiency and adequacy of human interfaces.

Hurlburt, Allen. *The Grid: A Modular System for the Design and Production of Newspapers, Magazines, and Books*. John Wiley & Sons, 1997. This is an excellent starting text about graphical page layout. Although originally intended for print design, this book contains many guidelines that are applicable to software design.

IBM Human-Computer Interaction Group. "IBM Ease of Use." Available: `http://www.ibm.com/ibm/easy`. This web site covers many fundamental aspects of human interface design.

Johnson, Jeff. *GUI Bloopers: Don'ts and Do's for Software Developers and Web Designers*. Morgan Kaufman, 2000. A new book that provides examples of poor design in windows, inconsistent use of labels, and lack of parallelism in visual layout and grammar. The writer develops principles for achieving lucidity and the harmony of look and feel.

Laurel, Brenda, ed. *Art of Human-Computer Interface Design*. Addison-Wesley, 1990. Begun as a project inside Apple, this collection of essays explores the reasoning behind human-computer interaction and looks at the future of the relationship between humans and computers.

Mullet, Kevin, and Darrell Sano. *Designing Visual Interfaces: Communication Oriented Techniques*. Prentice Hall, 1994. This volume covers fundamental design principles, common mistakes, and step-by-step techniques for handling the visual aspects of interface design.

Nielsen, Jakob. *Usability Engineering*. AP Professional, 1994. This is a classic book on design for usability. It gives practical advice and detailed information on designing for usability and on assessment techniques and also includes a chapter on international user interfaces.

Norman, Donald A. *The Design of Everyday Things*. Doubleday, 1990. A well-liked, amusing, and discerning examination of why some products satisfy while others only baffle or disappoint. Photographs and illustrations throughout complement the analysis of psychology and design.

Shneiderman, Ben. *Designing the User Interface: Strategies for Effective Human-Computer Interaction*, 3d ed. Addison-Wesley, 1997. The third edition of this best-seller adds new chapters on the World Wide Web, information visualization, and cooperative work and expands earlier work on development methodologies, evaluation techniques, and tools for building user interfaces.

Tognazzini, Bruce. *Tog On Software Design*. Addison-Wesley, 1995. A pivotal figure in computer design offers discerning, stimulating, argumentative, and amusing analysis for the lay reader and the computer professional. The work includes discussions of quality management and the meaning of standards.

Tufte, Edward R. *Envisioning Information*. Graphics Press, 1990. One of the best books on graphic design, this volume catalogues instances of superb information design (with an emphasis on maps and cartography) and analyzes the concepts behind their implementation.

Tufte, Edward R. *The Visual Display of Quantitative Information*. Graphics Press, 1992. Tufte explores the presentation of statistical information in charts and graphs with apt graphical examples and elegantly interwoven text.

Tufte, Edward R. *Visual Explanations: Images and Quantities, Evidence and Narrative*. Graphics Press, 1997. The third volume in Tufte's series on information display focuses on data that changes over time. Tufte explores the depiction of action and cause and effect through such examples as the explosion of the space shuttle Challenger, magic tricks, and a cholera epidemic in 19th-century London.

Design for Specific Platforms   The resources in this section cover application
design for the CDE, IBM, Java, Macintosh, and Microsoft Windows platforms.

CDE   Three volumes address the needs of designers and related professionals who
create applications using CDE and Motif 2.1.

The Open Group, 1997. *CDE 2.1/Motif 2.1--Style Guide and Glossary*.

The Open Group, 1997. *CDE 2.1/Motif 2.1--Style Guide Reference*.

The Open Group, 1997. *CDE 2.1/Motif 2.1--Style Guide Certification Check List*.

These titles can be ordered from the Open Group at
`http://www.opengroup.org/public/pubs/catalog/mo.htm`.

IBM   *Object-Oriented Interface Design: IBM Common User Access Guidelines*. Que
Corp, 1992. Available: `http://www-3.ibm.com/ibm/easy/`
`eou_ext.nsf/publish/586#143`. This book is out of print but available
from most IBM branch offices. A small portion of the printed book is
intertwined with a modest amount of more current material at the IBM web
site cited above.

Java   Campione, Mary, and Kathy Walrath. *The Java Tutorial: Object-Oriented
Programming for the Internet*, 2d ed. Addison-Wesley, 1998. Full of examples,
this task-oriented book introduces you to fundamental Java concepts and
applications. Walrath and Campione describe the Java language, applet
construction, and the fundamental Java classes and cover the use of multiple
threads and networking features.

Campione, Mary, and Kathy Walrath. *The JFC Swing Tutorial: A Guide to
Constructing GUIs*. Addison-Wesley, 1999. This readable technical description
of some difficult subjects includes material on layout managers, events,
listeners, and container hierarchy.

Campione, Mary, et al. *The Java Tutorial Continued: The Rest of the JDK*.
Addison-Wesley, 1998. The experts describe features added to the original
core Java platform with many self-paced, hands-on examples. The book
focuses on Java 2 APIs but also contains the information you need to use the
JDK 1.1 version of the APIs.

Chan, Patrick. *The Java Developer's Almanac, 1999*. Addison-Wesley, 1999.
Organized to increase programming performance and speed, this book
provides a quick but comprehensive reference to the Java™ 2 Platform,
Standard Edition, v. 1.2.

Eckstein, Robert, Mark Loy, and Dave Wood. *Java Swing*. O'Reilly & Associates, 1998. An excellent introduction to the Swing components, this book documents the Swing and Accessibility application programming interfaces. An especially useful chapter explains how to create a custom look and feel.

Geary, David M. *Graphic Java 2: Mastering the JFC*. Volume 2, *Swing*. Prentice Hall, 1998. This comprehensive volume describes the skills needed to build professional, cross-platform applications that take full advantage of the JFC. The volume includes chapters on drag and drop, graphics, colors and fonts, image manipulation, double buffering, sprite animation, and clipboard and data transfer.

Sun Microsystems, Inc. *J2EE Platform Specification*. Available: `http://java.sun.com/j2ee/download.html#platformspec`. This web site provides a way to download current information on the Java 2 Platform, Enterprise Edition, v. 1.3 (J2EE).

Sun Microsystems, Inc. *Java 2 Platform, Standard Edition, Version 1.3 API Specification*. Available: `http://java.sun.com/j2se/1.3/docs/index.html#guide`. This web site provides up-to-date technical documentation on the Java 2 API.

Sun Microsystems, Inc. *Java Look and Feel Design Guidelines*, 2d ed. Available: `http://java.sun.com/products/jlf`. This web site contains the HTML version of this book.

Sun Microsystems, Inc. *The Java Tutorial: A Practical Guide for Programmers*. Available: `http://java.sun.com/docs/books/tutorial/index.html`. This web site is divided into four trails: a trail covering the basics of the Java language and writing applets; a trail on constructing graphical user interfaces with the Swing classes and the JFC; specialized trails addressing such topics as internationalization, 2D graphics, and security; and trails available only online—including a discussion of drag and drop.

Topley, Kim. *Core Java Foundation Classes*. Prentice Hall Computer Books, 1998. Topley explains how to build basic Swing applications, with an emphasis on layout managers and basic graphics programming. The book also describes the creation of multiple document interface (MDI) applications.

Walker, Will. "The Multiplexing Look and Feel." Available: `http://www.sun.com/access/articles/#articles`. This article describes a special look and feel that provides a way to extend the features of a Swing GUI without having to create a new look and feel design. Walker describes an example application that can simultaneously provide audio output, Braille output, and the standard visual output of ordinary Swing applications.

Macintosh   Apple Computer, Inc. *Macintosh Human Interface Guidelines*. Addison-Wesley, 1992. This volume is the official word on Macintosh user interface principles. It includes a superb bibliography with titles on animation, cognitive psychology, color, environmental design, graphic and information design, human-computer design and interaction, language, accessibility, visual thinking, and internationalization.

Apple Computer, Inc. *Mac OS 8 Human Interface Guidelines*. Available: `http://developer.apple.com/techpubs/mac/HIGOS8Guide/` `thig-2.html`. This web site offers a supplement to *Macintosh Human Interface Guidelines*.

Microsoft Windows   *Microsoft Windows User Experience*. Microsoft Press, 1999. Available: `http://www.msdn.microsoft.com/library/books/` `winguide/welcome.htm`. The official book on Microsoft interface design contains specifications and principles for designers who would like to create effective interfaces. It contains numerous examples of design successes and failures. These guidelines are available in print and on the web site.

Design for Multiple Platforms   The books in this section discuss the complex issues that arise when designing software that runs on many platforms.

McFarland, Alan, and Tom Dayton (with others). *Design Guide for Multiplatform Graphical User Interfaces* (LP-R13). Bellcore, 1995. Available: `http://telecom-info.telcordia.com/site-cgi/ido/` `index.html`. This is an object-oriented style guide with extensive guidelines and a good explanation of object-oriented user interface style from the user's perspective.

Marcus, Aaron, Nick Smilonich, and Lynne Thompson. *The Cross-GUI Handbook: For Multiplatform User Interface Design*. Addison-Wesley, 1995. This source describes the graphical user interfaces of Microsoft Windows and Windows NT, OSF/Motif, NeXTSTEP, IBM OS/2, and Apple Macintosh. The text includes design recommendations for portability and migration and recommendations for handling contradictory or inadequate human interface guidelines.

Design for Internationalization   The books in this section describe software design for the global marketplace.

Fernandes, Tony. *Global Interface Design: A Guide to Designing International User Interfaces*. AP Professional, 1995. Fernandes addresses developers of Internet software designed for a global market. He explains cultural differences, languages and their variations, taboos, aesthetics, ergonomic standards, and other issues designers must research and understand.

Guide to Macintosh Software Localization. Addison-Wesley, 1992. A thorough and thoughtful discussion of the internationalization and localization processes that should prove helpful for developers on any platform.

Kano, Nadine. *Developing International Software for Windows 95 and Windows NT*. Microsoft Press, 1993. Kano targets Microsoft's guidelines for creating international software to an audience with knowledge of Microsoft Windows coding techniques and C++. The work contains information on punctuation, sort orders, locale-specific code-page data, DBCS/Unicode mapping tables, and multilingual API functions and structures.

Luong, Tuoc V., James S.H. Lok, and Kevin Driscoll. *Internationalization: Developing Software for Global Markets*. John Wiley & Sons, 1995. The Borland internationalization team describes its procedures and methods with a focus on testing and quality assurance for translated software. This hands-on guide tells how to produce software that runs anywhere in the world without requiring expensive recompiling of source code.

Nielsen, Jakob, and Elisa M. Del Galdo, eds. *International User Interfaces*. John Wiley & Sons, 1996. This book discusses what user interfaces can and must do to become commercially viable in the global marketplace. Contributors discuss issues such as international usability engineering, cultural models, multiple-language documents, and multilingual machine translation.

O'Donnell, Sandra Martin. *Programming for the World: A Guide to Internationalization*. Prentice Hall, 1994. This theoretical handbook explains how to modify computer systems to accommodate the needs of international users. O'Donnell describes many linguistic and cultural conventions used throughout the world and discusses how to design with the flexibility needed for the global marketplace.

Uren, Emmanuel, Robert Howard, and Tiziana Perinotti. *Software Internationalization and Localization: An Introduction*. Van Nostrand Reinhold, 1993. This guide to software adaptation encourages developers to aim at producing localized software with the same capabilities as the original software while meeting local requirements and conventions.

Design for Accessibility   These resources explore how to design software that
supports all users, including those with physical and cognitive limitations.

Bergman, Eric, and Earl Johnson. "Towards Accessible Human Interaction." In
Advances in Human-Computer Interaction, edited by Jakob Nielsen, vol. 5.
Ablex Publishing, 1995. Available: `http://www.sun.com/access/`
`developers/updt.HCI.advance.html`. This article discusses the
relevance of accessibility to human interface designers and explores the
process of designing for ranges of user capabilities. It provides design
guidelines for accommodating physical disabilities such as repetitive strain
injuries (RSI), low vision, blindness, and hearing impairment. It also contains
an excellent list of additional sources on accessibility issues.

Dunn, Jeff. "Developing Accessible JFC Applications." Available:
`http://www.sun.com/access/developers/developing-`
`accessible-apps`. This article covers the specifics of accessibility in Swing
classes, including an assistive technology primer, nuts-and-bolts information,
and test cases.

Schwerdtfeger, Richard S. *Making the GUI Talk*. BYTE, 1991. Available:
`ftp://ftp.software.ibm.com/sns/sr-os2/sr2doc/`
`guitalk.txt`. This speech deals with off-screen model technology and GUI
screen readers.

Schwerdtfeger, Richard S. *Special Needs Systems Guidelines*. IBM Corporation,
1998. Available: `http://www.austin.ibm.com/sns/access.html`.
This web site presents principles of accessibility, a checklist for software
accessibility, and a list of references and resources. In addition, it provides
discussions of accessibility for the web and for Java applications.

Sun Microsystems, Inc. *Accessibility Quick Reference Guide*. Available:
`http://www.sun.com/access/developers/`
`access.quick.ref.html`. This site defines accessibility, lists steps to
check and double-check your product's accessibility, and offers tips for
making applications more accessible.

Sun Microsystems, Inc. "Opening New Doors: Enabling Technologies."
Available: `http://www.sun.com/access`. This web site includes a
primer on the Java platform and accessibility and describes the support for
assistive technologies now provided by the Swing components of the JFC.

Design for Applets   These books provide a range of information on designing
applets.

Gulbransen, David, Kenrick Rawlings, and John December. *Creating Web
Applets With Java*. Sams Publishing, 1996. An introduction to Java applets,
this book addresses nonprogrammers who want to incorporate
preprogrammed Java applets into web pages.

Hopson, K.C., Stephen E. Ingram, and Patrick Chan. *Designing Professional
Java Applets*. Sams Publishing, 1996. An advanced reference for developing
Java applets for business, science, and research.

PART I: OVERVIEW

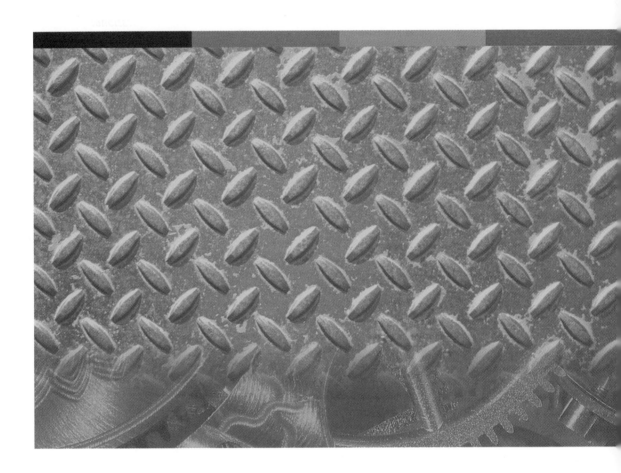

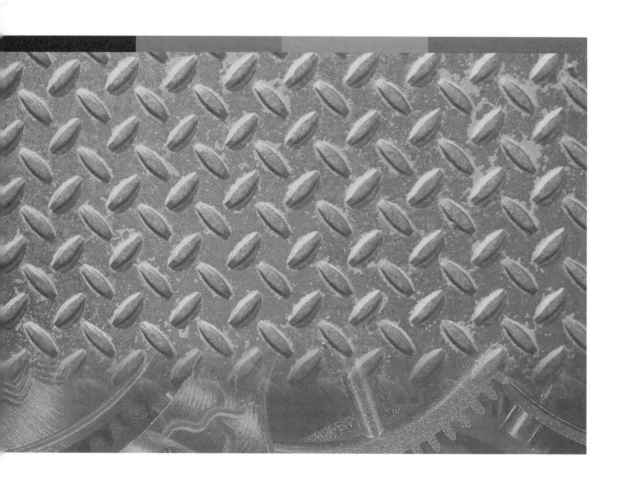

1: THE JAVA LOOK AND FEEL

As the Java platform has matured, designers and developers have recognized the need for consistent, compatible, and easy-to-use Java applications. The Java look and feel meets that need by providing a distinctive platform-independent appearance and standard behavior. The use of this single **look and feel** reduces design and development time and lowers training and documentation costs for all users.

This book sets standards for the use of the Java look and feel. By following these guidelines, you can create Java applications that effectively support all users worldwide, including those with physical and cognitive limitations.

Fundamentals of the Java Look and Feel

The Java look and feel is the default interface for applications built with the JFC. The Java look and feel is designed for cross-platform use and can provide:

- Consistency in the appearance and behavior of common design elements
- Compatibility with industry-standard components and interaction styles
- Aesthetic appeal that does not distract from application content

Three distinctive visual elements are the hallmarks of the Java look and feel components: the **flush 3D style**, the drag texture, and the color model.

In the Java look and feel, component surfaces with beveled edges appear to be at the same level as the surrounding canvas. This "flush 3D" style is illustrated in the following figure.

FIGURE 1   Consistent Use of the Flush 3D Style

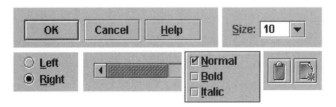

The clean, modern appearance reduces the visual noise associated with beveled edges. Flush 3D components fit in with a variety of applications and operating systems. For details on the flush 3D style, see "Producing the Flush 3D Effect" on page 90.

A textured pattern, used throughout the Java look and feel, indicates items that users can drag. Such an indication cues cross-platform users in a reliable way. The following figure demonstrates several uses of the drag texture.

FIGURE 2   Consistent Use of the Drag Texture

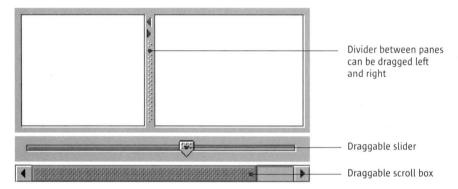

Divider between panes can be dragged left and right

Draggable slider

Draggable scroll box

A simple and flexible color model ensures compatibility with platforms and devices capable of displaying quite different color depths. The default colors provide an aesthetically pleasing and comfortable scheme for interface elements, as shown in the following figure. For more on the Java look and feel default color theme, see "Themes" on page 55.

FIGURE 3   Consistent Use of Color Across Design Elements

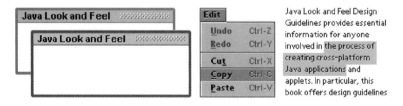

Visual Tour of the Java Look and Feel
The Java look and feel implements widely understood interface elements (windows, icons, menus, and pointers) and works in the same way on any operating system that supports the JFC. The visual tour in this section shows off two JFC applications

with the Java look and feel: MetalEdit and Retirement Savings Calculator. MetalEdit is a standalone, text-editing application; Retirement Savings Calculator is an applet displayed in a browser window.

The following figure shows a Microsoft Windows desktop with MetalEdit and Retirement Savings Calculator (a Java applet). MetalEdit has a menu bar and toolbar as well as a text-editing area. As an applet, Retirement Savings Calculator is displayed inside a web browser within an HTML page. Other Microsoft Windows applications are also present; some are represented by minimized windows.

Although the windows of many applications can be open on the desktop, only one can be the active window. In the figure, MetalEdit is the active window (indicated by the color of the title bar), whereas the Netscape Navigator™ browser, which contains Retirement Savings Calculator, is inactive.

FIGURE 4   Typical Desktop With Applications on the Microsoft Windows Platform

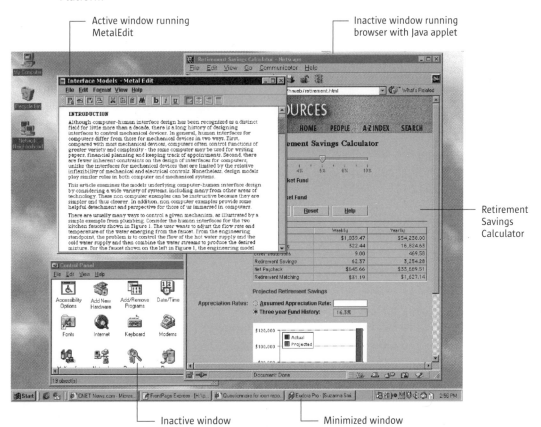

MetalEdit Application   This section uses the MetalEdit application to illustrate some of the most important visual characteristics of the Java look and feel, including its windows, menus, toolbars, editor panes, dialog boxes, and alert boxes.

Example Windows   The windows in Java look and feel applications use the borders, title bars, and window controls of the platform they are running on. For instance, the MetalEdit document window shown in Figure 4 on page 19 is running on a Microsoft Windows desktop and uses the standard Microsoft window frame and title bar.

In Figure 5, the contents of the document window (menu bar, toolbar, and editor pane) use the Java look and feel. However, the window borders, title bars, and window controls have a platform-specific appearance.

⊙ The corresponding code for Figure 5 is available on the companion CD-ROM.

FIGURE 5   Exploded Document Window on Three Platforms

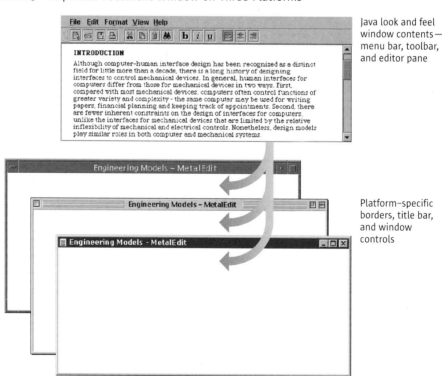

Java look and feel window contents— menu bar, toolbar, and editor pane

Platform–specific borders, title bar, and window controls

Example Menus   The menu bar, which is the horizontal strip under the window title, displays the titles of application menus, called "drop-down menus." Drop-down menus provide access to an application's primary functions. They also enable users to survey the features of the application by looking at the menu items. Chapter 9 contains discussions of drop-down menus, submenus, and contextual menus and provides guidelines for the creation of menus and menu items for your application.

FIGURE 6   Example Menu Bar

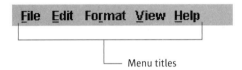

Menu titles

The menu items in Figure 7 (which shows the contents of the Edit and Format menus from the MetalEdit menu bar) are divided into logical groupings by menu separators (in the flush 3D style). For instance, in the Edit menu, the Cut, Copy, and Paste commands, which are related to the clipboard, are separated from Undo and Redo commands, which respectively reverse or restore changes in the document. For more information, see "Typical Edit Menu" on page 183. Titles of menus that are activated are highlighted in blue in the default Java look and feel theme.

⊙ The corresponding code for Figure 7 is available on the companion CD-ROM.

FIGURE 7   Example Drop-down Menus

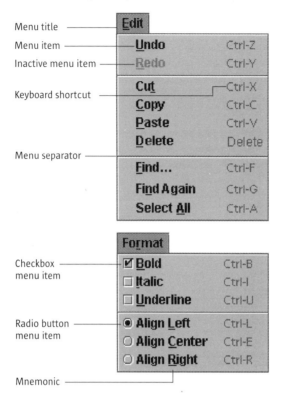

Keyboard shortcuts offer an alternative to using the mouse to choose a menu item. For instance, to copy a selection, users can press Control-C. For details, see "Keyboard Shortcuts" on page 115.

Mnemonics provide yet another way to access menu items. For instance, to view the contents of the Edit menu, users press Alt-E. Once the Edit menu has keyboard focus, users can press C (or Alt-C) to copy a selection. These alternatives are designated by underlining the "E" in Edit and the "C" in Copy. For details, see "Mnemonics" on page 118.

The menus shown in Figure 7 illustrate two commonly used menu titles, menu items, and menu item arrangements for Java look and feel applications. For details, see "Drop-down Menus" on page 175 and "Menu Items" on page 176.

Example Toolbar   A toolbar displays command and toggle buttons that offer immediate access to the functions of many menu items.

In Figure 8, the MetalEdit toolbar is divided into four areas for functions relating to file management, editing, font styles, and alignment. Note the flush 3D style of the command and toggle buttons and the textured drag area to the left of the toolbar. For details, see "Toolbars" on page 186. For a collection of toolbar buttons designed using the Java look and feel guidelines, see Appendix B.

⊙ The corresponding code for Figure 8 is available on the companion CD-ROM.

FIGURE 8   Example Toolbar

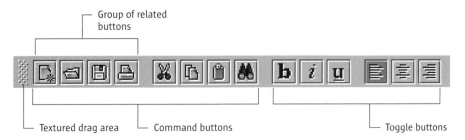

Example Editor Pane   The document text in the following figure is displayed in an editor pane with a styled text editor plug-in kit, which is embedded in a scroll pane. (Note the use of the drag texture in the scroll box.) For more on styled text editor plug-in kits, see "Editor Panes" on page 221. For details on scroll panes, see "Scroll Panes" on page 142.

FIGURE 9   Example Editor Pane

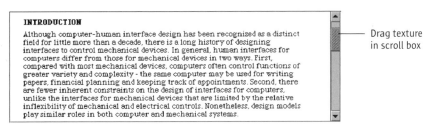

Example Dialog Boxes   In the Java look and feel, dialog boxes use the borders and title bars of the platform they are running on. However, the dialog box contents have the Java look and feel. Chapter 8 describes dialog boxes in the Java look and feel and contains recommendations for their use.

Figure 10 shows a preferences dialog box with the title bars, borders, and window controls of several platforms. The dialog box enables users to specify options in the MetalEdit application. Noneditable combo boxes are used to select ruler units and a font. Text fields are used to specify the margins. An editable combo box enables users to specify font size. Radio buttons and checkboxes are used to set other preferences. Clicking the Browse command button displays a file chooser in which users can select a stationery folder.

Note the flush 3D borders of the combo boxes, text fields, radio buttons, checkboxes, and command buttons. Labels use the primary 1 color, one of eight colors in the default Java look and feel theme. (For more, see "Colors" on page 55.) For a thorough treatment of basic controls (including combo boxes, radio buttons, checkboxes, and command buttons), see Chapter 10. For a detailed discussion of text fields and labels, see Chapter 11.

MetalEdit provides mnemonics and keyboard navigation and activation sequences for each of the interactive controls in the preferences dialog box. The dialog box in Figure 10 illustrates two ways to create a mnemonic: directly in a component, indicated by an underlined letter in the component text, or in a label associated with the component, indicated by an underlined letter in the label.

⊙ The corresponding code for Figure 10 is available on the companion CD-ROM.

FIGURE 10   Example Dialog Boxes on Microsoft Windows, Macintosh, and CDE Platforms

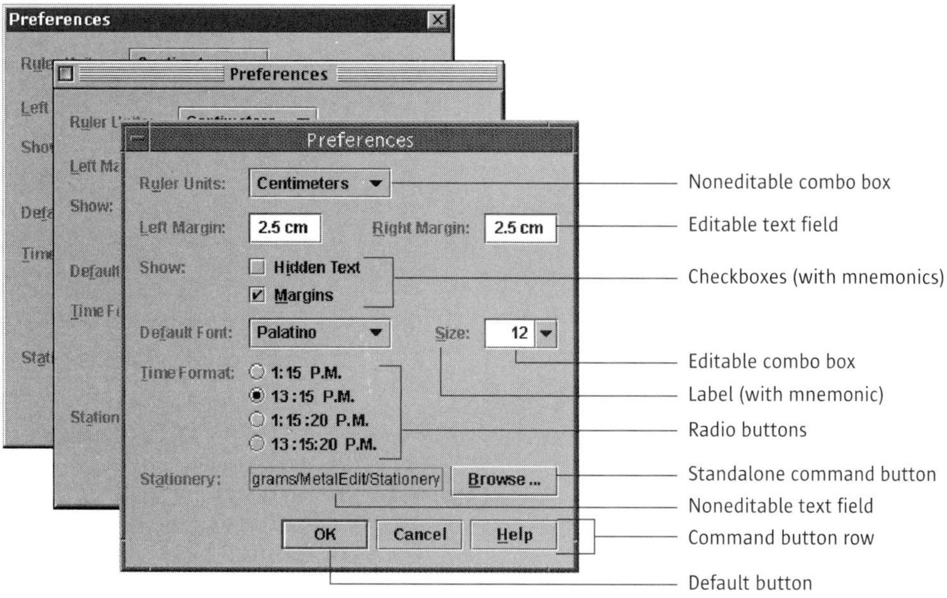

Example Alert Boxes   The alert boxes in a Java look and feel application use the borders, title bars, and window controls of the platform they are running on. However, the symbols, messages, and command buttons supplied by the JFC use the Java look and feel. (You provide the actual message and specify the number of command buttons and the button text. The JFC provides layouts for the symbol, the message, and the command buttons.)

In Figure 11, MetalEdit's warning box asks users if they would like to save changes when they try to close a window that has unsaved changes. Of the three command buttons in the alert box, the default command button is Save. The Don't Save button closes the window without saving changes. The Cancel button closes the dialog box but leaves the unsaved document open. For details, see "Alert Boxes" on page 169.

⊙   The corresponding code for Figure 11 is available on the companion CD-ROM.

FIGURE 11   Example Alert Boxes on CDE, Microsoft Windows, and Macintosh Platforms

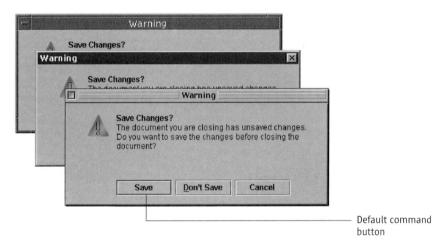

Default command button

Retirement Savings Calculator Applet   The sample applet shown in Figure 12, Retirement Savings Calculator, is part of a web page displayed in the Netscape Navigator browser.

This human resources applet enables employees of a fictitious company to determine their contributions to a retirement savings plan. To make it easy for all employees to access information on their retirement savings, the company provides the applet in a web page. (Note the boundaries of the applet. The HTML page also includes a banner in the GIF format as well as an

HTML header with the title of the page.) All of the JFC components use the Java look and feel. However, the browser, its menu bar, toolbar, and scrollbars all use the platform's native look and feel (Microsoft Windows, in this case).

⊙ The corresponding code for Figure 12 is available on the companion CD-ROM.

FIGURE 12   Applet on an HTML Page in a Browser

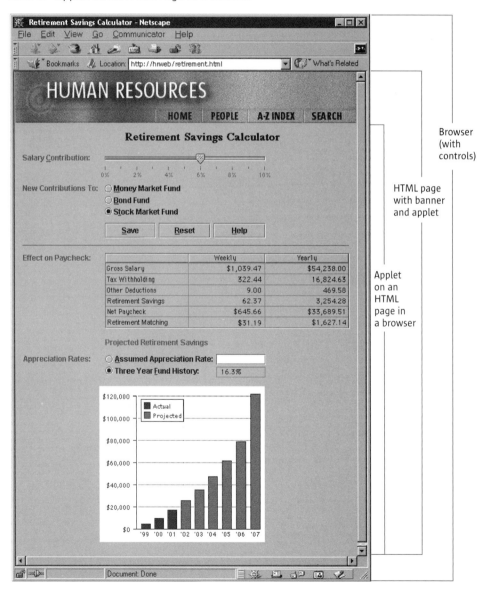

The applet obtains an employee's current retirement savings contribution and other salary data from a database and fills a table with the relevant data. The employee can drag a slider to specify a salary contribution and click a radio button to specify whether new contributions go to a money market, bond, or stock market fund. A row of command buttons offers a choice of whether to save changes, reset the salary contribution and fund contributed to, or display help.

Using the employee's input and databases, the applet calculates the employee's weekly and yearly gross salary, tax withholding, other deductions, retirement savings contribution, net paycheck, and the company's matching funds. Results are displayed in a table. Finally, the employee can type an assumed appreciation rate in an editable text field to see accumulated future savings or instruct the applet to use the nine-month fund history to project savings in the chart at the bottom of the applet.

⊙ The corresponding code for Figure 13 is available on the companion CD-ROM.

FIGURE 13   Retirement Savings Calculator Applet

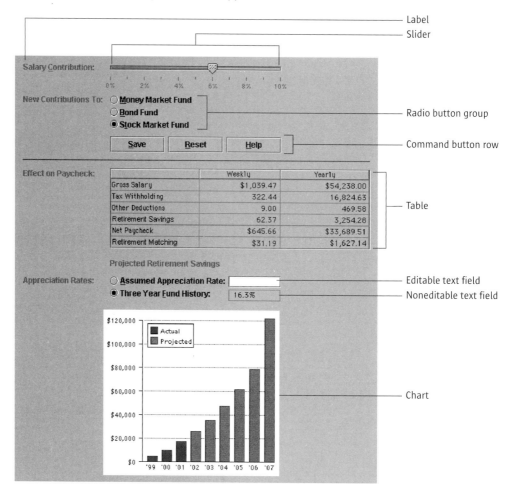

For more information on the components used in this applet, see "Text Fields" on page 217, "Sliders" on page 210, "Radio Buttons" on page 203, "Command Buttons" on page 196, and "Tables" on page 228.

2: THE JAVA FOUNDATION CLASSES

This book assumes that you are designing software based on the Java Foundation Classes (**JFC**) and utilizing the Java look and feel. This chapter provides an overview of that technology: the Java™ 2 SDK (software development kit), the user interface components of the Java Foundation Classes, the pluggable look and feel architecture, and available look and feel designs.

Java 2 Software Development Kit

The APIs and tools that developers need to write, compile, debug, and run Java applications are included in the **Java 2 SDK**.

The guidelines in this book pertain to GUI applications built with the Java 2 SDK, Standard Edition, v. 1.3 (**J2SE**), and the Java 2 SDK, Enterprise Edition, v. 1.3 (**J2EE**), (both referred to hereafter as "Java 2 SDK"). The guidelines do not apply to applications built with the Java 2 SDK, Micro Edition.

Java Foundation Classes

The JFC includes the **Swing classes**, which define a complete set of GUI components for JFC applications. An extension to the original Abstract Window Toolkit (**AWT**), the JFC includes the Swing classes, pluggable look and feel designs, and the Java Accessibility API, which are all implemented without **native code** (code that refers to the functions of a specific operating system or is compiled for a specific processor). The JFC components include windows and frames, panels and panes, dialog boxes, menus and toolbars, buttons, sliders, combo boxes, text components, tables, list components, and trees.

All the components have look and feel designs that you can specify. The cross-platform, default look and feel is the **Java look and feel**. For details on the design principles and visual elements underlying the Java look and feel, see Chapter 1.

⊟⊃   In code, the Java look and feel is referred to as "Metal."

The Java 2 SDK contains the AWT, the class library that provides the standard application programming interfaces for building GUIs for Java programs.

In the Java 2 SDK, the JFC also includes the Java 2D API, drag and drop, and other enhancements. The **Java 2D API** provides an advanced two-dimensional imaging model for complex shapes, text, and images. Features include enhanced font and color support and a single, comprehensive rendering model.

Support for Accessibility   Several features of the Java 2 SDK support people with special needs: the Java Accessibility API, the Java Accessibility Utilities, keyboard navigation, mnemonics, keyboard shortcuts (also called "accelerators"), customizable colors and fonts, and dynamic GUI layout.

The **Java Accessibility API** provides ways for an assistive technology to interact and communicate with JFC components. A Java application that fully supports the Java Accessibility API is compatible with technologies such as screen readers and screen magnifiers.

A separate set of utility classes, **Java Accessibility Utilities**, provides support in locating the objects that implement the Java Accessibility API. (These utilities are necessary for developers who develop only assistive technologies, not mainstream applications.)

A pluggable look and feel architecture is used to build both visual and nonvisual designs, such as audio and tactile user interfaces. For more on the pluggable look and feel, see "Pluggable Look and Feel Architecture" on page 31.

Keyboard navigation enables users to use the keyboard to move between components, open menus, highlight text, and so on. This support makes an application accessible to people who find it difficult or impossible to use a mouse. For details on keyboard operations, see Appendix A.

Mnemonics show users which key to press (in conjunction with the Alt key) in order to activate a command or navigate to a component. (For details on mnemonics, see "Mnemonics" on page 118.)

Keyboard shortcuts are keystroke combinations (usually a modifier key and a character key, like Control-C) that activate menu items from the keyboard even if the relevant menu is not currently displayed. (For more on keyboard shortcuts, see "Keyboard Shortcuts" on page 115.)

Support for Internationalization   The Java 2 SDK provides internationalized text handling and resource bundles. Text handling features include support for the bidirectional display of text lines—important for displaying documents that mix languages with a left-to-right text direction (for instance, English, German, or Japanese) and languages with a right-to-left direction (for instance, Arabic or Hebrew).

The Java 2 SDK also provides resource bundles, locale-sensitive sorting, and support for localized numbers, dates, times, and messages.

User Interface Components of the JFC   The JFC includes Swing, a complete set of user interface components, including windows, dialog boxes, alert boxes, panels and panes, and basic controls. Each JFC **component** contains a model (the data structure) and a user interface (the presentation and behavior of the component), as shown in the following illustration.

FIGURE 14   Structure of the JFC Components

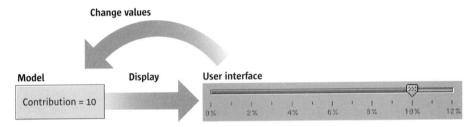

Pluggable Look and Feel Architecture   Because both presentation and behavior are separate and replaceable ("pluggable"), you can specify any of several look and feel designs for your application—or you can create your own look and feel. The separation of a component's model (data structure) from its user interface (display and interaction behavior) is the empowering principle behind the **pluggable look and feel architecture** of the JFC. A single **JFC application** can present a Java look and feel, a platform-specific look and feel, or a customized interface (for example, an audio interface).

Example Model and Interfaces   Consider the slider and the editable text field in the following figure as an example. The underlying model contains information about the current value as well as the minimum and maximum values. The slider's interface determines how users see or interact with the slider. The slider enforces the idea of a range of choices. However, an editable text field would be easier for keyboard users. The editable text field shares the data model with the slider. The text field's interface contains data about the position and color of the label and the text field and the response when users type in a new value.

FIGURE 15   Pluggable Look and Feel Architecture of a Slider

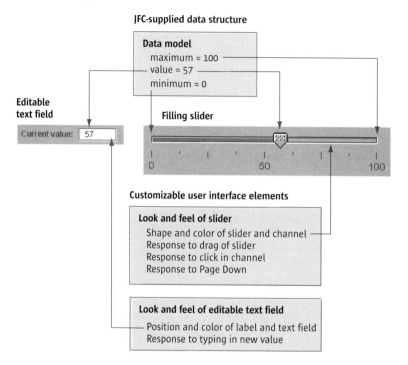

Client Properties   You can use the client properties mechanism to display an alternate form of a specific Java user interface component. If a look and feel design does not support a property, it ignores the property and displays the component as usual. You can set alternate appearances for sliders, toolbars, trees, and internal windows. For instance, a nonfilling slider might be displayed by default. However, by using the client properties mechanism, you can display a filling slider, as shown in the preceding figure.

Major JFC User Interface Components   The following table illustrates (with icons intended for use in a GUI builder) the major user interface components in the JFC. Components are listed alphabetically by their names in code. Their

English names are provided, followed by the location of more detailed
information on each component.

TABLE 1   Names of the JFC User Interface Components

Component	Code Name	Common Name	For Details
	JApplet	Applet	page 43
	JButton	Command button and toolbar button	page 196 and page 189
	JCheckBox	Checkbox	page 202
	JCheckBoxMenuItem	Checkbox menu item	page 180
	JColorChooser	Color chooser	page 167
	JComboBox	Noneditable and editable combo boxes	page 207
	JDesktopPane	Backing window	page 149
	JDialog	Dialog box, secondary window, and utility window	page 156, page 138, and page 140
	JEditorPane	Editor pane	page 221

TABLE 1   Names of the JFC User Interface Components *(Continued)*

Component	Code Name	Common Name	For Details
	JFrame	Primary window	page 135
	JInternalFrame	Internal window, minimized internal window, and internal utility window	page 150 and page 151
	JLabel	Label	page 214 and page 226
	JList	List components (list boxes and selectable lists)	page 204 and page 226
	JMenu	Drop-down menu and submenu	page 175
	JMenuBar	Menu bar	page 174
	JMenuItem	Menu item	page 176
	JOptionPane	Alert box	page 169
	JPanel	Panel	page 141
	JPasswordField	Password field	page 219
	JPopupMenu	Contextual menu	page 185

TABLE 1   Names of the JFC User Interface Components *(Continued)*

Component	Code Name	Common Name	For Details
	JProgressBar	Progress bar	page 122
	JRadioButton	Radio button	page 203
	JRadioButtonMenuItem	Radio button menu item	page 181
	JScrollBar	Scrollbar	page 143
	JScrollPane	Scroll pane	page 142
	JSeparator	Separator	page 179
	JSlider	Slider	page 210
	JSplitPane	Split pane	page 147
	JTabbedPane	Tabbed pane	page 145
	JTable	Table	page 228
	JTextArea	Plain text area	page 220
	JTextField	Noneditable and editable text fields (single line)	page 217

TABLE 1   Names of the JFC User Interface Components *(Continued)*

Component	Code Name	Common Name	For Details
T	JTextPane	Editor pane with the styled editor kit plug-in	page 222
ON	JToggleButton	Toggle button and toolbar toggle button	page 200 and page 189
	JToolBar	Toolbar	page 186
tip	JToolTip	Tool tip	page 191
	JTree	Tree component	page 240
	JWindow	Plain (unadorned) window	page 139

In the JFC, the typical primary windows that users work with are based on the JFrame component. Unadorned windows that consist of a rectangular region without any title bar, close control, or other window controls are based on the JWindow component. Designers and developers typically use the JWindow component to create windows without title bars, such as splash screens.

For details on the use of windows, panels, and panes, see Chapter 7.

Look and Feel Options
You, the designer, have the first choice of a look and feel design. You can determine the look and feel you want users to receive on a specific platform, or you can choose a **cross-platform** look and feel.

Java Look and Feel—the Recommended Design   With a cross-platform look and feel, your application will appear and perform the same everywhere, simplifying the application's development and documentation.

☕ Do not specify a look and feel explicitly. This way, the Java look and feel, which is a cross-platform look and feel, is used by default.

▤▭ If an error occurs while specifying the name of any look and feel, the Java look and feel is used by default.

Supplied Designs   If you do not specify the Java look and feel, you can specify another look and feel—one that ships with the JFC or one that someone else has made. Note, however, that not all look and feel designs are available on every platform. For example, the Microsoft Windows look and feel is available only on the Microsoft Windows platform.

Because there is far more to the design of an application than the look and feel of components, it is unwise to give end users the ability to swap look and feel designs while working in your application. Switching look and feel designs in this way only swaps the look and feel designs of the components from one platform to another. The layout and vocabulary do not change. Since layout conventions vary from platform to platform, this situation can result in an interface that looks inappropriate. For instance, swapping look and feel designs does not change the titles of the menus. (If you must provide users with the ability to switch look and feel designs, see Appendix D.)

The look and feel designs available in the Java 2 SDK are:

- **Java look and feel.** (Called "Metal" in the code.) The Java look and feel is designed for use on any platform that supports the JFC. This book provides recommendations on the use of the Java look and feel.

- **Microsoft Windows.** (Called "Windows" in the code.) The Microsoft Windows style look and feel can be used only on Microsoft Windows platforms. It follows the behavior of components in applications that ship with Windows NT 4.0. For details, see *Microsoft Windows User Experience*, which is described in "Microsoft Windows" on page 11.

- **CDE.** (Called "CDE/Motif" in the code.) The CDE style look and feel is designed for use on UNIX® platforms. It emulates OSF/Motif 1.2.5, which ships with the Solaris™ 2.6 operating system. For details, see the *CDE 2.1/Motif 2.1—Style Guide and Glossary*, which is described in "CDE" on page 9.

PART II: FUNDAMENTAL JAVA APPLICATION DESIGN

3: DESIGN CONSIDERATIONS

When you begin a software project, ask yourself these three questions:

- How do I want to deliver my software to users?

- How can I design an application that is accessible to all potential users?

- How can I design an application that suits a global audience and requires minimal effort to localize?

Choosing an Application or an Applet

Early in the development process, you must decide if you want to create a standalone **application** or an **applet** that is displayed in a web **browser**. The following figure shows the different environments for running applications and applets.

FIGURE 16 Environments for Applications and Applets

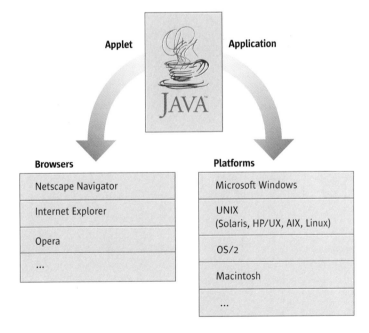

When deciding between an application and an applet, the two main issues you need to consider are distribution and security, including read and write permissions. If you decide to use an applet, you must also decide whether to display your applet in the user's current browser window or in a separate browser window. (It is possible, with a moderate amount of effort, to ship a program as both an applet and an application.)

For an example of an application that uses the Java look and feel, see "MetalEdit Application" on page 20. For an example of an applet, see "Retirement Savings Calculator Applet" on page 25. For a list of additional reading on applets, see "Design for Applets" on page 14.

Distribution

When deciding how to distribute your software, weigh the needs of both end users and administrators. Don't forget to consider ease-of-use issues for:

- Initial distribution and installation of the software
- Maintenance of the software
- Updates to the software
- Regular access to the software

One solution is the standalone application, distributed on a CD-ROM disc or a floppy disk and installed on the end user's local hard disk. Once the application is installed, users can easily access it. In an enterprise environment, however, maintenance can be complicated because separate copies of the application exist on each user's local computer. Distribution of the original application and subsequent updates require shipment of the software to, and installation by, multiple users.

In contrast, applets are simpler to distribute and maintain because they are installed on a central web server. Using a web browser on their local machines, users can access the latest version of the applet from anywhere on the intranet or Internet. Users, however, must download the applet over the network each time they start the applet.

If you are creating an applet, make sure that your users have a browser that contains the JFC or that they are using Java™ Plug-In. That way, users will not have to download the JFC every time they run the applet. (The HTML required to run an applet differs for plug-in and non-plug-in configurations. Consider providing both options to the user.)

Security Issues   Another issue to consider is whether your software needs to read and write files. Standalone Java applications can read or write files on the user's hard disk just as other applications do. For example, the MetalEdit application reads and writes documents on the user's local disk.

In contrast, applets usually cannot access a user's hard disk because they are intended for display on a web page. Generally, a user doesn't know the source of an applet that has been downloaded from the web, so standard security procedures include preventing all applets from reading and writing to the hard disk. Thus, applets are better suited for tasks that do not require access to the hard disk. For example, a web page for a bank might offer an applet that calculates home mortgage payments and prints results, but does not save files on the customer's hard disk.

You can also use an applet as a front end to a central database. For example, the Retirement Savings Calculator applet enables company employees to select funds for their retirement contribution and update the amount of their contribution in the company database.

Placement of Applets   If you decide to design an applet, you can display your applet in the user's current browser window or in a separate browser window.

Applets in the User's Current Browser Window   The current browser window is well suited for displaying applets in which users perform a single task. This approach enables users to perform the task and then resume other activities in the browser, such as surfing the web.

An applet displayed in the current browser window should not include a menu bar—having a menu bar in both the applet and the browser confuses users.

Applets generally cannot predict which mnemonics are (or are not) in use in the browser itself. Therefore, determine which top-level mnemonics are used in expected browsers and in their associated environments and avoid their use, so no conflicts occur. Examples of top-level mnemonics are menu title names (such as File and Edit).

Applets in Separate Browser Windows   If your applet involves more than one task or if users might want to visit other web pages before completing the task, launch a separate browser window and display the applet there. This approach enables users to interact with the applet and maintain the original browser window for other activities. Users can open multiple browser windows to do several tasks simultaneously. Navigating to another web page in the original browser window, however, does not affect the applet in its separate browser window.

Designing an applet for a separate browser window is simpler if you remove the browser's normal menu and navigation controls. Doing so avoids confusion between the browser's menu and controls and the applet's menus and controls. You also avoid potential conflicts between mnemonics in the two windows.

Designing for Accessibility
Accessibility refers to the removal of barriers that prevent people with disabilities from participating in social, professional, and practical life activities. In software design, **accessibility** requires taking into account the needs of people with functional differences: for example, users who are unable to operate a conventional mouse or keyboard or users who cannot process information using traditional output methods.

⊙ Java Accessibility Helper, a utility to aid you in assessing how well your application supports the needs of people with disabilities, is available on the companion CD-ROM.

Benefits of Accessibility
Accessibility provides a competitive advantage, increasing sales as well as the opportunities for employment, independence, and productivity for the approximately 750 million people worldwide with disabilities. Moreover, designing for accessibility provides potential benefits beyond enabling people with disabilities:

- Mnemonics and keyboard shortcuts, which are significantly faster than navigating using the mouse, make all users more productive.

- Keyboard navigation is preferred by a significant number of users and is good for users with even minor RSI (repetitive stress injury) issues.

- Customizable fonts enable users to pick fonts that reduce eye strain and display effectively on widely varying monitors.

- Customizable colors enable applications to fit into the desktop seamlessly and work properly on systems with limited available colors.

Consider the concept of electronic curb cuts: In the real world, cuts made in the sidewalk at intersections enable wheelchairs to exit the sidewalk and cross the intersection. Those curb cuts are also great for baby strollers, skateboards, and elderly people with only minor disabilities. In the same way, many software accessibility features make everyone more productive.

Many countries are instituting legislation (such as the Americans With Disabilities Act in the United States) that makes access to information, products, and services mandatory for individuals with special needs. In these countries, government and academic institutions are required to purchase and support technologies that maximize accessibility. For example, in the United States, Section 508 of the Federal Rehabilitation Act requires all federal contracts to include solutions for employees with disabilities. The international community of people with disabilities is also successfully pressuring companies to sell accessible software.

Accessible Design   Five steps will put you on a path to an accessible product:

- Follow the standards in this book
- Provide accessible names and descriptions for your components
- Employ mnemonics and keyboard shortcuts throughout your application
- Provide proper keyboard navigation and activation
- Perform usability studies with disabled users

For a list of additional reading, see "Design for Accessibility" on page 13.

Java Look and Feel Standards   The Java look and feel standards in this book take into account the needs of users with functional limitations. The standards cover how to use colors, fonts, animation, and graphics. By following these standards, you will be able to meet the needs of most of your users.

☕ Java look and feel standards are identified throughout the book by this symbol.

Accessible Names and Descriptions   An accessible name and description property should be provided for each component in your application. These properties enable an **assistive technology**, such as a screen reader, to interact with the component.

As a developer, you usually do not have to set these properties directly. Commonly, the accessible name and descriptions are picked up automatically from a component's label or tool tip. (Furthermore, Java Accessibility Helper, the utility provided on the companion CD-ROM, checks for this information.)

For details, see "Developing Accessible JFC Applications" at
`http://www.sun.com/access/developers/developing-`
`accessible-apps`.

Whenever possible, use tool tips and labels instead of setting accessibility
properties directly. This practice makes it easy to extract accessibility
information and localize the accessibility properties. If you set accessibility
properties directly and add unique strings to your application, be sure to
store the new information in your application's resource bundle. When the
bundle is localized, the accessibility values are included.

▦⟲ The `accessibleName` property provides a name for a component
and distinguishes it from other components of the same type. It enables
assistive technologies to provide users with the name of the component that
has input focus.

▦⟲ For components such as labels, buttons, and menu items that contain
noneditable text, the `accessibleName` property is set automatically to the
text. Other types of components should have corresponding `JLabel` objects.
Use the `JLabel.setLabelFor` method to instruct the target object to
inherit its accessible name from the label.

▦⟲ All components should have tool tips. They automatically set the
components' `accessibleDescription` property, which provides
information such as how a component works.

▦⟲ The Java Accessibility Helper utility can be used to determine whether
`accessibleName` properties and other API information are properly
implemented in your application. Java Accessibility Helper v.0.3 is included on
the companion CD-ROM.

For more information on the Java Accessibility API and the Java Accessibility
Utilities package, see "Support for Accessibility" on page 30.

Mnemonics and Keyboard Shortcuts   You should provide mnemonics and keyboard
shortcuts throughout your application. A mnemonic is an underlined
alphanumeric character that shows users which key to press (in conjunction
with the Alt key) to activate a command or navigate to a component.

The dialog box in Figure 17 shows the use of mnemonics for a text field,
checkboxes, radio buttons, and command buttons. For example, if keyboard
focus is within the dialog box, pressing Alt-W moves keyboard focus to the
Whole Word checkbox and selects it.

⊙ The corresponding code for Figure 17 is available on the companion CD-ROM.

FIGURE 17   Mnemonics in a Dialog Box

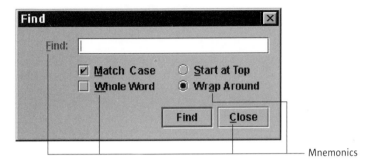

In cases where you can't add a mnemonic to the component itself, as in the text field in the preceding figure, you can place the mnemonic in the component's label. For more information on mnemonics, see "Mnemonics" on page 118.

⊟⊃ The `labelFor` property should always be used to associate a label with another component so that the component becomes active when the label's mnemonic is activated. This practice eliminates the need to set an `accessibleName` property programmatically.

Keyboard shortcuts are keystroke combinations (usually a modifier key and a character key, like Control-C) that activate menu items from the keyboard even if the relevant menu is not currently displayed. (For more on keyboard shortcuts, see "Keyboard Shortcuts" on page 115.)

Keyboard Focus and Tab Traversal   You can also assist users who navigate via the keyboard by assigning initial keyboard focus and by specifying a tab traversal order. Keyboard focus indicates where the next keystrokes will take effect. For more information, see "Keyboard Focus" on page 111.

Tab traversal order is the sequence in which components receive keyboard focus on successive presses of the Tab key. In most cases, the traversal order follows the reading order of the users' locale. For more information on tab traversal order, see "Tab Traversal Order" on page 158.

Make sure you test your application to see if users can access all functions and interactive components from the keyboard. Unplug the mouse and use only the keyboard when you perform your test.

Usability Studies   You should try out the application with a variety of users to see how well it provides for accessibility. Low-vision users, for example, are sensitive to font sizes and color, as well as layout and context problems. Blind users are affected by interface flow, tab order, layout, and terminology. Users with mobility impairments can be sensitive to tasks that require an excessive number of steps or a wide range of movement.

Planning for Internationalization and Localization

In software development, **internationalization** is the process of writing an application that is suitable for the global marketplace, taking into account variations in regions, languages, and cultures. A related term, **localization**, refers to the process of customizing an application for a particular language or region. The language, meaning, or format of the following types of data can vary with locale:

- Colors
- Currency formats
- Date and time formats
- Graphics
- Icons
- Labels
- Messages
- Number formats
- Online help
- Page layouts
- Personal titles
- Phone numbers
- Postal addresses
- Reading order
- Sounds
- Units of measurement

Figure 18 shows a notification dialog box in both English and Japanese. Much of the localization of this dialog box involves the translation of text. The Japanese dialog box is bigger than the English dialog box because some text strings are longer. Note the differences in the way that mnemonics are displayed. In English, the mnemonic for the Sound File text field is S. In Japanese, the same mnemonic (S) is placed at the end of the label.

⊙ The corresponding code for Figure 18 is available on the companion CD-ROM.

FIGURE 18   English and Japanese Notification Dialog Boxes

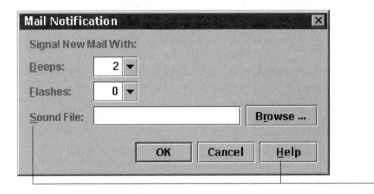

Benefits of Global Planning   The main benefit of designing an application for the global marketplace is more customers. Many countries require that companies purchase applications that support their language and culture. Global planning ensures that your application is easier to translate and maintain. A well-designed application functions the same way in all locales.

Global Design   You can incorporate support for localization into your design by using JFC-supplied layout managers and resource bundles. In addition, you should take into account that differences exist around the world in reading order, word order, mnemonics, graphics, formats, sorting orders, and fonts.

⊕ Internationalization guidelines are identified throughout the book by this symbol. For a list of additional reading, see "Design for Internationalization" on page 12.

Layout Managers   You can use a **layout manager** to control the size and location of the components in your application. For example, Figure 18 on page 49 shows that the Sound File label becomes longer when it is translated from English to Japanese. The spacing between the Sound File label and its text field, however, is the same in both dialog boxes. For more information on layout managers, see *The Java Tutorial* at `http://java.sun.com/docs/books/tutorial`.

Resource Bundles   You should use resource bundles to store locale-specific data, such as text, colors, graphics, fonts, and mnemonics. A **resource bundle** makes your application easier to localize by isolating locale-specific data so that it can be translated without changing the application source code.

If your application has a Cancel button, for example, the resource bundles in English, German, and Chinese would include the text shown in Figure 19.

⊙ The corresponding code for Figure 19 is available on the companion CD-ROM.

FIGURE 19   Cancel Buttons in English, German, and Chinese

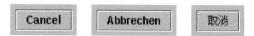

For translations of interface elements and concepts used in Java look and feel applications into selected European and Asian languages, see Appendix C. For more information on creating resource bundles, see *The Java Tutorial*. (*The Java Tutorial* is described in "Java" on page 9.)

Reading Order   When you lay out your application, place the components according to your users' reading order. This order will help users understand the components quickly as they read through them. Reading order varies among locales. The reading order in English, for example, is left to right and top to bottom. The reading order in Middle Eastern languages, on the other hand, is from right to left and top to bottom.

In this book, you will find standards such as "put labels before the component they describe." The term "before" is determined by the reading order of the user's language. For example, in English, labels appear to the left of the component they describe.

⊞⊃ In the JFC, component orientation features can be used to adapt your application to different reading orders.

⊞⊃ In the Java 2 SDK, the layout managers `FlowLayout` and `BorderLayout` are sensitive to the reading order of the locale.

Word Order Keep in mind that word order varies among languages, as shown in the following figure. A noneditable combo box that appears in the middle of an English sentence does not translate properly in French, where the adjective should come after the noun. (The correct French sentence is "Utilisez une Flèche Rouge.")

FIGURE 20 Incorrect Adaptation of English Word Order into French

The following figure corrects the problem by using a label before the noneditable combo box. This format works well in both English and French.

FIGURE 21 Correct Adaptation of English Word Order into French

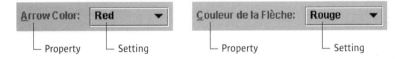

Mnemonics You must be careful when choosing mnemonics, which might change in different languages. Store mnemonics in resource bundles with the rest of your application's text. In addition, make sure that the characters you choose for your mnemonics are available on keyboards in the target countries for your application.

Graphics You can make localization easier by using globally understood graphics whenever possible. Many graphics that are easily understood in one locale are puzzling in another locale. For example, using a mailbox to represent an email application is problematic because the shape and size of mailboxes vary by locale. Graphics that represent everyday objects, holidays, and seasons are difficult to localize, as are graphics that include text.

Avoid using graphics that might be offensive in some locales, including:

- Images that contain text. For example, if an image contains English text, the text (and graphic) must be localized for each locale.
- Images that contain numbers. Numbers have different connotations in different locales. For example, just as the number 13 has an unlucky connotation in the United States, the number 4 connotes death in both Japan and Hong Kong.
- Images containing hand gestures. A gesture that is appropriate or meaningful in one locale can be offensive or meaningless in another locale.
- Images that represent a play on words. For instance, puns don't translate well.
- Images of animals. Just as the image of a dog to represent food would be unsettling to most people in the United States, the image of a cow in the same context can offend people in India.
- Images of people or faces. Depictions of certain facial expressions, nontraditional gender dynamics, and uncovered skin can be offensive to users in some locales.

An example of a symbol that works well in all cultures is the use of an airplane to denote an airport.

Like text, you can place graphics in resource bundles so that translators can change them without changing the application source code.

Test your graphics by showing them to users in the target locales. A low-cost way to test graphics is to solicit feedback on the proposed icons from salespeople in different locales.

Formats You can use the formatting classes provided in the Java 2 SDK to format numbers, currencies, dates, and times automatically for a specific locale. For example, in English, a date might appear as July 26, 1987, and the time as 3:17 p.m. In German, the same date is written as 26. Juli 1987 and the time is 15:17 Uhr.

For numbers and currencies, the class is `NumberFormat`; for dates and times, the class is `DateFormat`; and for strings that contain variable data, the class is `MessageFormat`. The formatting classes are part of the `java.text` package.

Sort Order   You can use the collator classes provided in the Java 2 SDK to enable the sorting of strings by locale. For example, in Roman languages, sorting is commonly based on alphabetical order (which might vary from one language to another). In other languages, sorting might be based on phonetics, character radicals, the number of character strokes, and so on.

⊞⊃ The Collator class in the java.text package enables locale-sensitive string sorting.

Fonts   You can place fonts in resource bundles so that they can be changed by the localizers. With the Java 2 SDK, the Lucida font (a cross-platform font) is available for use in your applications.

☕ The size of fonts is also an important consideration for users with visual limitations (that is, anyone over the age of thirty). Be sure to provide user control over font size in your application.

Usability Studies   Two kinds of studies done early in the design process can show you how well your application works in the global marketplace. First, you can send draft designs of your application to your translators. Second, you can try out your application with users from the locales you are targeting (for example, test a Japanese version of the application with Japanese users). This research will help you to determine whether users understand how to use the product, if they perceive the graphics and colors as you intended them, and if there is anything offensive in the product.

4: VISUAL DESIGN

Visual design and aesthetics affect user confidence in and comfort with your application. A polished and professional look without excess or oversimplification is not easy to attain. This chapter discusses these high-level, visual aspects of Java look and feel applications:

- Use of themes to control and change the colors and fonts of components to suit your requirements

- Layout and alignment of interface elements to enhance clarity, ease of use, and aesthetic appeal

- Capitalization of text in interface elements to ensure consistency and readability

- Use of animation to provide effective emphasis and meaningful feedback

Themes

As a software developer, you can use the **theme mechanism** to control many of the fundamental attributes of the Java look and feel design, including colors and fonts. For instance, you might want to change the colors and fonts in your application to match your corporate identity. The theme mechanism enables you to specify alternative colors and fonts across an entire Java look and feel application.

For more information on using themes, see the description of the `javax.swing.plaf.metal.DefaultMetalTheme` class.

Colors

If you want to change the color theme of your application, be sure that your interface elements remain visually coherent. The Java look and feel uses a simple color model so that it can run on a variety of platforms and on devices capable of displaying various depths of color. Eight colors are defined for the interface:

- Three primary colors to give the theme a color identity and to emphasize selected items

- Three secondary colors, typically shades of gray, for neutral drawing and inactive or unavailable items

- Two additional colors, usually defined as black and white, for the display of text and highlights

Within the primary and secondary color groups in the default theme, there is a gradation from dark (primary 1 and secondary 1) to lighter (primary 2 and secondary 2) to lightest (primary 3 and secondary 3).

Default Java Look and Feel Theme   The following table summarizes the eight colors defined in the default Java look and feel theme. It provides swatches and numerical parameters representing each color in the default theme. It also gives details about the roles each color plays in basic drawing, three-dimensional effects, and text.

TABLE 2   Colors of the Default Java Look and Feel Theme

Name	Basic Drawing	3D Effects	Text
Primary 1 RGB 102-102-153 Hex #666699	Active internal window borders	Shadows of activated items	System text (for example, labels)
Primary 2 RGB 153-153-204 Hex #9999CC	Highlighting to indicate activation (for example, of menu titles and menu items); indication of keyboard focus	Shadows (color)	
Primary 3 RGB 204-204-255 Hex #CCCCFF	Large colored areas (for example, the active title bar)		Text selection
Secondary 1 RGB 102-102-102 Hex #666666		Dark border for flush 3D style	
Secondary 2 RGB 153-153-153 Hex #999999	Inactive internal window borders; dimmed button borders	Shadows; highlighting of toolbar buttons upon mouse button down	Dimmed text (for example, inactive menu items or labels)

TABLE 2   Colors of the Default Java Look and Feel Theme *(Continued)*

Name	Basic Drawing	3D Effects	Text
Secondary 3 RGB 204-204-204 Hex #CCCCCC	Canvas color (that is, normal background color); inactive title bar		Background for noneditable text fields
Black RGB 000-000-000 Hex #000000			User text and control text (including items such as menu titles)
White RGB 255-255-255 Hex #FFFFFF		Highlights	Background for user text entry area

☕ Unless you are defining a reverse-video theme, maintain a dark-to-light gradation like the one in the default theme so that interface objects are properly rendered. To reproduce three-dimensional effects correctly, make the secondary 1 color darker than secondary 2, which should be darker than secondary 3 (the background color).

☕ Ensure that primary 1 (used for labels) has enough contrast with the background color (secondary 3) to make text labels easily readable.

Primary Colors   The visual elements of Java look and feel applications use the primary colors as follows:

- Primary 1 for active internal window borders, shadows of activated items, and system text, such as labels

- Primary 2 for highlighting of activated items, such as menu titles and menu items; keyboard focus; active scroll boxes; and progress bar fill

- Primary 3 for large colored areas, such as the title bar of active internal windows and the background of selected text

The usage is illustrated in the following figure.

FIGURE 22   Primary Colors in Default Color Theme

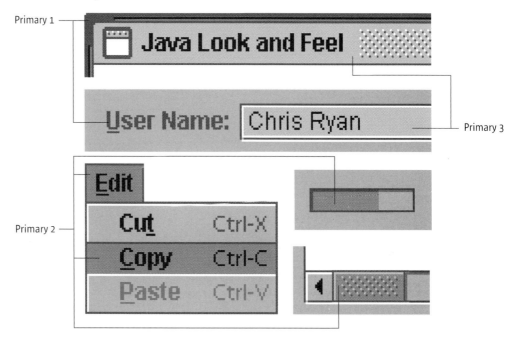

Secondary Colors   The visual elements of Java look and feel applications use the secondary colors as follows:

- Secondary 1 for the dark border that creates flush 3D effects for items such as command buttons

- Secondary 2 for inactive internal window borders, shadows, pressed buttons, and dimmed command button text and borders

- Secondary 3 for the background canvas, the background of noneditable text fields, and inactive title bars for internal windows

The usage is shown in the following figure.

FIGURE 23   Secondary Colors in Default Color Theme

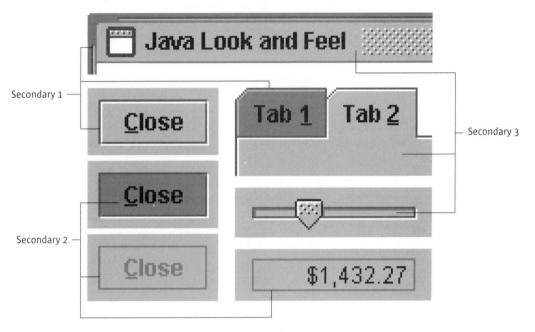

Black and White   Black and white have defined roles in the Java look and feel color model. In particular, black appears in:

- User text, such as the entry in an editable text field
- Control text, such as menu titles and menu items
- Title text in an internal window
- Button text in command buttons
- Tab text in tabbed panes
- Text in noneditable text fields

White is used for:

- Highlighting the flush 3D appearance of such components as command buttons

- Background of editable text fields

Redefinition of Colors   The simplest modification you can make to the color theme is to redefine the primary colors. For instance, you can substitute greens for the purple-blues used in the default theme, as shown in the following figure.

FIGURE 24   Green Color Theme

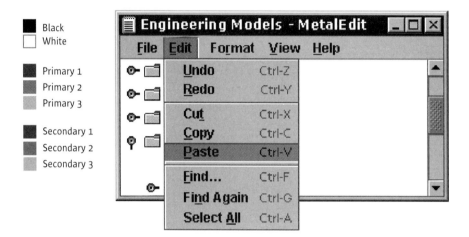

You can use the same value for more than one of the eight colors—for instance, a high-contrast theme might use only black, white, and grays. The following figure shows a theme that uses the same grays for primary 2 and secondary 2. White functions as primary 3 and secondary 3 as well as in its normal role.

FIGURE 25   High-Contrast Color Theme

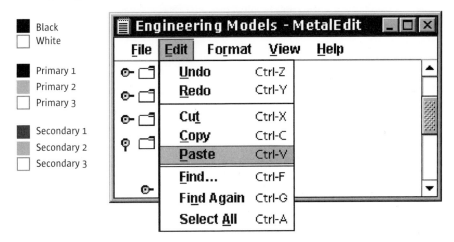

- Black
- White

- Primary 1
- Primary 2
- Primary 3

- Secondary 1
- Secondary 2
- Secondary 3

Fonts   As part of the theme mechanism and parallel to the color model, the Java look and feel provides a default font style model for a consistent look. You can use themes to redefine font typefaces, sizes, and styles in your application. The default Java look and feel theme defines four font categories, called "type styles": the control font, the system font, the user font, and the small font. The actual fonts used vary across platforms.

The following table shows the mappings to Java look and feel components for the default theme.

TABLE 3   Type Styles Defined by the Java Look and Feel

Type Style	Default Theme	Use
Control	12-point bold	Buttons, checkboxes, menu titles, labels, and window titles
Small	10-point plain	Keyboard shortcuts in menus and tool tips
System	12-point plain	Tree components and tool tips
User	12-point plain	Text fields and tables

To ensure consistency, ease of use, and visual appeal, use the supplied default fonts unless there is compelling reason for an application-wide change (such as higher readability). Use the theme mechanism if you do make modifications.

☕ Do not write font sizes or styles directly into your application source code (a programming practice that is also called "hardcoding"). Store font sizes and styles in resource bundles.

☕ Use layout managers to ensure that the layout of your application can handle different font sizes.

🖥 Ensure that the font settings you choose are legible and can be rendered well on your target systems.

🔲 In the Java look and feel, six methods are used to return references to the four type styles. The `getControlTextFont`, `getMenuTextFont`, and `getWindowTitleFont` methods return the control font; `getSystemTextFont` returns the system font; `getUserTextFont` returns the user font; and `getSubTextFont` returns the small font.

🔲 All fonts in the Java look and feel are defined in the default Java look and feel theme as Dialog, which maps to a platform-specific font.

Layout and Visual Alignment

Give careful consideration to the layout of components in your windows and dialog boxes. A clear and consistent layout streamlines the way users move through an application and helps them utilize its features efficiently. The best designs are aesthetically pleasing and easy to understand. They organize components in the direction in which people read them, and they group together logically related components. When you lay out your components, remember that users might use the mouse, keyboard, or assistive technologies to navigate through them.

The following sections specify the layout of text and components in your applications, including between-component spacing.

NOTE – Throughout this book, the spacing illustrations for all user interface elements use pixels as the unit of measurement. A screen at approximately 72 to 100 pixels per inch is assumed.

☕ Use a logical order when you lay out your components (for instance, place the most important elements within a dialog box first in reading order).

🌐 Use layout managers to allow for internationalized titles and labels in panels that use the JFC components.

Design Grids

The most effective method for laying out user interface elements is to create a design grid that uses blank space to set apart logically related sets of components. The rows and columns in a grid divide the available space into areas that can help you to arrange and align components in a pleasing layout. Grids make it easy for users to see the logical sequence of tasks and to understand the relationships between sets of components.

You can develop your grid with a pencil and paper, with a software tool, or even with a piece of graph paper. Once you have established the basic spatial relationships of your components, implement the design with a layout manager.

Developing a grid is an ongoing process. Once you have figured out which components you need, their relationships, and the available space, work with the components to discover the most effective use of space and alignment. You might need to readjust your grid again and again, trying different arrangements until you find one that works well and has a polished appearance.

A grid can also help you to determine how much space to allocate to a given set of components, for instance, choosers and dialog boxes, across the application. If you can define a grid that will work for a number of layouts, your application will have a more consistent appearance.

▦⊃ Design grids should not be confused with the AWT Grid Layout Manager.

Layout and Spacing of a Simple Dialog Box   This section illustrates how to use a grid to lay out a find dialog box.

1. Determine the functional requirements for your dialog box and the type and importance of the dialog box components.

2. Create 12-pixel margins between the border of the dialog box and its components. For example, in a find dialog box, you might need two command buttons, an editable text field and associated label, a set of checkboxes, and a set of radio buttons.

3. Arrange the command button row and separate it vertically from the rest of the components.

4. Use the number and width of the rest of the components to decide the number of columns and the column width for your design grid. (You might try several possibilities before you find the best horizontal separation.)

5. Add the components to the dialog box in logical sequence. The components that you determined were most important in Step 1 should appear first in reading order. Add rows of blank space between the component groups.

6. Align the related components using the columns as a guide.

The following illustration shows the recommended 12-pixel margins around a dialog box.

FIGURE 26   Spacing Between Border and Components of a Dialog Box

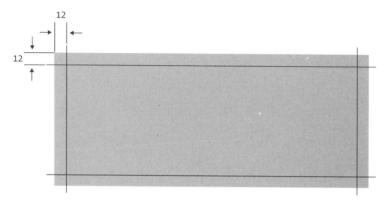

Include 12 pixels between the top and left borders of a dialog box and its components.

The following figure shows the recommended spacing between the borders of the dialog box and the command button row in the dialog box. It also illustrates the vertical separation of the command buttons from the other components.

FIGURE 27   Vertical Separation of Command Buttons

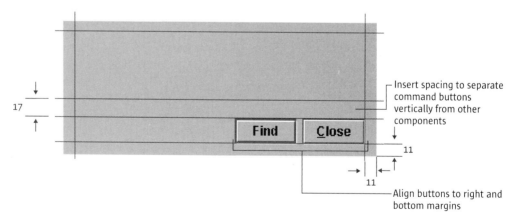

Include 11 pixels between the bottom and right borders of a dialog box and its command buttons. (To the eye, the 11-pixel spacing appears to be 12 pixels because the white borders on the lower and right edges of the button components are not visually significant.)

☕ In dialog boxes, right-align command buttons along the bottom margin.

☕ In dialog boxes, place 17 pixels of vertical space between the command button row and the other components.

You can use the number and width of components and their associated labels to determine the number of columns in your grid. At the beginning of the design process, vertical divisions are more difficult to set because they depend on the depth and grouping of component sets, which are not yet determined. In the following illustration, five columns have been created in the grid to accommodate the editable text field and its label, the checkbox and radio button sets, and the command buttons. Note the 11-pixel interval between the lines that delineate the columns.

FIGURE 28   Horizontal Separation of User Interface Elements

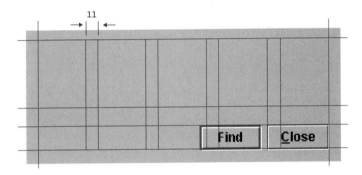

☕ Use the number and width of dialog box components and labels to determine the number of columns in the design grid.

In Figure 29, the most important option—the text field for the search string—has been placed first. Component groups are set off in multiples of 6 pixels minus one. For instance, a row of 11 pixels of empty space separates the editable text box and the checkbox and radio button sets. Spacing between components (and groups of components) follows the Java look and feel standards. For details, see "Between-Component Spacing Guidelines" on page 68.

Related options (for instance, the Match Case and Whole Word checkboxes) are aligned along a column guide. Additional options (for instance, the Start at Top and Wrap Around radio buttons) have been aligned with a secondary column guide.

FIGURE 29   Alignment of Related Options and Vertical Separation of Component Groups

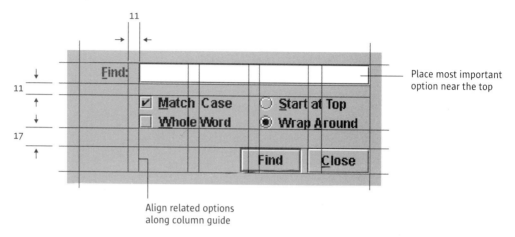

When designing a dialog box, place the most important options, or those you expect users to complete first, prior to others (in reading order).

For spacing between rows and columns of dialog box components, use multiples of 6 pixels minus 1, to allow for the flush 3D border.

Align related dialog box components using a design grid column.

See "Between-Component Spacing Guidelines" on page 68 for details.

Text Layout   Text is an important design element in your layouts. The way you align and lay out text is vital to the appearance and ease of use of your application. The most significant layout issues with respect to text are label placement and alignment.

Label Placement   You indicate a label's association with a component when you specify its relative position. In the following figure, the label appears before and at the top of the list in reading order.

FIGURE 30   Label Placement

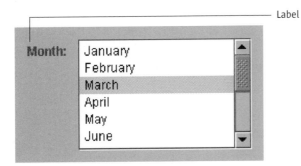

Label

☕ In general, place labels before the component to which they refer, in reading order for the current locale. For instance, in the U.S. locale, place labels above or to the left of the component. Positioning to the left is preferable, since it allows for separation of text and components into discrete columns. This practice helps users read and understand the options.

Label Alignment and Spacing   Between components, alignment of multiple labels becomes an issue. Aligning labels to a left margin can make them easier to scan and read. It also helps to give visual structure to a block of components, particularly if there is no immediate border (such as a window frame) surrounding them. If labels vary greatly in length, the use of right alignment can make it easier to determine the associated component; however, this practice also introduces large areas of negative space, which can be unattractive. The use of concise wording in labels can help to alleviate such difficulties.

☕ Insert 12 pixels between the trailing edge of a label and any associated components. Insert 12 pixels between the trailing edge of a label and the component it describes when labels are right-aligned. When labels are left-aligned, insert 12 pixels between the trailing edge of the longest label and its associated component.

☕ Align labels with the top of associated components.

⊕ Since the length and height of translated text varies, use layout managers to allow for differences in labels.

The following figure shows the recommended spacing of labels in relationship to their associated components.

FIGURE 31   Spacing Between a Label and a Component

⊞▭   The `JLabel.setLabelFor()` method should always be used to specify which component a label is associated with. This practice facilitates the setting of mnemonics and accessible names.

For more information on capitalization, see "Text in the Interface" on page 75. For more information on labels, see "Labels" on page 214.

Between-Component Spacing Guidelines

Use multiples of 6 pixels for perceived spacing between components. If the measurement involves a component edge with a white border, subtract 1 pixel to arrive at the actual measurement between components (because the white border on **available** components is less visually significant than the dark border). In these cases, you should specify the actual measurement as 1 pixel less—that is, 5 pixels between components within a group and 11 pixels between groups of components.

NOTE – Exceptions to these spacing guidelines are noted in the relevant component sections that follow. For instance, the perceived spacing between toolbar buttons is 3 pixels, and the actual spacing is 2 pixels.

In the following figure, a perceived 6-pixel vertical space is actually 5 pixels between checkbox components. The figure also shows how the perceived spacing between **unavailable** objects is preserved. Note that the dimensions of unavailable components are the same as those of available objects, although the white border of available objects is replaced by an invisible 1-pixel border on the bottom and right side of unavailable objects.

FIGURE 32   Perceived and Actual Spacing of Available and Unavailable
Components

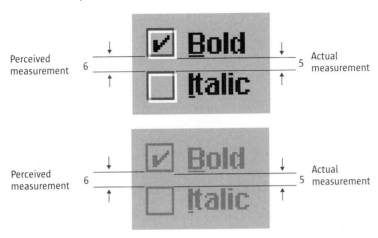

Insert 5 pixels (6 minus 1) between closely related items such as
grouped checkboxes. Insert 11 pixels (12 minus 1) for greater separation
between sets of components (such as between a group of radio buttons and a
group of checkboxes). Insert 12 pixels between items that don't have the
flush 3D border highlight (for instance, text labels and titled borders).

FIGURE 33   Spacing of Multiple Groups of Components

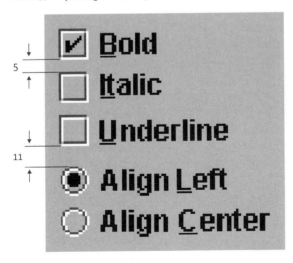

For guidelines on the spacing of specific JFC components with the Java look
and feel, see the following section.

Spacing Guidelines for Specific JFC Components   This section specifies the
horizontal and vertical spacing for individual instances and groups of:

- Toolbar buttons
- Command buttons
- Toggle buttons
- Checkboxes
- Radio buttons

▤⬯ Struts and glue in the `javax.swing.Box` component can be used to
adjust component spacing.

Toolbar Button Spacing   This section contains the vertical and horizontal spacing
measurements for toolbar buttons. Figure 34 shows the spacing between
individual toolbar buttons and groups of toolbar buttons.

☕ Space individual toolbar buttons 2 pixels apart. Space groups of toolbar
buttons 11 pixels apart.

☕ Include 3 pixels of space above and below toolbar buttons. This actually
means 2 pixels of space below the toolbar because of the white border on the
buttons.

FIGURE 34   Toolbar Button Spacing

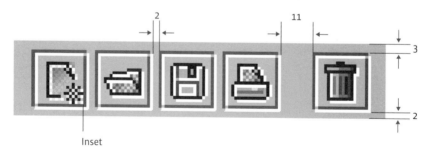

Inset

☕ When you use mouse-over feedback, space individual toolbar buttons
zero pixels apart within a group. Space groups of toolbar buttons 11 pixels
apart.

▤⬯ The inset (that is, the padding between the button graphic and the
button border) on toolbar buttons should be zero.

For details on toolbars, see "Toolbars" on page 186.

Toggle Button Spacing   Spacing recommendations differ for independent and exclusive toggle buttons in toolbars and outside of toolbars.

☕ When toggle buttons are independent (like checkboxes) and used outside a toolbar, separate them with 5 pixels. Within a toolbar, separate independent toggle buttons by 2 pixels.

FIGURE 35   Spacing Between Independent Toggle Buttons

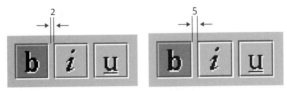

Within toolbar   Outside of toolbar

☕ When toggle buttons are exclusive (that is, they form a radio button set), separate them with 2 pixels. This rule applies whether the toggle buttons appear in a toolbar or elsewhere in the interface.

FIGURE 36   Spacing of Exclusive Toggle Buttons

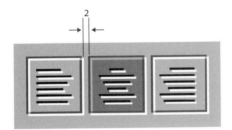

For details on independent and exclusive toggle buttons, see "Toggle Buttons" on page 200.

Command Button Spacing and Padding   For a consistent appearance, follow the guidelines described in this section to create space within and between command buttons. The following figure shows button text (Help) centered in a command button.

☕ Space buttons in a group 5 pixels apart. (Because of the white border on the right side of a button, the apparent spacing will be 6 pixels.)

☕ Center the text within buttons.

FIGURE 37   Command Button With Centered Text

⊕ Since the length and height of translated text varies, use layout managers to allow for differences in button text.

The blank space between the button text and the button border is referred to as command button **padding**. Often command buttons appear in groups within a dialog box or an applet. In such a case, the button in the group with the widest text determines the inner padding, as shown in Figure 38. Here the Cancel button has the widest text. The perceived padding is 12 pixels on either side of the button text. The other buttons in the group (OK and Help) have the same width as the Cancel button. A space of 17 pixels should be left above command button rows in dialog boxes (see Figure 29).

☕ Determine which button has the widest button text and insert 12 pixels of padding on either side of the text. Make all the remaining buttons in the group the same size as the button with the longest text.

☕ Use the default height for whatever font size you select for your command buttons.

☕ Make all command buttons in a group (including buttons that contain graphics) the same width and height.

⊕ Since the button with the longest text might vary from locale to locale, enable any of the command buttons to determine the width of all the other buttons.

FIGURE 38   Spacing and Padding in Command Button Groups

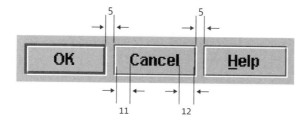

For details on command buttons, see "Command Buttons" on page 196.

Checkbox and Radio Button Layout and Spacing   This section provides layout and spacing guidelines for checkbox and radio button components.

Align the leading of edge of checkboxes with that of other components.

FIGURE 39   Checkbox Layout

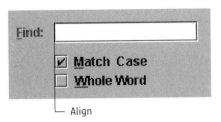

As shown in the following figure, the height of the checkbox square doesn't change in an unavailable checkbox even though the white highlight border is not drawn. Although the checkbox is the same size, the last row and column of pixels on the bottom and right are the same color as the background canvas. The apparent spacing is 6 pixels between components; the actual spacing is 5 pixels.

FIGURE 40   Checkbox and Radio Button Spacing

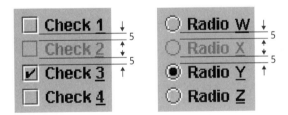

Space checkboxes in a group 5 pixels apart.

Use a layout manager to achieve consistent spacing in checkbox button groups.

For details on checkboxes, see "Checkboxes" on page 202.

The height of the radio button is 12 pixels, not counting the white highlight border. Unavailable radio buttons do not have white borders. Although the unavailable radio button is 12 pixels high, the last row and column of pixels on the bottom and right are the same color as the background canvas. As shown in the preceding figure, the apparent spacing is 6 pixels between components; the actual spacing is 5 pixels.

Space radio buttons in a group 5 pixels apart.

☕ Use the appropriate layout manager to achieve consistent spacing in radio button groups.

For more on radio buttons, see "Radio Buttons" on page 203.

Titled Borders for Panels   Sometimes you can group components using simple spacing and alignment, as described in "Layout and Spacing of a Simple Dialog Box" on page 63. Other times, particularly when you want to display multiple groupings of components, you might want to place the related sets into a labeled box. The JFC enables you to specify a titled border for panels (and many other components), which serves this purpose.

FIGURE 41   Spacing for a Panel With Titled Border

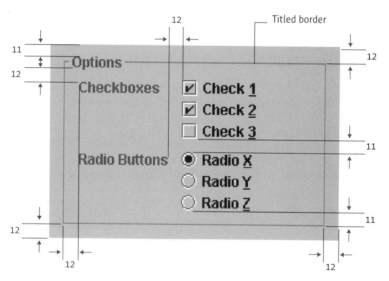

☕ Since titled borders take up considerable space, do not use them to supply titles for individual components; use labels instead.

☕ Use a titled border in a panel to group two or more sets of related components, but do not draw titled borders around a *single* set of checkboxes or radio buttons. Use labels instead.

☕ Use titled borders sparingly: they are best when you must emphasize one group of components or separate one group of components from other components in the same window. Do not use multiple rows and columns of titled borders; they can be more confusing than simply grouping the elements with a design grid.

☕ Never nest titled borders—that is, do not insert one titled border inside another. It becomes difficult to see the organizational structure of the panel and too many lines cause distracting optical effects.

☕ Insert 12 pixels between the edges of the panel and the titled border. Insert 11 pixels between the top of the title and the component above the titled border. Insert 12 pixels between the bottom of the title and the top of the first label in the panel. Insert 11 pixels between component groups and between the bottom of the last component and the lower border.

Text in the Interface

Text is an important design element and appears throughout your application in such components as command buttons, checkboxes, radio buttons, alert box messages, and labels for groups of interface elements. Strive to be concise and consistent with language.

☕ Use language that is clear, consistent, and concise throughout your application text. Moreover, ensure that the wording of your labels, component text, and instructions is readable and grammatically correct.

☕ For all text that appears in the interface elements of your application, follow one of two capitalization conventions: headline capitalization or sentence capitalization. Use headline capitalization for most names, titles, labels, and short text. Use sentence capitalization for lengthy text messages.

☕ Do not capitalize words automatically. You might encounter situations in your interface when capitalization is not appropriate, as in window titles for documents that users have named without using capitalization.

🌐 Use standard typographical conventions for sentences and headlines in your application components. Let translators determine the standards in your target locales.

🌐 Place all text in resource bundles so that localization experts don't have to change your application's source code to accommodate translation. See Appendix C for lists of localized terms and phrases that might appear in your interface.

Headline Capitalization in English

Most items in your application interface should use headline capitalization, which is the style traditionally used for book titles (and the section titles in this book). Capitalize every word except articles ("a," "an," and "the"), coordinating conjunctions (for example, "and," "or," "but," "so," "yet," and "nor"), and prepositions with fewer than four letters (like "in"). The first and last words are always capitalized, regardless of what they are.

Use headline capitalization for the following interface elements (examples are in parentheses):

- Checkbox text (Automatic Save Every Five Minutes)
- Combo box text (Centimeters)
- Command button text (Don't Save)
- Icon names (Trash Can)
- Labels for buttons or controls (New Contribution To:)
- Menu items (Save As...)
- Menu titles (View)
- Radio button text (Start at Top)
- Slider text (Left)
- Tab names (RGB Color)
- Titles of windows, panes, and dialog boxes (Color Chooser)
- Tool tips (Cut Selection)

If your tool tips are longer than a few words, sentence capitalization is acceptable. Be consistent within your application.

Sentence Capitalization in English

When text is in the form of full sentences, capitalize only the first word of each sentence (unless the text contains proper nouns, proper adjectives, or acronyms that are always capitalized). Observe proper punctuation within and at the end of full sentences. Avoid the use of long phrases that are not full sentences. If you determine that you must use a phrase that is not a full sentence, no punctuation is required at the end.

Use sentence capitalization in the following interface elements (examples are in parentheses):

- Alert box text (The document you are closing has unsaved changes.)
- Error or help messages (The printer is out of paper.)
- Labels that indicate changes in status (Operation is 75% complete.)

Animation

Animation can provide effective emphasis if used correctly, but give careful thought to whether animation is warranted. The human eye is attracted to animated elements. If the user's attention needs to be elsewhere, animation might increase user errors.

Do not use animation when it:

- Detracts from more important screen elements
- Interferes with the user's work
- Dazzles without purpose

Useful animations include progress or status animations. For details, see "Progress Animation" on page 122 and "Status Animation" on page 123. Other uses of animation include an animated graphic that activates when the user empties the trash or when the system state changes.

You can also animate application graphics to call attention to user actions.

☕ Limit animation to situations that provide meaningful feedback to the user.

The following figure shows an interesting use of animation in a process control application. The progress bar does not track the progress of the operation; rather, it acts as a gauge to show the temperature of a vat in a candy factory. The progress bar indicates what proportion of the maximum temperature has been reached (more than three-quarters), and the text message within the progress bar specifies the exact temperature (114 degrees) of the vat's contents.

FIGURE 42   Text Inside a Progress Bar

☕ If you write a message to display inside a progress bar, make it concise. Otherwise, localized text might outgrow the progress bar.

5: APPLICATION GRAPHICS

This chapter provides details on:

- The use of cross-platform color

- The design of application graphics, such as icons, button graphics, and symbols

- The use of graphics to enhance your product and corporate identity

Because the quality of your graphics can affect user confidence and even the perceived stability of your application, it is wise to seek the advice of a professional visual designer.

Working With Cross-Platform Color

In a cross-platform delivery environment, you need to ensure that the visual components of your application reproduce legibly and aesthetically on all your target systems. You do not have control over which platforms will be used to run your software or what display capabilities users might have.

Online graphics consist of the visual representations of JFC components in the Java look and feel, which are drawn for you by the toolkit, and application graphics such as icons and splash screens, which you supply.

The Java look and feel components use a simple color model that reproduces well even on displays with a relatively small number of available colors.

Use themes to control the colors of Java look and feel components—for instance, to provide support for display devices with minimal available colors (fewer than 16 colors).

You need to supply icons, button graphics, pictures and logos for splash screens and About boxes. Since these graphics might be displayed on a number of different platforms and configurations, you must develop a strategy for ensuring a high quality of appearance. In addition, you need to ensure that your graphics are meaningful to color-blind users. Strategies for addressing color blindness are similar to those used for handling limited display colors.

☕ Use color only as a secondary means of representing important information. Make use of other characteristics (shape, texture, size, or intensity contrast) that do not require color vision or a color monitor.

Working With Available Colors

The number of colors available on a system is determined by the **bit depth**, which is the number of bits of information used to represent a single pixel on the monitor. The lowest number of bits used for modern desktop color monitors is usually 8 bits (256 colors); 16 bits provide for thousands of colors (65,536, to be exact); and 24 bits, common on newer systems, provide for millions of colors (16,777,216). The specific colors available on a system are determined by the way in which the target platform allocates colors. Available colors might differ from application to application.

Designers sometimes use predefined color palettes when producing images. For example, some web designers work within a set of 216 "web-safe" colors. These colors reproduce in many web browsers without **dithering** (as long as the system is capable of displaying at least 256 colors). Dithering occurs when a system or application attempts to simulate an unavailable color by using a pattern of two or more colors from the system palette. The main drawback of dithering is the striped (moiré) patterns that can result.

Outside web browsers, available colors are not so predictable. Individual platforms have different standard colors or deal with palettes in a dynamic way. The web-safe colors might dither when running in a standalone application, or even in an applet within a browser that usually does not dither these colors. Since the colors available to a Java application can differ each time it is run, especially across platforms, you cannot always avoid dithering in your images.

🖳🖳 Identify and understand the way that your target platforms handle colors at different bit depths. To achieve your desired effect, test your graphics on all target platforms at depths of 8 bits (that is, 256 colors).

Choosing Graphic File Formats

You can use two graphic file formats for images on the Java platform: **GIF** (Graphics Interchange Format) and **JPEG** (named after its developers, the Joint Photographic Experts Group).

GIF is the common format for application graphics in the Java look and feel. GIF files tend to be smaller on disk and in memory than JPEG files. A GIF file includes a color table (or palette) of up to 256 colors. The number of colors in the table and the complexity of the image are two factors that affect the size of the graphic file.

On 8-bit systems, some of the colors specified in a GIF file will be unavailable if they are not part of the system's current color palette. These unavailable colors will be dithered by the system. On 16-bit and 24-bit systems, more colors are available and different sets of colors can be used in different GIF files. Each GIF image, however, is still restricted to a set of 256 colors.

JPEG graphics are generally better suited for photographs than for the more symbolic style of icons, button graphics, and corporate type and logos. JPEG graphics use a compression algorithm that yields varying image quality depending on the compression setting, whereas GIF graphics use lossless compression that preserves the appearance of the original 8-bit image.

Choosing Colors   At monitor depths greater than 8 bits, most concerns about how any particular color reproduces become less significant. Any system capable of displaying thousands (16 bits) or millions (24 bits) of colors can find a color very close to, or exactly the same as, each value defined in a given image. Newer systems typically display a minimum of thousands of colors. Since each system renders colors slightly differently, different monitors and different platforms might display the same color differently, however. For instance, a given color in one GIF file might look different to the eye from one system to another.

Many older monitors or systems still display only 256 colors. For users with these systems, it might be advantageous to use colors known to exist in the system palette of the target platforms. Most platforms include a small set of "reserved" colors that are always available. Unfortunately, these reserved colors are often not useful for visual design purposes or for interface elements because they are highly saturated (the overpowering hues one might expect to find in a basic box of crayons). Furthermore, there is little overlap between the reserved color sets of different platforms, so reserved colors are not guaranteed to reproduce without dithering across platforms.

☕ Select colors that do not overwhelm the content of your application or distract users from their tasks. Stay away from saturated hues. For the sake of visual appeal and ease of use, choose groups of muted tones for your interface elements.

Since there is no lowest-common-denominator solution for choosing common colors across platforms (or even colors that are guaranteed to reproduce on a single platform), some of the colors in your application graphics will dither when running in 8-bit color. The best strategy is to design images that dither gracefully, as described in the following section.

Maximizing Color Quality   Images with fine color detail often reproduce better on 8-bit systems than those images that are mapped to a predefined palette (such as the web-safe palette) and use large areas of solid colors. Dithering is less noticeable in small areas, and, for isolated pixels of a given color, dithering simply becomes color substitution. Often colors in the system palette can provide a fair-to-good match with those specified in a GIF file. The overall effect of color substitution in small areas can be preferable to the dithering patterns produced for single colors, or to the limited number of colors resulting from pre-mapping to a given color palette.

There are no absolutely safe cross-platform colors. Areas of solid color often dither, producing distracting patterns. One effective way to avoid coarse dithering patterns is to "pre-dither" your artwork intentionally. This approach minimizes obvious patterned dithering on 8-bit systems while still permitting very pleasing effects on systems capable of displaying more than 256 colors.

To achieve this effect, overlay a semitransparent checkerboard pattern on your graphics. The following figure shows how to build a graphic using this technique.

FIGURE 43   Adding a Pattern to Avoid Coarse Dithering Patterns

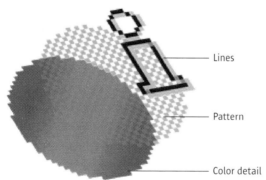

— Lines

— Pattern

— Color detail

To build the graphic:

1. Use a graphics application with layers.

2. Make a 1 x 1 pixel checkerboard pattern with the default secondary 3 color (RGB 204-204-204).

3. Apply the pattern only to areas that might dither badly. Leave borders and other detail lines as solid colors.

4. Adjust the transparency setting for the pattern layer until the pattern is dark enough to mix with the color detail without overwhelming it visually. A 25% transparency with the default secondary 2 color (RGB 153-153-153) produces a good result for most graphics.

5. Test your results on your target 8-bit platforms.

6. If a pattern does not solve your problems, try using additional graphics techniques, such as a gradient.

The following table shows the results of graphic reproduction in 8-bit color on different operating systems.

TABLE 4   Variations in Reproduction of 8-Bit Color

Styles	Original Graphic	Microsoft Windows (8 bits)	Mac OS (8 bits)	CDE (8 bits)
Plain				
Dithering added				
Gradient added				
Dithering added to gradient				

The plain graphic in the preceding table, which uses a large area of a single web-safe color, dithers badly on Microsoft Windows and CDE. A gradient effect is added to the original graphic to add some visual interest; this produces a banding effect on Mac OS. Adding the dithered pattern along with the gradient produces good results on all three platforms with 8-bit color. In 16-bit and 24-bit color, the graphic reproduction is very close to, or exactly the same as, the originals.

Categorizing Application Graphics   Application graphics that you
design fall into three broad categories:

- Icons, which represent objects that users can select, open, or drag

- Button graphics, which identify actions, settings, and tools (modes of the application)

- Symbols, which are used for general identification and labeling (for instance, as indicators of conditions or states)

TABLE 5   Examples of Application Graphics

Graphic Type	Examples	Flush 3D Style	Pre-Dithered (With Added Gradients)
Icons			
Button graphics			
Symbols			

☕ Use the GIF file format for application graphics. It usually results in a smaller file size than the JPEG format and uses lossless compression.

🌐 To facilitate localization, place all application graphics in resource bundles.

🌐 Where possible, use globally understood icons, button graphics, and symbols. Where none exist, create them with input from international sources. If you can't create a single symbol that works in all cultures, define appropriate graphics for different locales (but try to minimize this task).

Designing Icons
Icons typically represent containers, documents, network objects, or other data that users can open or manipulate within an application. An **icon** usually appears with identifying text.

Sizes for icons vary from platform to platform. Two common sizes are 16 x 16 pixels and 32 x 32 pixels. In the Java look and feel, the smaller size is used in the title bar of windows (to identify the contents of the window or minimized window) and inside tree components (for container and leaf nodes). You can use 32 x 32 icons for the desktop representation of Microsoft Windows applications and for components in applications designed for users with visual impairments, or for objects in a diagram, such as a network topology.

Design icons to identify clearly the objects or concepts they represent. Keep the drawing style symbolic, as opposed to photo-realistic. Too much detail can make it more difficult for users to recognize what the icon represents.

When designing large and small icons that represent the same object, make sure that they have similar shape, color, and detail.

Specify tool tips for each icon so that assistive technologies can use the `accessibleDescription` property to find out how to use the icon.

Specify the `accessibleName` property for each icon so that assistive technologies can find out what the icon is.

Consider providing an option that enables users to switch from smaller to larger icons.

Since sizes of icons vary across platforms, determine the size requirements of your target platform and provide suitably sized icons.

Working With Icon Styles
Icons can appear as flat drawings or as perspective drawings. The flush 3D style is a unique effect that can be applied to either flat (2D) or perspective (3D) icons.

The following figure shows flush 3D icons for files and folders drawn in the perspective and flat styles. Icons drawn in the flush 3D style fit best with the Java look and feel. For information on how to create the flush 3D style, see "Drawing Icons" on page 87 and "Producing the Flush 3D Effect" on page 90. Three visual elements appear in the sample icons: an interior highlight (to preserve the flush style used throughout the Java look and feel), a pattern to minimize dithering (described in "Working With Available Colors" on page 80), and a dark border.

FIGURE 44   Two Families of Flush 3D Icons

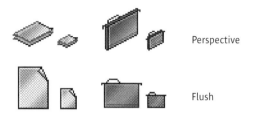

Perspective

Flush

☕ Use a single style to create a "family" of icons that utilize common visual elements to reflect similar concepts, roles, and identity. Icons in families might use a similar palette, size, and style.

☕ Don't mix two- and three-dimensional styles in the same icon family.

☕ Use the flush 3D style so that your icons suit the Java look and feel.

For more on the flush 3D style, see "Producing the Flush 3D Effect" on page 90.

Because icons must appear on various backgrounds across platforms, the borders of graphics must maintain consistent color. Changing the appearance of an object's border to look smoother at screen resolution in relationship to a specific color is called **anti-aliasing**. In most application development cases, anti-aliasing is not desirable because you are unlikely to be sure what background color the object will appear against. However, within an icon, anti-aliasing can provide smoother interior lines.

☕ For satisfactory display on a wide range of background colors and textures, use a clear, dark exterior border and ensure that there is no anti-aliasing or other detail around the perimeter of the graphic.

Drawing Icons   The following section uses a simple folder as an example of how to draw an icon. Before you start, decide on a general design for the object. In this example, a hanging file folder is used to represent a directory.

1. Draw a basic outline shape first.

   Icons can use as much of the available space as possible because they are displayed without borders. Icons should usually be centered horizontally in the available space.

   For vertical spacing, consider aligning to the lower edge of other icons in the set, or aligning with the baseline of text, as shown in the figure.

   If multiple sizes of an icon are required, work on them at the same time rather than trying to scale down a large icon later; all sizes then can evolve into designs that are recognizable as the same object.

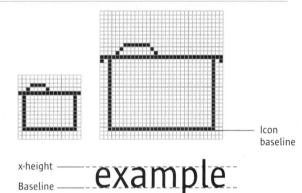

2. Add some basic color (green is used here).

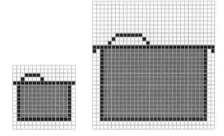

3. Draw a highlight on the inside top and left using white or a lighter shade of the existing color.

   This practice creates the flush 3D style of the Java look and feel.

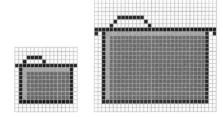

4. Add some detail to the icon.

   In this case, the crease or "fold" mark in the hanging folder is drawn.

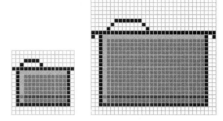

5. Try a gradient that produces a "shining" effect instead of the flat green.

   Here a dark green has replaced the black border on the right and bottom; black is not a requirement as long as there is a well-defined border.

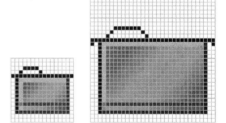

6. Add a pattern to prevent coarse dithering. This technique minimizes banding and dithering on displays with 256 or fewer colors (see "Maximizing Color Quality" on page 82).

   The first graphic is an exploded view of an icon that shows how the pattern is added.

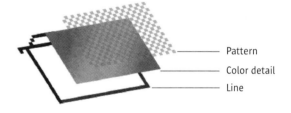

Pattern

Color detail

Line

   The next graphic shows an icon in which a pattern has been added to the color detail.

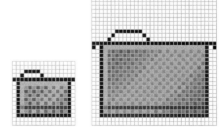

7. Define the empty area around the icon graphic (in which you have not drawn anything) as transparent pixels in the GIF file.

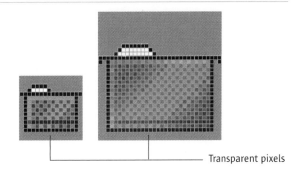

Transparent pixels

This practice ensures that the background color shows through; if the icon is dragged to or displayed on a different background, the area surrounding it matches the color or pattern of the rest of the background.

8. Test your icon on target platforms.

Designing Button Graphics

Button graphics appear inside buttons—most often in toolbar buttons. Such graphics identify the action, setting, mode, or other function represented by the button. For instance, clicking the button might carry out an action (creating a new file) or set a state (boldfaced text).

⊙ For a collection of button graphics designed in the Java look and feel, see Appendix B. The graphics in this repository can also be found on the companion CD-ROM.

The two standard sizes for button graphics are 16 x 16 pixels and 24 x 24 pixels. You can use either size (but not both at the same time) in toolbars or tool palettes, depending on the amount of space available. For details on toolbars, see "Toolbars" on page 186.

It might be appropriate to use toolbar buttons that display text in addition to or instead of graphics. Consider this approach if your usability studies establish that the action, state, or mode represented by the button graphic is difficult for users to comprehend.

If you include both text and graphics in a button, the size of the button will exceed 16 x 16 or 24 x 24 pixels. Consider using tool tips instead, or let users choose between displaying button text or using tool tips. For details, see "Tool Tips for Toolbar Buttons" on page 191.

☕ Use tool tips to help clarify the meaning of toolbar buttons.

☕ When designing your button graphics, clearly show the action, state, or mode that the button initiates.

☕ Keep the drawing style symbolic; too much detail can make it more difficult for users to understand what a button does.

☕ Use a flush 3D border to indicate that a button is clickable.

☕ Draw a distinct dark border without anti-aliasing or other exterior detail (except the flush 3D highlight) around the outside of a button graphic.

⊕ Do not include text as part of your button graphics (GIF files). Use button text instead. Keep the button text in a resource bundle to facilitate localization.

▤⌐ Setting tool tips automatically sets the `accessibleDescription` of an object, which in turn, greatly benefits users with physical and cognitive limitations.

Using Button Graphic Styles   The following figure shows sample button graphics designed for toolbars and for the contents of an internal utility window.

FIGURE 45   Button Graphics for a Toolbar and an Internal Utility Window

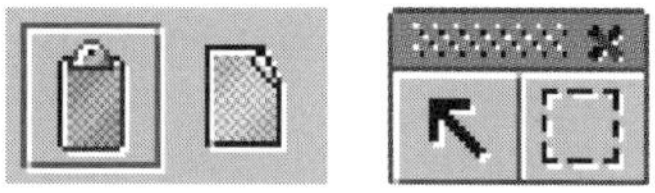

☕ Use a single style to create a "family" of button graphics with common visual elements. You might use a similar color palette, size, and style for all button groups across your GUI, such as toolbar buttons, toggle buttons, or command buttons. Review the graphics in context before finalizing them.

Producing the Flush 3D Effect   The flush 3D effect simulates the appearance of beveled buttons or shapes inset at the same level as the background. To achieve this effect, you need to create a shadow and a highlight for both the background and the button graphic. In smaller button graphics, you can achieve this effect by placing highlights at the correct locations along the edges of the icon. (The shadows are already provided by the darker outline of the button graphic.) In a larger 24 x 24 or 32 x 32 pixel graphic, you can use a graduated highlight within the button graphic to simulate a more smoothly rounded edge.

With the flush 3D effect, the button graphic appears to have a light beveling around the edges.

To produce the flush 3D effect on button graphics, add:

- An exterior white highlight on the outside right and bottom of the button graphic itself

- An interior white highlight on the inside left and top of the button graphic

- A dark shadow inside the exterior white highlight and outside of the interior white highlight (both shadows are already present if you created a button graphic with a dark outline in the first place)

FIGURE 46   Flush 3D Effect in a Button Graphic

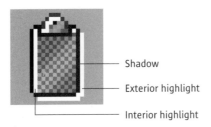

Shadow

Exterior highlight

Interior highlight

Working With Button Borders   The size of a button graphic includes all the pixels within the border. As shown in the following illustration, horizontal and vertical dimensions are both either 16 or 24 pixels. The border abuts the button graphic (that is, there are no pixels between the border and the graphic).

FIGURE 47   Button Graphics With Borders

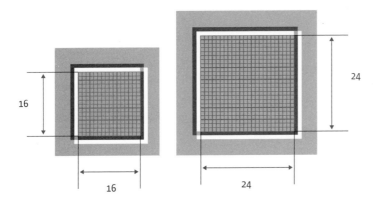

Determining the Primary Drawing Area   Leave an apparent two pixels between
the button border and the graphic. Because the white pixels in both the
button border and the button graphic are less visually significant than the
darker borders, the area used for most of the drawing is offset within the
16 x 16 or 24 x 24 space. Actually, 1 pixel is reserved on the left and top, and
2 pixels are reserved on the right and bottom (but highlights are allowed to
extend in this area). The following illustration shows the standard drawing
area for both button sizes.

FIGURE 48   Primary Drawing Area in Buttons

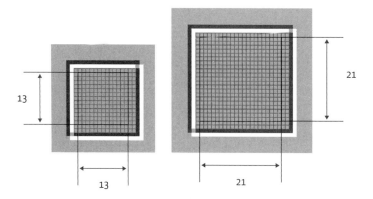

The following illustration shows 16 x 16 and 24 x 24 button graphics that
use the maximum recommended drawing area. On all four sides, there are
2 pixels between the dark border of the button graphic and the dark portion
of the button border.

FIGURE 49   Maximum-Size Button Graphics

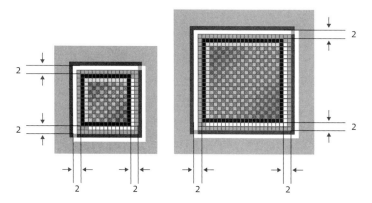

Drawing the Button Graphic When drawing a button graphic, first decide on a general design that represents the action or setting activated by the button. In the following examples, a clipboard represents the Paste command.

1. Decide which sizes you want to use for the button or toolbar graphic and identify your primary drawing area.

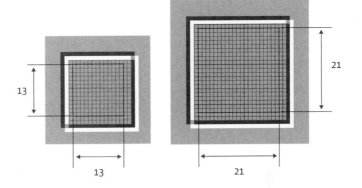

2. Draw a basic outline shape, taking care to remain within the primary drawing area.

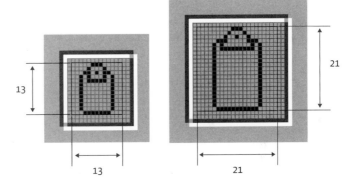

3. Add some basic color.

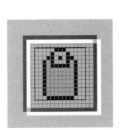
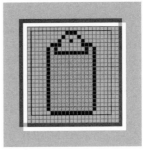

4. Add the flush 3D effect by drawing highlights on the inside left and top, and on the outside bottom and right of the outline. Note that the highlights can extend beyond the primary drawing area.

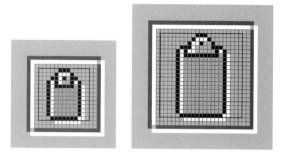

This is a good basic design, but because of the large area using a single color, the graphic lacks visual interest and might not reproduce well on some systems.

5. Try a gradient instead of the flat color.

6. Add a pattern. This technique minimizes banding and dithering on displays with 256 or fewer colors (see "Maximizing Color Quality" on page 82).

— Pattern

— Color detail

— Line

Here is an exploded view of the button graphic and its color overlay.

This figure shows the effect of the pattern on the color detail of the button graphic.

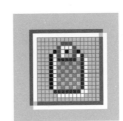

7. Define the empty area around your button graphic (in which you have not drawn anything) as transparent pixels in the GIF file.

   This practice ensures that the background color shows through; if the theme changes, the area around the button graphic will match the rest of the background canvas in the interface.

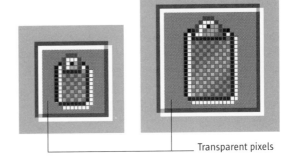

Transparent pixels

8. Test your button graphic on target platforms.

Using Badges in Button Graphics

Badges are a kind of visual shorthand used extensively in toolbar button design. The presence of a menu, the creation of a new object, the addition of an object to a collection, and the review or editing of properties and settings are typically represented by incorporating a **badge** into an existing button graphic. This section suggests standard ways for you to incorporate badges into the design of your toolbar button graphics.

⊙ The badges in the button graphics in this chapter appear in several of the graphics discussed in Appendix B and are included in the graphics on the companion CD-ROM.

Menu Indicators   An arrow in a button graphic indicates that a click (or a press) of the mouse button displays a menu of choices. The following illustration shows the volume toolbar button with a menu indicator.

FIGURE 50   Menu Indicator in a Volume Toolbar Button

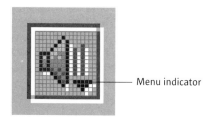

—— Menu indicator

☕ To indicate that a click or press of the mouse button displays a menu, provide an arrow menu indicator in the lower-right corner of toolbar button graphics.

Badges can extend as far as one pixel from the button border, and their highlights can touch the border. Use a 1-pixel-wide transparent area between a badge and the main button graphic to set off the badge visually. The following illustration shows the buffer area around the menu indicator. The buffer area placed around the indicator shows the background of the toolbar button, not the background of the volume graphic. For details, see "Drawing the Button Graphic" on page 93.

FIGURE 51   Menu Indicator and Transparent Buffer Area

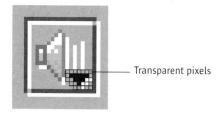

—— Transparent pixels

☕ Use transparent pixels around the menu indicator arrow to set it off from the rest of the button graphic.

☕ Add the standard highlight below or to the right of the badge in a button graphic.

The following figure shows the volume toolbar button with the menu
indicator at actual size (16 x 16 pixels).

FIGURE 52   Volume Toolbar Button (Actual Size)

The lower-right corner is the standard location for the arrow graphic (in
locales with left-to-right reading order). The following illustration shows the
arrows for 16 x 16 and 24 x 24 pixel graphics.

FIGURE 53   Position and Space Around Menu Indicators

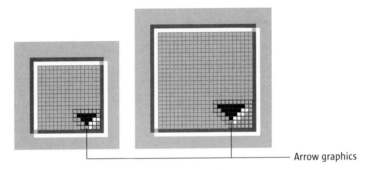

New Object Indicators   Some buttons create new objects. You can use a twinkle
graphic to indicate this button feature. In 16 x 16 pixel graphics, the
twinkle graphic might touch the lower edge of the button border, as shown in
the following illustration.

FIGURE 54   New Object Indicator and Transparent Buffer Area

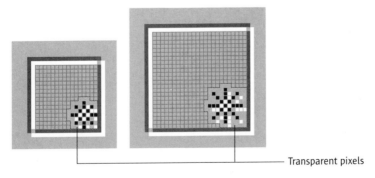

To indicate the creation of a new object, provide a twinkle graphic in
the lower-right corner of toolbar button graphics.

The following illustration shows a twinkle graphic incorporated into a document toolbar button to indicate that clicking the button creates a new document.

FIGURE 55   Document Toolbar Button With a New Object Indicator

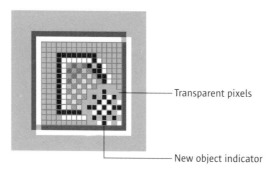

The following figure shows the toolbar button with the new object indicator at its actual size (16 x 16 pixels).

FIGURE 56   New Document Toolbar Button (Actual Size)

Add Object Indicators

Some buttons add objects to a group. You can incorporate an addition symbol into your button, as shown in the following figure, to indicate this aspect of the button's features.

FIGURE 57   Add Object Indicator and Transparent Buffer Area

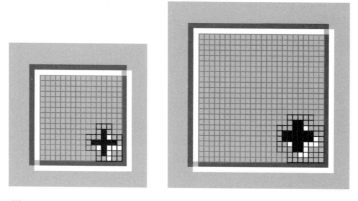

To indicate the addition of a new object to a group, provide an addition symbol in the lower-right corner of toolbar button graphics.

The following figure provides an example of the symbol incorporated into a document toolbar button.

FIGURE 58   Document Toolbar Button With an Add Object Indicator

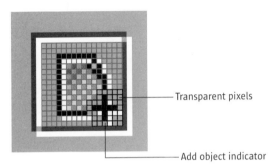

——— Transparent pixels

——— Add object indicator

The following figure shows the toolbar button with the add object indicator at its actual size (16 x 16 pixels).

FIGURE 59   Add Document Toolbar Button (Actual Size)

Properties Indicators   Some buttons open a properties or settings window for the object or action indicated by the main part of the button graphic. You can use a small check mark to represent this action, as shown in the following illustration.

FIGURE 60   Properties Indicator and Transparent Buffer Area

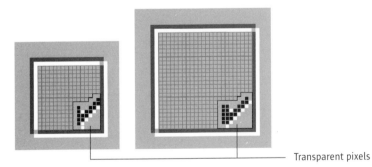

——— Transparent pixels

To indicate the opening of a properties or settings window or panel for the object or action represented by the main part of a button graphic, provide a small check mark in the lower-right corner of toolbar button graphics.

The following figure shows a page setup button with the properties indicator at its actual size (16 x 16 pixels).

FIGURE 61   Page Setup Toolbar Button (Actual Size)

Combining Indicators   As a general rule, you should not need to combine the functions represented by these indicators.

☕ Design toolbar buttons with badges individually rather than adding badges programmatically. This practice ensures that the transparent buffer area is tuned for each indicator.

☕ Do not use more than one of the Java look and feel badges (that is, the menu, new object, add object, or properties indicators) in a single button graphic.

☕ If the button graphic needs to indicate that more choices are available, use a menu indicator and drop-down menu. Ensure that menu items are closely related and parallel.

☕ Do not overload toolbar buttons with features. Ensure that the button graphic and its tool tip clearly indicate the function of the toolbar button.

Designing Symbols   Symbols include any graphic (typically 48 x 48 pixels or smaller) that stands for a state or a concept but has no directly associated action or object. Symbols might appear within dialog boxes, system status alert boxes, and event logs.

The examples in the following figure show the graphics from an Info alert box and a Question alert box and a caution symbol superimposed on a folder icon to indicate a hypothetical state.

The style for symbols is not as narrowly defined as that for icons and button graphics. The examples in the following figure use a flush effect for interior detail but not for the border of the graphic.

FIGURE 62   Symbols

Information   Caution   Question
symbol   symbol   symbol

The question symbol is used in an input alert box, as shown in the following figure.

FIGURE 63   Question Symbol in Alert Box

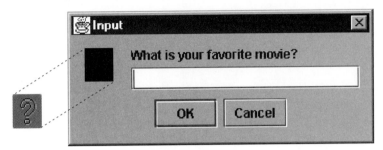

☕ Ensure adequate contrast between a caution symbol and the icon or background it appears against.

Designing Graphics for Corporate and Product Identity

Application graphics present an excellent opportunity for you to heighten your corporate or product identity. This section presents information about splash screens, About boxes, and login splash screens.

NOTE – The examples presented in this section use the sample text-editing and mail applications, MetalEdit and MetalMail. They are not appropriate for third-party use.

☕ Use the JPEG file format for any photographic elements in your splash screens and About boxes.

Designing Splash Screens   A **splash screen** is a plain window that appears briefly in the time between the launch of a program and the appearance of its main application window. Splash screens disappear when the application is ready to run. Nothing other than a blank space is included with a JFC-supplied plain window; you must provide the border and the contents of the splash screen. For instance, the black border on the window in the following figure is part of the file supplied by the splash screen designer.

FIGURE 64   Splash Screen for MetalEdit

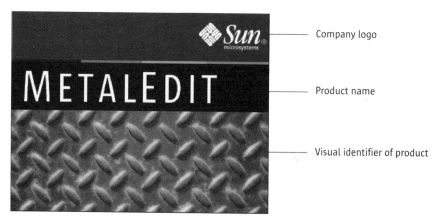

Although not required, splash screens are included in most commercial products. Splash screens typically have the following elements:

- Company logo
- Product name (trademarked, if appropriate)
- Visual identifier of the product or product logo

Check with your legal adviser about requirements for placing copyright notices or other legal information in your splash screens.

To get the black border that is recommended for splash screens, you must include a 1-pixel black border as part of the image you create. (You can get a black border with a border object instead of putting a black line in the image itself.)

The JWindow component, not the JFrame component, is typically used to implement the plain window that provides the basis for splash screens.

Designing Login Splash Screens   If your application requires users to log in, you might consider replacing the traditional splash screen with a simple login window or a combination login and splash screen.

Figure 65 shows the login splash screen for the MetalMail application.

The corresponding code for Figure 65 is available on the companion CD-ROM.

FIGURE 65   Login Splash Screen for MetalMail

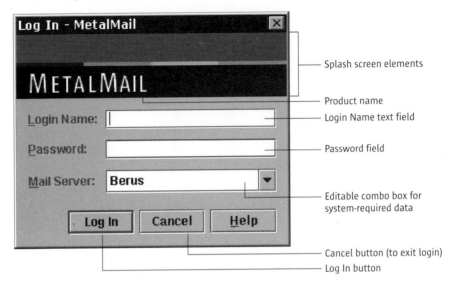

The elements of this screen might include:

- Label and text field for a login user name

- Label and password field

- Labels and interactive components (such as editable combo boxes) for any other information required by the system

- Buttons for logging in and canceling the login splash screen

If you want to increase the chance of users viewing your splash screen, it is a good idea to combine the login window and splash screen.

☕ Provide a way for users to exit the login splash screen without first logging in (if it is possible for users to do anything on the system without first logging in).

▤☞ The JDialog component, not the JWindow component, is typically used to implement a login splash screen.

Designing About Boxes   An About box is a dialog box that contains basic
information about your application.

Figure 66 shows the About box for the MetalMail application.

FIGURE 66   About Box for MetalEdit

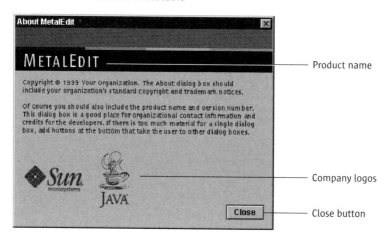

An About box might contain the following elements:

- Product name (trademarked, if appropriate)
- Version number
- Company logo
- Product logo or a visual reminder of the product logo
- Copyright, trademarks, and other legal notices
- Names of contributors to the product

Users typically display About boxes by choosing the About Application item
from the Help menu.

🖳🖳 Because the dialog box title bar might not include a Close button on
all platforms, always include a Close button in your About boxes so that users
can dismiss them after reading them. Follow the guidelines for button
placement described in "Command Buttons in Dialog Boxes" on page 159.

6: BEHAVIOR

Users interact with the computer by means of the mouse, the keyboard, and the screen. (Throughout this book, "mouse" refers to any pointing device, including standard mouse devices, trackballs, track pads, and so forth.) Such interaction constitutes the "feel" portion of the Java look and feel.

This chapter describes mouse operations, pointers, and drag-and-drop operations. It discusses keyboard operations, including the use of keyboard focus, keyboard shortcuts, and mnemonics in Java look and feel applications. It also offers guidance on how to provide feedback regarding application progress or status.

Mouse Operations

In Java look and feel applications, the following common mouse operations are available to users:

- Moving the mouse changes the position of the onscreen **pointer** (often called the "cursor").

- Clicking (pressing and releasing a mouse button) selects or activates the object beneath the pointer. The object is usually highlighted when the mouse button is pressed and then selected or activated when the mouse button is released. For example, users **click** to activate a command button, to select an item from a list, or to set an insertion point in a text area.

- Double-clicking (clicking a mouse button twice in rapid succession without moving the mouse) is used to select larger units (for example, to select a word in a text field) or to select and open an object.

- Triple-clicking (clicking a mouse button three times in rapid succession without moving the mouse) is used to select even larger units (for instance, to select an entire line in a text field).

- Pressing (holding down a mouse button) is used to display drop-down menus, including those marked by menu indicators on buttons.

- Dragging (pressing a mouse button, moving the mouse, and releasing the mouse button) is used to select a range of objects, to choose items from drop-down or contextual menus, or to move objects in the interface. For example, users **drag** to select a range of text in a document.

☕ In your design, assume a two-button mouse. Use **mouse button 1** (usually the left button) for selection, activation of components, dragging, and the display of drop-down menus. Use **mouse button 2** (usually the right button) to display contextual menus. Do not use the **middle mouse button**; it is not available on most target platforms.

☕ Provide keyboard equivalents for all mouse operations, including multiple selections.

🖳🖥 Be aware that Macintosh systems usually have a one-button mouse, other personal computers and network computers usually have a two-button mouse, and UNIX systems usually have a three-button mouse. Macintosh users can simulate mouse button 2 by holding down the Control key while mousing.

The following figure shows the relative placement of mouse buttons 1 and 2 on Macintosh, PC, and UNIX mouse devices.

FIGURE 67   Mouse Buttons and Their Default Assignments

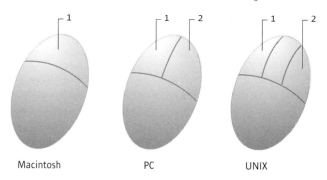

Macintosh   PC   UNIX

Pointer Feedback   The pointer can assume a variety of shapes. For instance, in a text-editing application, the pointer might assume an I-beam shape (called a "text pointer" in the Java 2 platform) to indicate where the insertion point will be if the user presses the mouse button. The **insertion point** is the location where typed text or a dragged or pasted selection will appear. When the pointer moves out of the editor pane, its appearance changes in accordance with the new component the pointer rests over.

The Java look and feel defines a set of pointer types that map to the corresponding native platform pointers; therefore, the appearance of pointers can vary from platform to platform, as shown in the following table. When no corresponding pointer exists in the native platform toolkit, the pointer is supplied by the JFC.

TABLE 6   Pointer Types Available for the Java 2 Platform

Pointer	Macintosh	Microsoft Windows	CDE	Usage in Java Look and Feel Applications
Default				Pointing or selecting
Crosshair	+	+	+	Interacting with graphic objects
Hand				Panning objects by direct manipulation
Move				Moving objects
Text	I	I	I	Selecting or inserting text
Wait				Indicating that an operation is in progress and the user cannot do other tasks
N Resize				Adjusting the upper (northern) border of an object
S Resize				Adjusting the lower (southern) border of an object
E Resize				Adjusting the right (eastern) border of an object
W Resize				Adjusting the left (western) border of an object
NW Resize				Adjusting the upper-left (northwest) corner of an object
NE Resize				Adjusting the upper-right (northeast) corner of an object
SE Resize				Adjusting the lower-right (southeast) corner of an object
SW Resize				Adjusting the lower-left (southwest) corner of an object

In addition to the shapes in Table 6, a pointer graphic can be defined as an image and created using Toolkit.createCustomCursor if you are using the Java 2 platform.

Mouse-over Feedback   Mouse-over feedback is a visual effect that occurs when users move the pointer over an area of an application window without pressing the mouse button.

In the Java look and feel, **mouse-over feedback** can be used to show borders on toolbar buttons when the pointer moves over them. A slightly different effect is used to display tool tips. For details, see "Toolbars" on page 186 and "Tool Tips" on page 191.

Clicking and Selecting Objects   In the JFC, the selection of objects with the mouse is similar to the standard practice for other graphical user interfaces. Users **select** an object by clicking it. Clicking an unselected object also deselects any previous selection.

☕ Follow the general JFC-provided rules for text selection:

- A single click deselects any existing selection and sets the insertion point.

- A double click on a word deselects any existing selection and selects the word.

- A triple click in a line of text deselects any existing selection and selects the line.

- A Shift-click extends a selection using the same units as the previous selection (character, word, line, and so forth).

- Dragging (that is, moving the mouse while holding down mouse button 1) through a range of text deselects any existing selection and selects the range.

☕ Follow the general JFC-provided rules for selection in selectable lists and tables:

- A click on an object deselects any existing selection and selects the object.

- A Shift-click on an object extends the selection from the most recently selected object to the current object.

- A Control-click on an object toggles its selection without affecting the selection of any other objects. This operation can result in disjoint selections.

Displaying Contextual Menus   It can be difficult for users to find and access desired features given all the commands in the menus and submenus of a complex application. Contextual menus (sometimes called "pop-up menus") enable you to make functions easily accessible by associating them with appropriate objects.

Users can open contextual menus in two ways:

■ To pull down the menu, users can press and hold mouse button 2 over a relevant object. Then they can drag to the desired menu item and release the mouse button to choose the item.

■ To post the menu (that is, to pull down the menu and leave it open), users can click mouse button 2 over a relevant object. Then they can click the desired menu item to choose it. The menu is dismissed when a menu item is chosen or the area outside the menu is clicked.

⊙   The corresponding code for Figure 68 is available on the companion CD-ROM.

FIGURE 68   Contextual Menu for a Text Selection

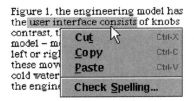

⎕⎕ Because users often have difficulty knowing whether contextual menus are available and what is in them, ensure that the items in your contextual menu also appear in the menu bar or toolbar of the primary windows in your application.

⎕⎕ Users on the Microsoft Windows and UNIX platforms display a contextual menu by clicking or pressing mouse button 2. Macintosh users hold down the Control key while clicking.

Drag-and-Drop Operations   Drag-and-drop operations include moving, copying, or linking selected objects by dragging them from one location and dropping them over another. These operations provide a convenient and intuitive way to perform many tasks using direct manipulation. Common examples of **drag and drop** in the user interface are moving files by dragging file icons between folders or dragging selected text from one document to another. The Java 2 platform supports drag and drop

within an application, between two Java applications, or between a Java application and a native application. For example, on a Microsoft Windows system, users can drag a text selection from a Java application and drop it into a Microsoft Word document.

☕ Provide keyboard equivalents for all drag-and-drop operations (such as Cut, Copy, and Paste).

Typical Drag and Drop

Drag and drop in Java applications is similar to dragging behavior on other platforms. Users press mouse button 1 while the pointer is over a source object and then drag the object by moving the pointer while holding down the mouse button. To drop the object, users release the button when the pointer is over a suitable destination. A successful drop triggers an action that depends on the nature of the source and destination. If the drag source is part of a range selection, the entire selection (for example, several file icons or a range of text) is dragged. To cancel a drag-and-drop operation after it has started, users drop the object over an invalid destination or press the Escape key.

Pointer and Destination Feedback

During any drag-and-drop operation, your Java look and feel application needs to give visual feedback using the pointer and the destination.

☕ Provide the user with feedback that a drag operation is in progress by changing the shape of the pointer when the drag is initiated. Use different pointers to distinguish operations (such as copying or moving).

☕ Provide destination feedback so users know where the dragged object can be dropped. Use one or both of the following methods to provide destination feedback:

- Change the shape of the pointer to reflect whether the object is over a possible drop target.

- Highlight drop targets when the pointer is over them to indicate that they can accept the selection or source.

⊟⊏⊃ Java objects are specified by their **MIME** (Multipurpose Internet Mail Extensions) types, and the Java™ runtime environment automatically translates back and forth between MIME types and system-native types as needed. As an object is dragged over potential targets, each potential target can query the drag source to obtain a list of available data types and then compare that with the list of data types that it can accept. For example, when dragging a range of text, the source might be able to deliver the text in a number of different encodings such as plain text, styled text, or HTML text. If there is a match in data types, potential targets should be highlighted as the pointer passes over them to indicate that they can accept the dragged object.

Keyboard Operations

The Java look and feel assumes a PC-style keyboard. The standard ASCII keys are used, along with the following modifier keys: Shift, Control, and Alt (Option on the Macintosh); the function keys F1 through F12; the four arrow keys; Delete, Backspace, Home, End, Page Up, and Page Down. Enter and Return are equivalent. (Return does not appear on PC keyboards.)

A **modifier key** is a key that does not produce an alphanumeric character but can be used in combination with other keys to alter the meaning of those keys. Typical modifier keys in Java look and feel applications are Shift, Control, and Alt.

This section provides recommendations for the use of **keyboard operations**, which include keyboard shortcuts, mnemonics, and other forms of navigation, selection, and activation that utilize the keyboard instead of the mouse. (See Appendix A for more on keyboard operations.)

A **mnemonic** is an underlined letter that typically appears in a menu title, menu item, or the text of a button or other component. The underlined letter reminds users how to activate the equivalent command by pressing the Alt key and the character key that corresponds to the underlined letter. For instance, you could use a mnemonic to give keyboard focus to a text area or to activate a command button. A **keyboard shortcut** (sometimes called an "accelerator") is a keystroke combination (such as Control-A) that activates a menu item from the keyboard even if the relevant menu is not currently displayed.

Keyboard Focus

The **keyboard focus** (sometimes called "input focus") designates the active window or component where the user's next keystrokes will take effect. Focus typically moves when users click a component with a pointing device or move to the next component using keyboard equivalents. Either way, users designate the window, or component within a window, that receives input. (Many toolbar buttons are exceptions: for instance, a left-alignment button on a toolbar should not take focus away from the text area where the actual work is taking place.)

☕ When a window is first opened, assign initial keyboard focus to the
component that would normally be used first. Often, this is the component
appearing in the upper-left portion of the window. If keyboard focus is not
assigned to a component in the active window, the keyboard navigation and
control mechanisms cannot be used. The assignment of initial keyboard focus
is especially important for people who use only a keyboard to navigate
through your application—for instance, those with visual or mobility
impairments and many power users.

In the Java look and feel, many components (including command buttons,
checkboxes, radio buttons, toggle buttons, list boxes, combo boxes, tabbed
panes, editable cells, and tree components) indicate keyboard focus by
displaying a rectangular border (blue, in the default color theme).

FIGURE 69   Keyboard Focus Indicated by Rectangular Border

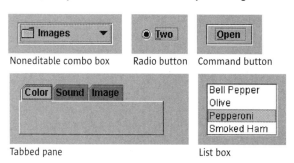

Editable text components, such as text fields, indicate keyboard focus by
displaying a blinking bar at the insertion point.

FIGURE 70   Keyboard Focus Indicated by Blinking Bar at Insertion Point

Menus indicate focus with a colored background for menu titles or menu items (blue, in the default color theme).

⊙ The corresponding code for Figure 71 is available on the companion CD-ROM.

FIGURE 71   Keyboard Focus Indicated by Colored Background

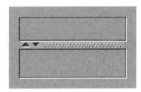

Drop-down menu

Split panes and sliders indicate focus by darkening the zoom buttons and slider indicator (blue, in the default color theme) respectively.

FIGURE 72   Keyboard Focus Indicated by Drag Texture

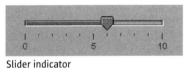

Slider indicator

Split pane zoom buttons

Keyboard Navigation and Activation   Keyboard **navigation** enables users to move keyboard focus from one user interface component to another using the keyboard. Navigation does not necessarily affect the selection and does not, by itself, cause activation. Keyboard **activation**, on the other hand, enables users to cause an action by using the keyboard.

In general, pressing the Tab key moves focus through the major components; Shift-Tab moves through the components in the reverse direction. Control-Tab and Control-Shift-Tab work in a similar fashion and are necessary when keyboard focus is in an element that accepts tabs, such as a text area. Arrow keys are often used to move within groups of components—for example, Tab puts focus in a list box and then the arrow keys move focus among the list box items. The Tab key is used to move among checkboxes.

Once an element has focus, pressing the spacebar typically activates its function, such as selecting or deselecting a checkbox. In a list component, pressing Shift-spacebar extends the selection; pressing Control-spacebar toggles the selection state of the current item without affecting any other selections. (Using the up and down arrow keys actually changes the selection in a list component.)

Some components do not need explicit keyboard focus to be operated. For example, users activate the default button in a dialog box by pressing the Enter or Return key. Similarly, scrollbars can be operated from the keyboard using keys such as Page Up and Page Down if focus is anywhere within the scroll pane.

Keyboard navigation can be useful not only for accessibility purposes but also for power users or users who choose alternative input methods like voice input or touch screens.

Ensure that all application functions are accessible from the keyboard by unplugging the mouse and testing the application's keyboard operations.

Some of the keyboard operations in the tables in Appendix A are temporarily incomplete or unimplemented. However, the key sequences listed in this appendix should be reserved for future versions of the JFC and the Java 2 platform.

Common keyboard navigation and activation operations are summarized in the following table.

TABLE 7   Common Navigation and Activation Keys

Keyboard Operation	Action
Tab[1]	Navigates to the next focusable component
Control-Tab[1]	Navigates to the next focusable component (works even if the component that previously had focus accepts tabs)
Left arrow	Moves focus left one character or component
Right arrow	Moves focus right one character or component
Up arrow	Moves focus up one line or component
Down arrow	Moves focus down one line or component
Page Up	Moves up one pane of information
Page Down	Moves down one pane of information

TABLE 7   Common Navigation and Activation Keys *(Continued)*

Keyboard Operation	Action
Home	Moves to the beginning of the data; in a table, moves to the beginning of a row
End	Moves to the end of the data; in a table, moves to the last cell in a row
Enter or Return	Activates the default command button
Escape	Dismisses a menu or dialog box without changes; cancels a drag-and-drop operation in progress
Spacebar	Activates the component that has keyboard focus

1. With Shift key, reverses direction

NOTE – The keyboard operations described in the previous table generally have separate actions for navigation and activation. For the keyboard shortcuts and mnemonics described in the following sections, however, the same action performs both navigation and activation.

Keyboard Shortcuts   Keyboard shortcuts are keystroke combinations that activate a menu item from the keyboard even if the menu for that command is not currently displayed. Keyboard shortcuts usually consist of a modifier key and a character key, like Control-Z, plus a few special keys such as F1 and Delete. Unlike mnemonics, keyboard shortcuts do not post menus; rather, they perform the indicated actions directly. Since all keyboard shortcuts are available at all times, you cannot reuse them as you do mnemonics.

Figure 73 shows an example of keyboard shortcuts and mnemonics on a typical Edit menu.

⊙ The corresponding code for Figure 73 is available on the companion CD-ROM.

FIGURE 73   Edit Menu With Keyboard Shortcuts and Mnemonics

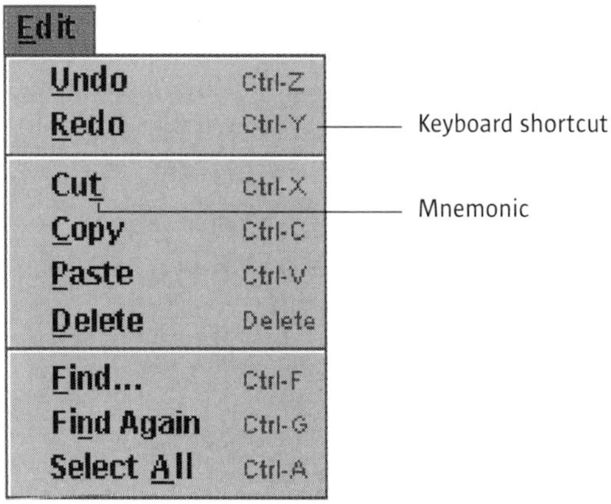

To use a keyboard shortcut in Java look and feel applications, users typically hold down the Control key (and optionally, an additional modifier key, such as Shift) and press the character key that is shown after the menu item; in some cases, they press the single key that corresponds to the shortcut, such as the Delete key in the previous figure. Typing a keyboard shortcut has the same effect as choosing the corresponding menu item. For instance, to undo an action, users can either choose the Undo item from the Edit menu or hold down the Control key and press Z.

Specify keyboard shortcuts for frequently used menu items to provide an alternative to mouse operation. You do not need to provide a shortcut for all commands.

Display keyboard shortcuts using the standard abbreviations for key names (such as Ctrl for the Control key), separated by hyphens.

Be aware of and use the common shortcuts across platforms. If your application doesn't use a particular command, you can use that common shortcut for some other command. However, if a later version of your application is likely to contain the common command, reserve the shortcut so future users won't have to relearn your shortcuts.

Do not use the Meta key (the Command key on the Macintosh platform) for a keyboard shortcut, except as an alternate for Control. It is not available on some target platforms.

The common keyboard shortcuts (in the order of their use in menus) are summarized in the following table. For an alphabetical listing of the shortcuts in this table, see "Common Keyboard Shortcuts" on page 246.

TABLE 8   Common Keyboard Shortcuts (Organized by Menus)

Sequence	Equivalent
Ctrl-N	New (File menu)
Ctrl-O	Open (File menu)
Ctrl-W	Close (File menu)
Ctrl-S	Save (File menu)
Ctrl-P	Print (File menu)
Ctrl-Z	Undo (Edit menu)
Ctrl-Y	Redo (Edit menu)
Ctrl-X	Cut (Edit menu)
Ctrl-C	Copy (Edit menu)
Ctrl-V	Paste (Edit menu)
Delete	Delete (Edit menu)
Ctrl-F	Find (Edit menu)
Ctrl-G	Find Again (Edit menu)
Ctrl-A	Select All (Edit menu)
Ctrl-H	Replace (Edit menu)
Ctrl-B	Bold (Format menu)
Ctrl-I	Italic (Format menu)
Ctrl-U	Underline (Format menu)
Ctrl-L	Align Left (Format menu)
Ctrl-E	Align Center (Format menu)
Ctrl-R	Align Right (Format menu)
F1	Help
Shift-F1	Contextual help
F5	Refresh

🖥️ Because each platform has its own standard keyboard shortcuts, ensure that any new keyboard shortcuts you have created are compatible with existing shortcuts on all your target platforms.

🌐 To ease the localization process, place keyboard shortcuts in resource bundles. If it turns out that something needs to be localized because of a situation specific to a particular language, resource bundles facilitate the process.

Mnemonics   Mnemonics provide yet another keyboard alternative to the mouse. A mnemonic is an underlined alphanumeric character in a menu title, menu item, or other interface component. It reminds the user how to activate the equivalent command by simultaneously pressing the Alt key and the character key that corresponds to the underlined letter or numeral.

⊙ The corresponding code for Figure 74 is available on the companion CD-ROM.

FIGURE 74   File Menu With Mnemonics and Keyboard Shortcuts

When keyboard focus is not in a text element, the Alt modifier is not always required. Menus are an example. For instance, to choose the Exit command from the File menu, the user can hold down the Alt key and press F to post the File menu, release the Alt key, and then press X.

Unlike keyboard shortcuts, mnemonics can be reused from one context to another. Once users have displayed a menu with a keyboard sequence, the subsequent keypress can activate a command only from that menu. Hence, users can press Alt-F to display the File menu and then type A to activate the Save As command, or press Alt-E to display the Edit menu, and then type A to activate the Select All command.

You should provide mnemonics for components within the dialog boxes in your application. In dialog boxes, users must press a modifier key to activate the associated component. For instance, within a dialog box, you might have a mnemonic for the Help button. Once keyboard focus is within the dialog box, users press Alt and then H to activate the Help button.

☕ Provide a mnemonic for all menu titles, menu items, and dialog box components in your application.

☕ Do not associate mnemonics with the default button or the Cancel button in a dialog box. Use Enter or Return for the default button and Escape for the Cancel button instead.

☕ Choose mnemonics that avoid conflicts within a context. For instance, you should not use the letter P as the mnemonic for both the Print and Page Setup commands in the File menu.

☕ Ensure that the mnemonics associated with menu titles are not reused in any context in which the menus are active.

☕ When you assign mnemonics, follow these guidelines in the specified order.

1. Use common mnemonics as they appear in Table 9. (For an alphabetical listing of the mnemonics, see Table 13 on page 247.)

2. If the mnemonic does not appear in the table of common mnemonics, choose the first letter of the menu item. (For instance, choose J for Justify.)

3. If the first letter of the menu item conflicts with the mnemonics of other items, choose a prominent consonant. (For instance, the letter S may have already been designated as the mnemonic for the Style command. Therefore, choose the letter Z as the mnemonic for the Size command.)

4. If the first letter of the menu item and the prominent consonant conflict with those of other menu items, choose a prominent vowel.

⊕ Place mnemonics in resource bundles to facilitate the localization process.

TABLE 9   Common Mnemonics (Organized by Menu)

Menu Titles	Menu Items
<u>F</u>ile	<u>N</u>ew, <u>O</u>pen, <u>C</u>lose, <u>S</u>ave, S<u>a</u>ve As, Page Set<u>u</u>p, <u>P</u>rint, E<u>x</u>it
<u>E</u>dit	<u>U</u>ndo, <u>R</u>edo, Cu<u>t</u>, <u>C</u>opy, <u>P</u>aste, <u>D</u>elete, <u>F</u>ind, Fi<u>n</u>d Again, Select <u>A</u>ll
Fo<u>r</u>mat	<u>F</u>ont, <u>S</u>tyle, Si<u>z</u>e, <u>B</u>old, <u>I</u>talic, <u>U</u>nderline, Align <u>L</u>eft, Align <u>C</u>enter, Align <u>R</u>ight
<u>V</u>iew	Lar<u>g</u>e Icons, S<u>m</u>all Icons, <u>L</u>ist, <u>D</u>etails, <u>S</u>ort By, <u>F</u>ilter, <u>Z</u>oom In, Zoom <u>O</u>ut, <u>R</u>efresh
<u>H</u>elp	<u>C</u>ontents, <u>T</u>utorial, <u>I</u>ndex, <u>S</u>earch, <u>A</u>bout Application

☕ Enable users to use the Tab key navigate to components without their own text or labels. For instance, a text field might be dependent on a checkbox or a radio button, as shown in the following figure.

FIGURE 75   Navigating to a Component Without Associated Text

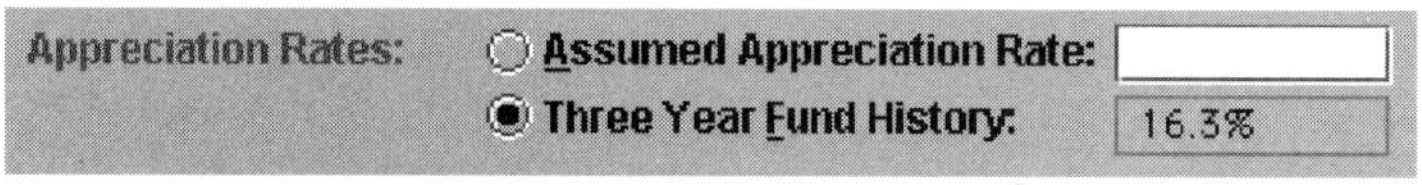

⊕ Mnemonics vary by locale, so use letters that occur in the localized strings. However, for nonalphabetic languages, use the English mnemonic at the trailing edge of the string. For an example, see Figure 18 on page 49.

▤▭ The setMnemonic method can be used to specify mnemonics for buttons, checkboxes, radio buttons, toggle buttons, and menu titles. For components such as text fields, list boxes, and combo boxes that do not have text of their own, mnemonics can be specified on associated labels. The setDisplayedMnemonic method can be used for labels, and the setMnemonic method for menu items. The labelFor property is used to associate the label and its mnemonic with the appropriate component.

▤▭ The Java language underlines the first instance of a letter that appears in the string regardless of whether that instance of the letter led the designer to choose it as the mnemonic. Hence, it would display the mnemonic for the Save As command as S<u>a</u>ve As, not Save <u>A</u>s.

Operational Feedback

Users interact more smoothly with your application if you keep them informed about the application's state. The information you provide can include a response to an action that a user is intentionally controlling (such as changing the shape of the pointer), or you can offer feedback about actions that the application is performing on its own (such as a long copying operation). This section focuses on feedback about operations that the application performs on its own once the user initiates them.

You can use three kinds of visual feedback for operations that take a long time to complete:

- Pointer feedback — changes the shape of the pointer (which tracks the mouse or other pointing device)

- Progress animation — an indicator such as a progress bar that shows what percentage of an operation is complete

- Status animation — an animation that shows an operation is ongoing

Animation is especially beneficial when you want to communicate that the system is busy. Progress indication shows users the state of an operation; status animation lets users know that an application or a part of an application is not available until an operation is done. For more about animation in your interface, see "Animation" on page 76.

When your application is processing a long operation and users can continue to work in other areas of the application, provide them with information regarding the state of the process.

During a long operation, when users must wait until the operation is complete, change the shape of the pointer. For example, an application's pointer might change to the wait pointer after the user selects a file and before the file opens.

For information on the JFC-supplied pointer shapes available in the Java look and feel, see Table 6 on page 107.

Use a wait pointer whenever users are (or could be) blocked from interaction with the application for more than 2 seconds.

Use a progress bar whenever users are blocked from interacting with the application for more than 6 seconds.

Use a progress bar when users want to know when or whether the operation has been completed, and the absolute or approximate proportion of completion can be determined.

☕ Use a status animation when an activity will take 6 or more seconds and you can communicate only whether the process is live or not.

Progress Animation   Progress animation consists of a progress bar or percentage indicator that is generated by an application. You can use progress animation to describe any job in progress.

The most useful form of progress animation, a **progress bar**, is an interface element that indicates one or more operations are in progress and shows users what proportion of the operation has been completed. The progress bar consists of a rectangular bar that fills as the operation progresses, as shown in the following figure.

FIGURE 76   Progress Bar

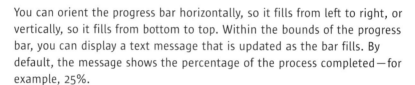

You can orient the progress bar horizontally, so it fills from left to right, or vertically, so it fills from bottom to top. Within the bounds of the progress bar, you can display a text message that is updated as the bar fills. By default, the message shows the percentage of the process completed—for example, 25%.

☕ If you know the estimated length of an operation (for example, if the user is copying files) or the number of operations, use the Java look and feel progress bar. This bar fills as the operation progresses.

☕ When the user performs an operation whose function can be accurately estimated, show the time remaining as part of the progress bar. For example, you might use the message, "Two hours and 18 minutes remaining." In most cases, you will need to base your estimate on typical throughput and adjust your estimate as you determine how the current system load or network delay affects throughput. These calculations sometimes result in an increase in the remaining time.

☕ When the user performs an operation on objects of known size, or when only the number of objects is known, equate the length of the progress bar to the total units of work to be performed.

☕ Update the progress bar to show the proportion completed at least every 4 seconds. If you overestimate how much is already done, the progress bar can remain at 99 percent until the task is complete. If you underestimate how much is already done, fill the remaining portion of the progress bar when the operation completes. The percentage done should never decrease.

⬛ Use the most accurate form of progress bar (time remaining, proportion remaining, objects remaining) available, given the data you are trying to time.

⬛ Users cannot interact with a progress bar. If you would like to enable users to set a value in a range, use the slider (implemented with the JSlider component).

Figure 77 shows the use of progress animation in a progress dialog box.

⊙ The corresponding code for Figure 77 is available on the companion CD-ROM.

FIGURE 77   Animation in a Progress Dialog Box

Progress bar

Status Animation   When you have no numeric information on which to base your progress estimates, use a status animation to reassure the user that an otherwise invisible activity is still in progress and the system has not crashed.

A status animation is a sequence of images designed to inform users that an operation is in progress. A status animation loops endlessly until the operation finishes or the user acts to stop the operation. The animation reassures users that an otherwise invisible activity is still in progress and the system has not crashed. Because the display duration of any status animation is often unknown, you should design the loop to run continuously until the operation completes.

For each status animation, include a still image and an animation. The still image indicates that a process has stopped or that the system is inactive. Make the still image different from the animation sequence so that users can easily tell whether an activity is in progress (though possibly stalled) or the system is quiescent.

⬛ When creating system status animation, consider the target users and their environment. If the animation needs to be visible from across the room, a bolder animation coupled with sound might be effective. On the other hand, that same animation viewed by a user sitting at the workstation would be annoying.

☕ When feasible, let users configure system status animation, so they can adapt their systems to the environment.

☕ In your status animations, provide two files, one an animation sequence to display the active status and the other a still image to display the inactive status.

⌨ Screen readers, which are used by people with visual impairments, do not recognize images. Use the `accessibleDescription` field to describe what is represented by the animation and change the description appropriately when the status of the animation changes. Make sure that this information results in a `propertyChange` event so that the user can be notified of the change.

Design for Smooth Interaction

As a human interface designer, you do more than assemble the proper interface components in a window. You also lay out the components to help users understand the tasks they face and to foster a natural flow through the activities. Good interface design frequently goes unnoticed because everything works as expected. Users notice a poorly designed application that puts GUI obstacles in their way. Thought, attention to detail, and testing with real users can eliminate these difficulties.

This section examines the interaction flow in a simple login dialog box, showing how careful attention to detail makes a significant difference in the user experience. For more information, see "Login Dialog Boxes" on page 165. For a discussion of password fields, see "Password Fields" on page 219.

Initial Focus

The login dialog box in Figure 78 is for MetalManage, a hypothetical management application. This particular application requires users to type both a login name and a password. When the dialog box initially appears, the Login Name and Password fields are empty, and keyboard focus is in the Login Name field, which is typically the first place that users type information. The Log In button is unavailable because the application requires a login name and password, and those fields are currently empty.

⊙ The corresponding code for Figure 78 is available on the companion CD-ROM.

FIGURE 78   Simple Login Dialog Box in Its Initial Configuration

☕ Whenever possible, design an interaction flow that prevents users from making errors. For instance, make the Log In button unavailable until the text fields of a login dialog box are filled in because pressing the button earlier would result in an error.

Navigation   This login dialog box is designed with a standard tab traversal order. As shown in the following figure, keyboard focus starts in the Login Name text field, progresses to the Password field, then moves to the buttons in the command button row, and finally loops back to the first text field. (The Log In button is automatically dropped from the traversal order when it is unavailable.) Users can navigate through the dialog box by:

- Using the mouse
- Pressing the Tab key (or Ctrl-Tab) to move forward through the components
- Pressing Shift-Tab (or Ctrl-Shift-Tab) to move backward through the components
- Using mnemonics

Most users find that their interaction with login dialog boxes becomes habitual.

FIGURE 79   Standard Tab Traversal in a Login Dialog Box

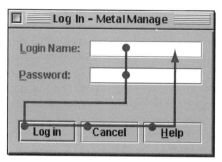

☕ Ensure that keyboard navigation works smoothly in all dialog boxes. Many users want to perform operations such as logging in using only the keyboard.

The typical login sequence for most users involves typing a login name, pressing Tab to advance focus to the Password field, typing a password, and pressing Enter (or Return) to activate the Log In button.

This sequence works work well if the Log In button is the default command button. However, making the Log In button the default button creates a possible annoyance. Some users, particularly in login dialog boxes, habitually press the Enter key to advance to the next text field.

In a quick usability study conducted with this dialog box, about 25 percent of users pressed the Enter key after typing their login names. Therefore, the design was changed so that if users press Enter in the Login Name field, keyboard focus advances to the Password field. Although this behavior is not standard for the Enter key, it allows for very smooth use by the minority of users who want to type their login names, press Enter, type their passwords, and press Enter to get logged in. Furthermore, it does not interfere with the typical use of the Tab key by most users.

If the Log In button had been the default button, pressing Enter after typing a login name would activate the Log In button. An error would occur because the user had not typed in a password. As a result, the new design made the Log In button unavailable until both the Login Name and Password fields contain text.

Password Field   As soon as both the Login Name and Password fields contain text, the Log In button becomes available and becomes the default button (as shown in the following figure). Users can then press Enter to activate the Log In button.

FIGURE 80   Standard Login Dialog Box With Filled-in Text Fields

If your application allows null passwords, the interaction is a little more complex. In that case, make the Log In button available as soon as users type a character in the Login Name field, so that they can attempt to log in without typing a password. However, do not make the Log In button the *default* button until keyboard focus moves to the Password field. Then users who press Enter to move to the Password field cannot activate the Log In button by mistake. Instead, move the focus to the Password field and only then make the Log In button the default command button. Users can type in a password, if any, and then press Enter to activate the Log In button.

FIGURE 81   Login Dialog Box With Null Passwords

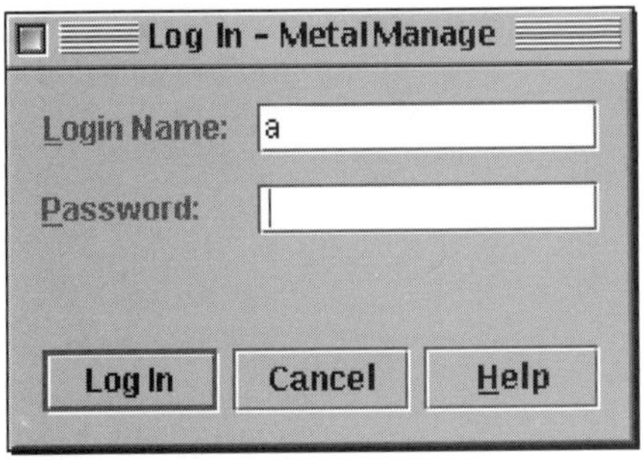

Status and Error Messages   The login dialog box has more than the recommended 17 pixels between the Password field and the command button row. That extra space is used for displaying status messages, such as the progress notification shown in the following figure.

FIGURE 82   Status Message in a Login Dialog Box

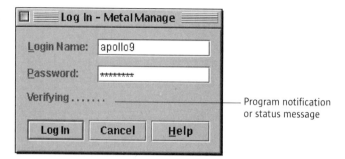

— Program notification or status message

A status message appears in the form of a label while the system is verifying the login attempt. Dots are added to the label at about 1 dot per second to indicate that the system is still working.

You can use this same extra space to display short error messages—for example, if the login attempt fails. You could display such error messages in a standard error alert box. However, as long as the error message is brief, as shown in the following figure, the status area in the login dialog box provides a simple alternative that doesn't require users to dismiss a separate dialog box.

FIGURE 83   Error Message in a Login Dialog Box

— Error message

Note that the text in the Login Name field is automatically selected when the login fails, enabling users to type in a new login name easily or to press Tab or Enter to navigate to the Password field (which then appears with its contents selected).

Users typically observe the status area during the login attempt, so an error message displayed there is easily seen, especially with the accompanying graphic. Nevertheless, it is also advisable to play a sound when the error message appears. The sound helps distracted users as well as visually impaired people. Be sure to offer users the option to turn off the sound.

Text Selection and Filled Text Fields   When keyboard focus enters a text field (unless it does so because of a user click in the field), select any existing text in the field and place the insertion point at the end of the text, as shown in the following figure. Users can then start typing characters to replace the existing text or they can press the Tab key to move to the next field, leaving the original text intact.

When the text is selected, pressing the left or right arrow key deselects the text and moves the insertion point (if possible), enabling users to correct the text using only the keyboard. Of course, if users click in a text field, place the insertion point as close to the click point as possible, without selecting text. For more information on editable text field navigation, see "Editable Text Fields" on page 218.

FIGURE 84   Entering a Filled Text Field

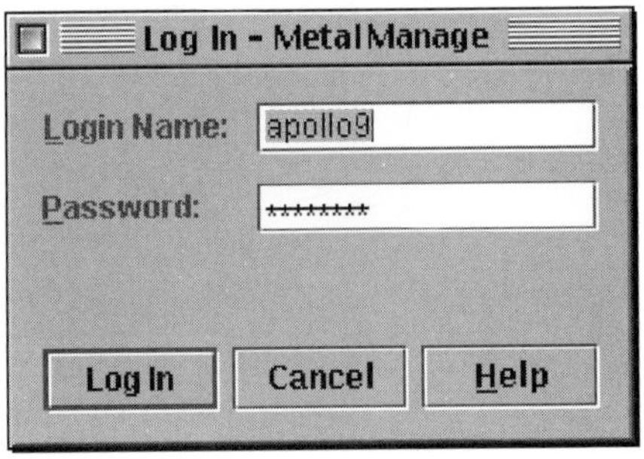

PART III: THE COMPONENTS OF THE JAVA FOUNDATION CLASSES

7: WINDOWS AND PANES

A window is a user interface element and **container** that designers use to organize the information that users see in an application. The information in a window consists of objects (and their properties) that enable users to perform actions or to report information about actions. Primary windows, secondary windows, utility windows, and plain windows provide the top-level containers for your application. A **primary window** is a window in which the user's main interaction with the data or document takes place. An application can use any number of primary windows, which can be opened, closed, minimized, or resized independently. A **secondary window** is a supportive window that is dependent on a primary window (or another secondary window). A **utility window** is a window whose contents affect an active primary window. Unlike secondary windows, utility windows remain open when primary windows are closed or minimized. An example of a utility window is a tool palette that is used to select a graphic tool. A **plain window** is a window with no title bar or window controls, typically used for splash screens.

FIGURE 85   Primary, Utility, Plain, and Secondary Windows

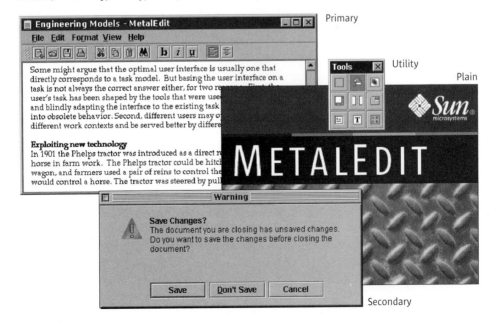

Panels, panes, and internal windows are lower-level containers for use within primary and secondary windows. A **panel** is a container for organizing the contents of a window, dialog box, or applet. A **pane** is a collective term for scroll panes, split panes, and tabbed panes, which are described in this chapter. (You can place panels in panes or panes in panels.) An **internal window** is a container used in MDI applications to create windows that users cannot drag outside of the main backing window.

FIGURE 86   Scroll Pane, Tabbed Pane, Split Pane, and Internal Window

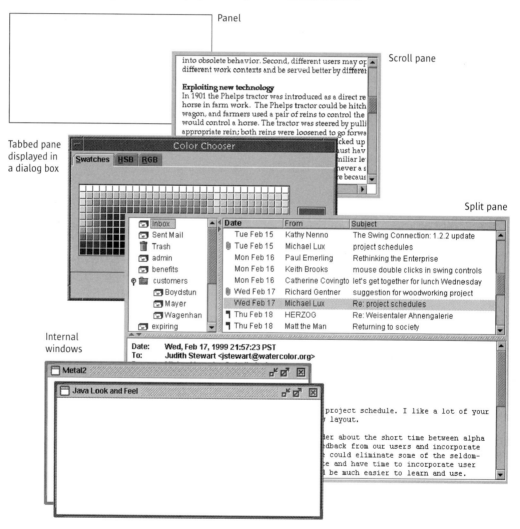

When you begin to organize the information in an application, ask yourself these questions:

- Should information appear in a primary window or a secondary window?
- Which information goes in which kind of window?
- How are different kinds of windows titled?

This chapter uses the concept of an **object**, an entity your application presents in its interface and that users manipulate. While an object can be logical to the user, it might have little relationship to the implementation of the application. Objects have properties or sets of values that users can view or change. Objects also have actions or operations that can be performed on them.

Objects might be documents, the computers that an application monitors, or even log entries—for example, a word processor works with documents, chapters, and paragraphs. A mail program works with mail servers, mailboxes, and mail messages.

Anatomy of a Primary Window

Primary windows act as top-level containers for the user interface elements that appear inside them. A primary window might hold a series of embedded containers. For example, a primary window in your application could have this organization:

- The window frame contains a menu bar and a panel
- The menu bar contains menus
- The panel contains a toolbar and a scroll pane and scrollbar
- The toolbar contains toolbar buttons
- The scroll pane contains an editor pane with a plug-in editor kit for styled text

FIGURE 87   Components Contained in a Primary Window

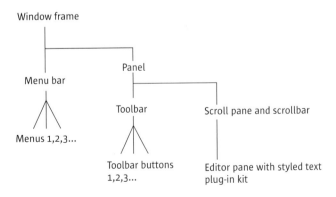

Note the appearance of the embedded containers in an actual primary window and their relationship to the underlying structure, as shown in Figure 88.

FIGURE 88 Anatomy of a Primary Window

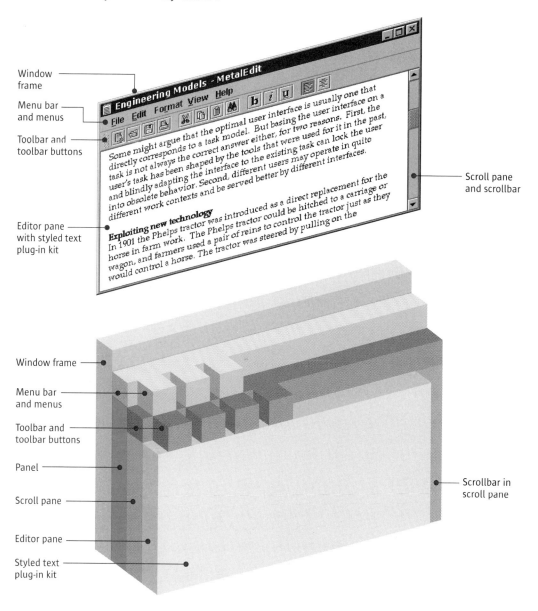

Constructing Windows

A primary window, secondary window, utility window, or plain window can serve as a **top-level container** for interface elements in your application.

FIGURE 89   Top-Level Containers

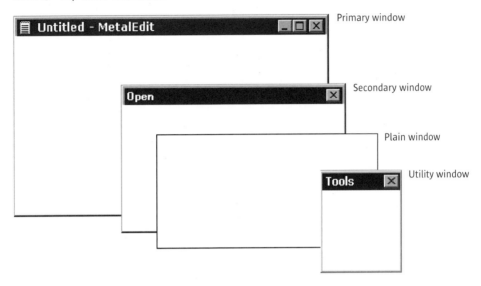

Primary windows are implemented using the JFrame component. Secondary windows and utility windows are implemented using the JDialog component (for dialog boxes and utility windows) or the JOptionPane component (for alert boxes). Plain windows are implemented using the JWindow component.

Primary Windows

Primary windows are provided by the operating system of the platform on which the application is running—for instance, UNIX, Microsoft Windows, OS/2, or Macintosh.

Specifically, you cannot alter the appearance of the window border and **title bar**, including the **window controls** that affect the state of a window (for example, the Maximize button in Microsoft Windows title bars). Window behavior, such as resizing, dragging, minimizing, positioning, and layering, is controlled by the operating system.

The content provided by your application, however, takes on the Java look and feel, as shown in Figure 90 (which depicts a MetalEdit document window as it appears on the Microsoft Windows platform).

 The corresponding code for Figure 90 appears on the companion CD-ROM.

FIGURE 90   Primary Window on the Microsoft Windows Platform

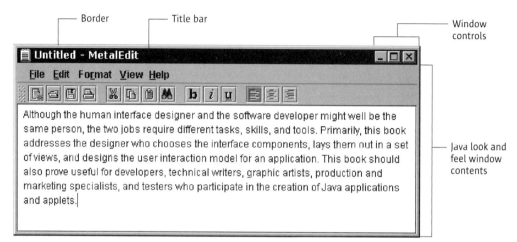

Typically, when users close or minimize a window, any associated secondary windows are closed as well. However, the operating system does not take care of this behavior automatically for JFC applications.

Keep track of the secondary windows in your application; close them if the primary window is closed or hide them if their primary window is minimized.

Although native operating systems typically display a close control on the title bar of windows, provide a Close item or Exit item in your File menu as well.

In the JFC, primary windows are created using the JFrame component. This component appears with the border, title bar, and window controls of the platform on which it is running. This is the JFC component you are most likely to use as the top-level container for a primary window.

Secondary Windows   Secondary windows (dialog boxes and alert boxes) are displayed in a window supplied by the native operating system. In the JFC, the component for dialog boxes is called JDialog, and the component for alert boxes is JOptionPane. These windows appear with the borders and title bars of the platform on which they are running. Chapter 8 provides more guidelines for the design of dialog boxes and alert boxes.

Figure 91 shows a JFC-supplied Warning alert box for the sample text-editing application, MetalEdit.

⊙ The corresponding code for Figure 91 appears on the companion CD-ROM.

FIGURE 91   Alert Box on the Macintosh Platform

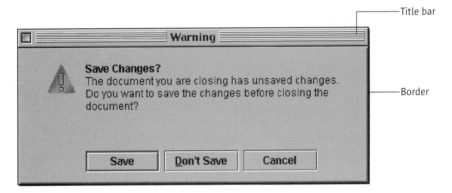

Dialog and alert box behavior, such as dragging and closing, is controlled by the native operating system. For keyboard operations that are appropriate to dialog and alert boxes, see Table 23 on page 254.

🖳🖥️ Keep in mind that some platforms do not provide close controls in the title bar for dialog boxes. Always provide a way to close the window in the dialog box or alert box itself.

▦⌐ The JOptionPane component is used to implement an alert box. If the box supplied by the JFC does not suit your needs, you can use the JDialog component.

Plain Windows   You can create a window that is a blank plain rectangle. The window contains no title bar or window controls, as shown in the following figure. (Note that the black border shown around this plain window is not provided by the JFC.)

FIGURE 92   Plain Window Used as the Basis for a Splash Screen

A plain window does not provide dragging, closing, minimizing, or maximizing. You can use a plain window as the container for a splash screen, which appears and disappears without user interaction, as shown in the preceding figure.

⊞◯   The JWindow component is used to implement plain windows. (The JFrame component is used to implement primary windows.)

Utility Windows   A utility window is often used to display a collection of tools, colors, or patterns. Figure 93 shows a utility window that displays a collection of objects.

FIGURE 93   Utility Window

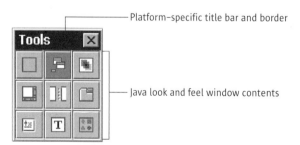

Platform-specific title bar and border

Java look and feel window contents

Unlike secondary windows, which should close automatically when their associated windows are closed, utility windows should remain open when primary windows are closed.

User choices made in a utility window refer to and affect the active primary window. A utility window remains on screen for an extended period of time while users go back and forth between the utility window and primary windows. In contrast, a secondary window is designed to enable users to resolve an issue in an associated primary window and is usually dismissed once users have resolved the issue.

The same keyboard operations that apply in dialog boxes and alert boxes apply to utility windows. For information on keyboard operations appropriate for utility windows, see Table 14 on page 249 and Table 23 on page 254.

☕ Because utility windows are not dependent on a primary window, do not automatically dismiss utility windows when primary windows are closed.

☕ Ensure that the same initial focus and keyboard navigation features available in secondary windows are available in utility windows.

🖉 Utility windows in a non-MDI application are implemented using the `JDialog` component, whereas in an MDI application, internal utility windows are a specific style of the `JInternalFrame` component. Therefore, internal utility windows can be used only within a backing window. Use the client properties mechanism to set the `JInternalFrame.isPalette` to true.

Organizing the Contents of Windows

The JFC provides a number of user interface elements you can use for organizing the contents of windows: panels, tabbed panes, split panes, and scroll panes. Panels and panes can be used to organize windows into one or more viewing areas. A panel is a JFC component that you can use for grouping other components inside windows or other panels.

A pane is a collective term used for scroll panes, split panes, and tabbed panes, among others. Panes provide a client area where you can offer control over which user interface elements users see. For instance, a scroll pane enables the viewing of different parts of a client area; a tabbed pane enables users to choose among screen-related client areas; and a split pane enables users to allocate the proportions of a larger viewing area between two client areas.

FIGURE 94   Lower-Level Containers

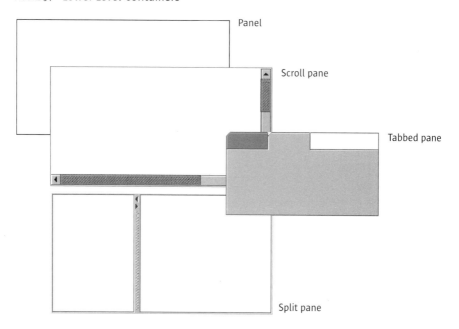

Panel

Scroll pane

Tabbed pane

Split pane

Panels   In contrast to scroll panes and tabbed panes, which typically play an
interactive role in an application, a panel simply groups components within a
window or another panel. Layout managers enable you to position
components visually within a panel. For a thorough treatment of the visual
layout and alignment of components, see "Layout and Visual Alignment" on
page 62. For more information on layout managers, see *The Java Tutorial* at
`http://java.sun.com/docs/books/tutorial`.

Scroll Panes   A **scroll pane** is a specialized container offering vertical or horizontal
scrollbars (or both) that enable users to change the visible portion of the
window contents.

Figure 95 provides an example of a scroll pane with a vertical scrollbar. The
size of the scroll box indicates the proportion of the content currently
displayed.

FIGURE 95   Scroll Pane in a Document Window

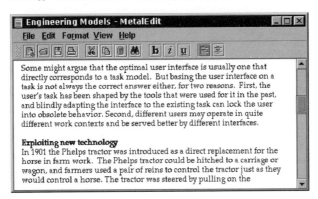

You can choose whether a scroll pane always displays scrollbars or whether they appear only when needed.

☕ Unless you have a compelling reason to do otherwise, use the default setting for horizontal scrollbars, which specifies that they appear only when needed.

☕ Display a horizontal scrollbar if users can't see all the information in the window pane—for instance, in a word-processing application that prepares printed pages, users might want to look at the margins as well as the text.

☕ If the data in a list is known and appears to fit in the available space (for example, a predetermined set of colors), you still need to place the list in a scroll pane. Specify that a vertical scrollbar should appear only if needed. For instance, if users change the font, the list items might become too large to fit in the available space, and a vertical scrollbar would be required.

☕ If the data in a scroll pane sometimes requires a vertical scrollbar in the normal font, specify that the vertical scrollbar always be present. This practice prevents the distracting reformatting of the display whenever the vertical scrollbar appears or disappears.

🖇 Scrollbars are obtained by placing the component, such as a text area, inside a scroll pane.

Scrollbars   A **scrollbar** is a component that enables users to control what portion of a document or list (or similar information) is visible on screen. In locales with left-to-right writing systems, scrollbars appear along the bottom and the right sides of a scroll pane, a list, a combo box, a text area, or an editor pane. In locales with right-to-left writing systems, such as Hebrew and Arabic, scrollbars appear along the bottom and left sides of the relevant component.

By default, scrollbars appear only when needed to view information that is not currently visible, although you can specify that the scrollbar is always present.

The size of the **scroll box** represents the proportion of the window content that is currently visible. The position of the scroll box within the scrollbar represents the position of the visible material within the document. As users move the scroll box, the view of the document changes accordingly. If the entire document is visible, the scroll box fills the entire channel.

Both horizontal and vertical scroll boxes have a minimum size of 16 x 16 pixels so that users can still manipulate them when viewing very long documents or lists.

At either end of the scrollbar is a **scroll arrow**, which is used for controlling small movements of the data.

The following figure shows horizontal and vertical scrollbars. Each scrollbar is a rectangle consisting of a textured scroll box, a recessed channel, and scroll arrows.

FIGURE 96   Vertical and Horizontal Scrollbars

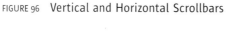
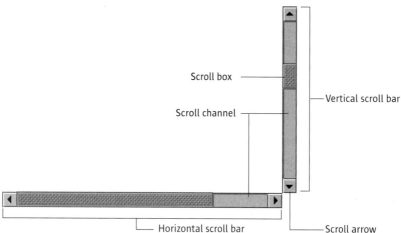

Do not confuse the scrollbar with a slider, which is used to select a value. For details, see "Sliders" on page 210.

Users drag the scroll box, click the scroll arrows, or click in the channel to change the contents of the viewing area. When users click a scroll arrow, more of the document or list scrolls into view. The contents of the pane or list move in increments based on the type of data. When users hold down the mouse button, the pane or list scrolls continuously.

For a description of keyboard operations for scrollbars, see Table 22 on page 253.

☕ Scroll the content approximately one pane at a time when users click in the scrollbar's channel. Leave one small unit of overlap from the previous information pane to provide context for the user. For instance, in scrolling through a long document, help users become oriented to the new page by providing one line of text from the previous page.

☕ Scroll the content one small unit at a time when users click a scroll arrow. (The smallest unit might be one line of text, one row in a table, or 10 to 20 pixels of a graphic.) The unit controlled by the scroll arrows should be small enough to enable precise positioning of the text or graphic but not so small that users must spend an impractical amount of time using the scroll arrow.

☕ Ensure that the scroll speed is fairly constant when users click the scroll arrows. Ensure that scrollbar controls run quickly yet enable users to perform the operation without overshooting the intended location. The best way to determine the appropriate scrolling rate is to test the scrolling rate with users who are unfamiliar with your application.

☕ Ensure that the scrolling rate is appropriate across different processor speeds.

⊕ Place scrollbars in the orientation that is suitable for the writing system of your target locale. For example, in the left-to-right writing systems (such as English and other European languages), the scrollbars appear along the right side of the scroll pane or other component. In other locales, they might appear along the left side of the scroll pane.

Tabbed Panes

A **tabbed pane** is a container that enables users to switch between several content panes that appear to share the same space on screen. (The panes are implemented as `JPanel` components.) The tabs themselves can contain text or images or both.

A typical tabbed pane appears with tabs displayed at the top, but the tabs can be displayed on any of the four sides. If the tabs cannot fit in a single row, additional rows are created automatically. Note that tabs do not change position when they are activated. For the first row of tabs, there is no separator line between the active tab and the pane.

The following figure shows the initial content pane in the JFC-supplied color chooser. Note that the tabbed pane is displayed within a dialog box that uses the borders, title bar, and window controls of the platform on which its associated application is running.

FIGURE 97   Swatches Content Pane in the JFC Color Chooser

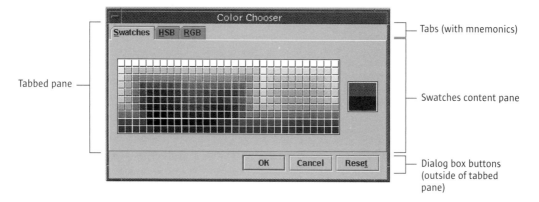

Users choose which content pane to view by clicking the corresponding tab. The content pane changes accordingly, as shown in the following figure of the content pane associated with the RGB tab.

For a list of keyboard operations appropriate for tabbed panes, see Table 26 on page 256.

FIGURE 98   RGB Content Pane in the JFC Color Chooser

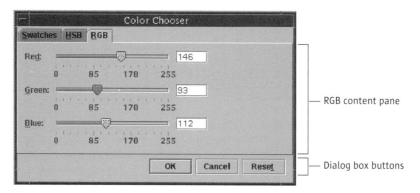

You can use tabbed panes to good advantage in secondary windows, such as a preferences dialog box, that require you to fit a lot of information into a small area.

You can also use tabbed panes to provide a way for users to switch between content panes that represent:

- Different ways to view the same information, like a color chooser's RGB and HSB panes

- Different parts of an informational unit, like worksheets that are part of a workbook in a spreadsheet application

☕ Use headline capitalization for tab names.

☕ Provide mnemonics so users can navigate from tab to tab and from tabs to associated content panes using keyboard operations.

☕ Do not nest tabbed panes.

☕ If your tabbed pane requires multiple rows of tabs, consider dividing the content among several dialog boxes or other components. Multiple rows of tabs can be confusing. You might also consider displaying the tabs vertically so more could be displayed in a single column.

☕ Place any dialog box buttons outside the tabbed pane because they apply to the whole dialog box (that is, all the panes) at once.

Split Panes

A **split pane** is a container that divides a larger pane into resizable panes. Split panes enable users to adjust the relative sizes of two adjacent panes. The Java look and feel drag texture (along with a pointer change when the pointer is over the splitter bar) indicates that users can resize split panes.

To adjust the size of the split panes, users drag the splitter bar, as shown in the following figure.

FIGURE 99   Split Pane (Horizontal Orientation)

Splitter bar

Users can also control the splitter bar by clicking one of the optional zoom buttons shown in the following figure. Clicking a button moves the splitter bar to its extreme (upper, lower, left, or right) position. If the splitter bar is already at its extreme position, clicking a zoom button in the direction of the split restores the panes to the size they had before the zoom operation (or before the user dragged the splitter bar to close one of the panes).

For a list of keyboard operations appropriate for split panes, see Table 25 on page 255.

FIGURE 100 Zoom Buttons in a Split Pane (Vertical Orientation)

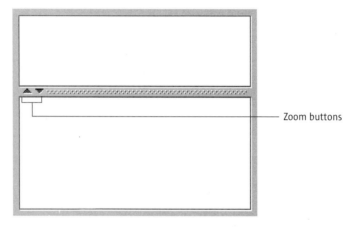

Zoom buttons

Include zoom buttons in split panes because they are very convenient for users.

Nested Split Panes   In addition to splitting panes either horizontally or vertically, you can nest one split pane inside another. The following figure portrays a mail application in which the top pane of a vertically split pane has a horizontally split pane (in blue in the lower schematic diagram) embedded in it.

FIGURE 101 Nested Split Panes

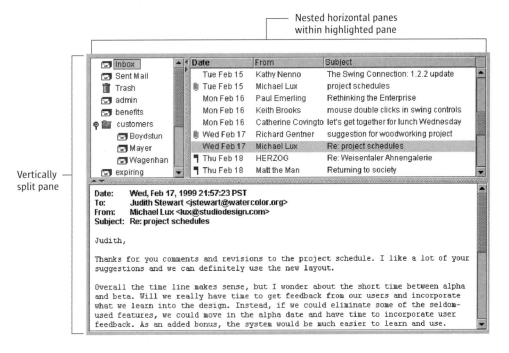

Nested horizontal panes
within highlighted pane

Vertically
split pane

Working With Multiple Document Interfaces   A multiple document interface (**MDI**) application provides a way to manage multiple windows that are confined inside a main window called a **backing window** (previously called a "desktop pane"). To support MDI designers, the JFC provides the internal window and internal utility window.

Backing Windows   In an MDI application, a large window, called the backing window, contains other windows. The menus and toolbars for the application are usually displayed in the backing window rather than in each internal (primary) window. For more on menus and toolbars, see Chapter 9.

The `JDesktopPane` component is used to implement backing windows.

Internal Windows   Primary windows in MDI applications must stay inside the main backing window and so are called "internal windows." The main backing window is a native platform window with the native look and feel. However, in an MDI that uses the Java look and feel, internal windows have window borders, title bars, and standard window controls with the Java look and feel.

The following figure shows examples of internal windows for an MDI application.

FIGURE 102   Internal Windows in an MDI Application

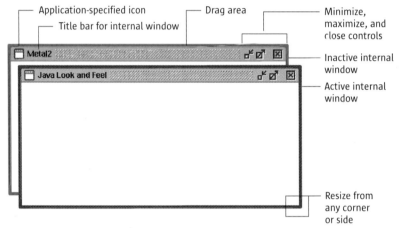

Users can use the mouse to:

- Activate a window (and deactivate the previously activated window) by clicking anywhere in the window

- Adjust the size of a resizable internal window by dragging from any side or corner

- Drag the internal window (by the title bar) within the backing window

- Minimize, maximize, restore, and close the internal window by clicking the appropriate window controls

For keyboard operations appropriate to internal windows, see Table 14 on page 249.

A **minimized internal window** is a horizontally oriented component (shown in the following figure) that represents an internal window that has been minimized. The width of these minimized internal windows is sized to accommodate the window title. Minimized internal windows consist of a drag area followed by an area containing an application-specific icon and the text of the window title.

FIGURE 103 Minimized Internal Window

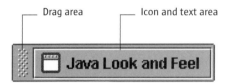

Users can rearrange minimized internal windows by dragging the textured area. Users can click the icon and text area in a minimized internal window to restore the window to its previous location and size.

For details on the keyboard operations appropriate for minimized internal windows, see Table 14 on page 249.

Secondary Windows

In MDI applications, secondary windows have the same appearance and behavior as they do in non-MDI applications. Unlike internal windows, secondary windows can move outside the backing window.

⊞⊃ If you are working with an MDI application using the Java look and feel, the JDialog component can be used to create secondary windows.

Internal Utility Windows

An **internal utility window** (previously called a "palette window") is a type of internal window that floats above other internal windows within the backing window for an MDI application.

The following figure shows an internal utility window from a hypothetical graphical interface builder. A set of buttons enables users to construct menus.

FIGURE 104 Internal Utility Window

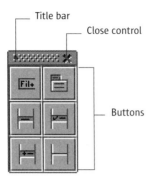

Internal utility windows can contain any component. Users can close internal windows, but they cannot resize, minimize, or maximize them. The title bars of internal utility windows cannot contain text.

For keyboard operations for internal utility windows, see Table 14 on page 249.

☕ Provide a close control on all internal utility windows.

▭⊃ An internal utility window is a specific style of `JInternalFrame` and, therefore, can be used only within a backing window. Use the client properties mechanism to set the `JInternalFrame.isPalette` to true.

Window Titles

This section discusses conventions for window titles of both primary and secondary windows. Italics indicate text you must replace; window titles themselves do not use the italic font style.

Title Text in Primary Windows

The title text in a primary window should use the format *Document* or *Object Name - Application Name*. Figure 105 shows the proper format for the window title, with the document title appearing first. If the title is truncated, the most important part of the title remains visible.

FIGURE 105 Proper Format for Window Title

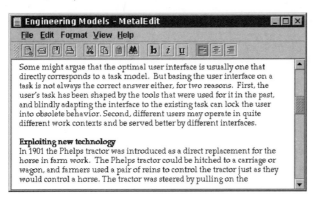

☕ In primary windows, begin the window title text with a name describing the contents of the window, followed by a space, a hyphen, another space, and the application name.

Title Text in Secondary Windows   The title text in secondary windows should use the format *Descriptive Name - Application Name*. The *Application Name* is optional but should be included if users might not otherwise recognize the source of the secondary window.

☕ In secondary windows, begin the window title with a name describing the contents of the window. Follow that text with the application name when users might be unclear which application is associated with the window.

The secondary window in the following figure is often displayed by the MetalButler calendar program while users are focused on some other task. Therefore, its window title includes the application name.

FIGURE 106 Secondary Window Title With Optional Application Name

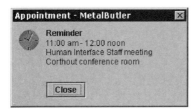

The secondary window shown in Figure 107 is displayed immediately after a user tries to save a new file with an existing name. The source of the alert box is clear. Therefore, the window title does not include the application name.

⊙ The corresponding code for Figure 107 appears on the companion CD-ROM.

FIGURE 107 Secondary Window Title Without Optional Application Name

Title Text in Internal Windows   The title text in internal windows should use the format *Descriptive Name* or *Descriptive Name - Tool Name*. For an example of the title text in an internal window, see Figure 102 on page 150.

☕ In an internal window, provide the window title with a name describing the contents of the window. Since the backing window makes the application name clear, you can omit the application name. If there is a tool within the application, you can use the format *Descriptive Name - Tool Name*.

8: DIALOG BOXES AND ALERT BOXES

A **dialog box** is a secondary window in which users perform a task that is supplemental to the task in the primary window. For example, a dialog box might enable users to set preferences or choose a file from the hard disk. A dialog box can contain panes and panels, text, graphics, controls (such as checkboxes, radio buttons, or sliders), and one or more command buttons. Dialog boxes use the native window frame of the platform on which they are running (in both non-MDI and MDI applications).

An **alert box** is a secondary window that provides for brief interaction with users. Alert boxes present error messages, warn of potentially harmful actions, obtain a small amount of information from users, or display messages. The basic alert box has a symbol that identifies the type of the alert, a textual message, and one or more command buttons. The layout of these components is determined by the JFC.

FIGURE 108 Dialog Box and Alert Box

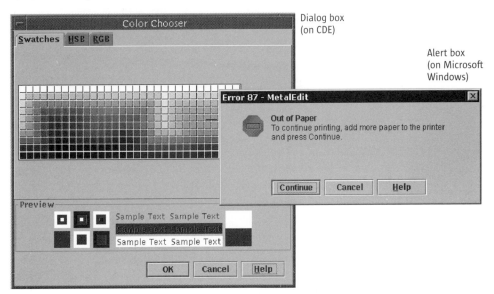

Dialog box
(on CDE)

Alert box
(on Microsoft
Windows)

☕ If you are designing an MDI application, use the JFC-supplied dialog boxes and alert boxes. Because these secondary windows use the platform's native windows (and not the JFC-supplied internal window), they are free to move outside the backing window.

Modal and Modeless Dialog Boxes

Dialog boxes can be modal or modeless. A **modal dialog box** prevents users from interacting with the application until the dialog box is dismissed. However, users can move a modal dialog box and interact with other applications while the modal dialog box is open. This behavior is sometimes called "application-modal."

A **modeless dialog box** does not prevent users from interacting with the application they are in or with any other application. Users can go back and forth between a modeless dialog box and other application windows.

☕ Use modeless dialog boxes whenever possible. The order in which users perform tasks might vary, or users might want to check information in other windows before dismissing the dialog box. Users might also want to go back and forth between the dialog box and the primary window.

☕ Use modal dialog boxes when interaction with the application cannot proceed while the dialog box is displayed. For example, a progress dialog box that appears while your application is loading its data might be a modal dialog box if users can do nothing useful during the loading process.

Dialog Box Design

Figure 109 illustrates dialog box design guidelines for the Java look and feel.

The dialog box in the figure has a title in the window's title bar, a series of user interface elements, and a row of command buttons. The default command button is the OK button, indicated by its heavy border. The underlined letters are mnemonics, which remind users how to activate components by pressing the Alt key and the appropriate character key. The Ruler Units noneditable combo box has initial keyboard focus, indicating that the user's next keystrokes will take effect in that component. For a discussion of the text that should appear in dialog box titles, see "Title Text in Secondary Windows" on page 153.

⊙ The corresponding code for Figure 109 is available on the companion CD-ROM.

FIGURE 109 Sample Dialog Box

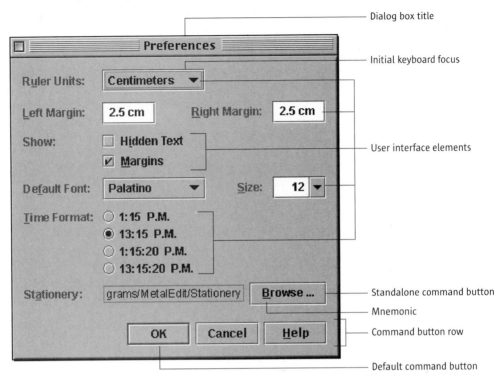

In dialog boxes, include mnemonics for all user interface elements except the default button and the Cancel button.

When opening a dialog box, provide initial keyboard focus to the component that you expect users to operate first. This focus is especially important for users who must use a keyboard to navigate your application.

Consider the effect of internationalization on your design. Use a layout manager, which allows for text strings to become bigger or smaller when translated to another language.

For guidelines for the spacing between JFC components, see "Layout and Visual Alignment" on page 62. For more information on internationalization, see "Planning for Internationalization and Localization" on page 48. For details on keyboard support for navigating through dialog boxes, see Table 23 on page 254. For information on how to capitalize text in dialog boxes, see "Text in the Interface" on page 75.

Tab Traversal Order   Tab traversal order is the order in which the components in a
dialog box receive keyboard focus on successive presses of the Tab key. If
users press the Tab key when keyboard focus is on the last component in the
dialog box, you should return keyboard focus to the first component.

Figure 110 shows the tab traversal order that the designer has set for this
preferences dialog box.

⊙ The corresponding code for Figure 110 is available on the companion
CD-ROM.

FIGURE 110 Tab Traversal Order in the Sample Dialog Box

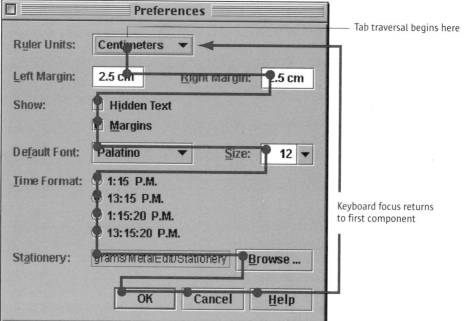

☝ Specify a logical tab traversal order for the user interface elements in a
dialog box. The traversal order should match the reading order for your
application's specified locale. For example, in English, the traversal order is
left to right, top to bottom. By default, the traversal order is the sequence in
which you added the components to the dialog box.

⊞⊃ The `setNextFocusableComponent` method from `JComponent`
can be used to specify the next component to receive keyboard focus. If a
component is unavailable, it is skipped in the tab traversal order.

Single-Use and Multiple-Use Dialog Boxes   Dialog boxes can be designed for single or multiple use. This usage determines the combinations of command buttons that should appear in the dialog box.

■ If users are likely to perform one operation with the dialog box and then dismiss it, a single-use dialog box is appropriate. The command buttons (except Help) in a single-use dialog box perform their operations and then close the window. An example of a single-use dialog box is a systems settings dialog box.

■ If users might want to perform several operations with the dialog box before dismissing it, a multiple-operation dialog box is appropriate. The command buttons (except Close) in a multiple-use dialog box perform their operations and leave the window open. An example of a multiple-use dialog box is a sophisticated find-and-replace dialog box that provides command buttons for Find, Find Next, Replace, and Replace All.

Command Buttons in Dialog Boxes   In dialog boxes, you can place command buttons alone or in a command button row at the bottom of the dialog box, as shown in Figure 109 on page 157. This section provides some general guidelines about the uses and placement of command buttons in dialog boxes.

☕ Place command buttons that apply to the dialog box as a whole in the command button row at the bottom of the dialog box. This includes all buttons that dismiss the dialog box as one of their actions.

☕ Align buttons in the command button row along the lower-right edge of the dialog box. (The alignment of the command button row in alert boxes, including those supplied by the JFC, is different from the alignment in dialog boxes.)

☕ Place command buttons that apply to one or a few components next to their associated components. For instance, place a Browse button at the trailing edge of the text field it fills in.

For general information on command buttons, see "Command Buttons" on page 196. For guidelines on the spacing of command buttons, see "Command Button Spacing and Padding" on page 71. For keyboard operations appropriate to command buttons, see Table 17 on page 250.

OK and Cancel Buttons   The OK and Cancel buttons work well in single-use dialog boxes (for instance, those in which users specify options or settings). OK instructs the system to apply and save the settings, whereas Cancel instructs the system to ignore any changed settings. In most cases, OK is the default button. OK and Cancel are appropriate in both modal and modeless dialog boxes. The following figure shows a preferences dialog box with OK, Cancel, and Help buttons.

FIGURE 111 Dialog Box With OK, Cancel, and Help Buttons

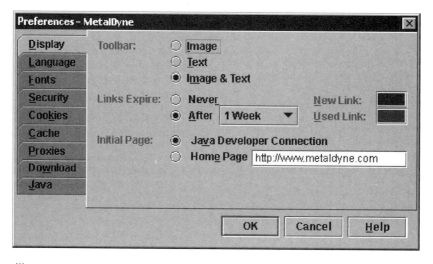

When users click the OK button in a dialog box, save the settings or carry out the commands specified and close the dialog box. Whenever possible, provide the button with a command name that describes the action (such as Print or Find) instead of OK.

When users click the Cancel button in a dialog box, close the window and restore the settings in the dialog box to the state they were in when the dialog box was opened.

Do not add a mnemonic to the Cancel button.

The Cancel button should be activated when users press the Escape key. The Cancel button does not need keyboard focus for this interaction. The Cancel button and its keyboard equivalent (Escape) are not built into the JFC; you must implement them yourself.

Apply and Close Buttons   The Apply and Close buttons work well in multiple-use dialog boxes (those that remain open for repeated use), as shown in the properties dialog box in the following figure. Apply and Close often appear together in modeless dialog boxes.

FIGURE 112 Dialog Box With Apply and Close Buttons

Use the Apply button to carry out the changes users specify in a dialog box without closing the window.

In a multiple-use dialog box that is used to perform an action, use a specific action name (such as "Find") instead of "Apply." More than one kind of action or apply button might be appropriate—for instance, "Find" and "Replace."

Use a Reset button to restore the values in a dialog box to the values specified by the last Apply command. If users have not activated Apply, restore the values in effect when the dialog box was opened. Do not close the dialog box when users choose Reset. Place a Reset button between the Apply and Close buttons.

Include a Close button in a dialog box with an Apply (or other action) button. Close dismisses the dialog box without applying changes.

Because a Cancel button might make users think they can apply changes temporarily and then rescind them, do not use a Cancel button in a dialog box that includes an Apply button. Use a Close button instead.

If the user has made changes in a dialog box and clicks Close before clicking the Apply button, display a Warning alert box. The alert box should ask the user whether to apply the changes before closing, discard changes, or cancel the close operation.

Close Buttons   The Close button is commonly used to dismiss simple secondary windows, such as an Info alert box. The Close button is also commonly used to dismiss dialog boxes in which user actions take effect immediately. A Close button is appropriate in both modal and modeless dialog boxes.

The following dialog box enables users to specify properties such as the width and height of a rectangle. Changes take effect immediately. The dialog box includes a Close button that users can click to dismiss the dialog box.

Even though the Close button has a mnemonic (usually C), you can also have the Close button respond to the Escape key.

FIGURE 113 Dialog Box With a Close Button

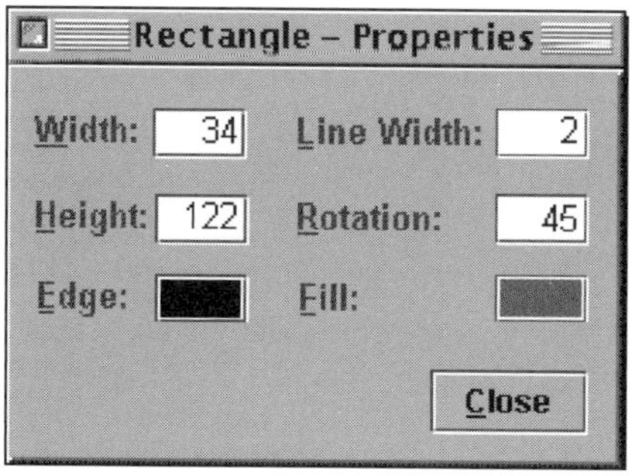

Never use an OK button in a window that has a Close button.

When users click the Close button, dismiss the dialog box and do not make additional changes to the system.

Help Buttons   You can include a Help button in any dialog box. A Help button enables users to obtain additional information about the dialog box. For example, when users click Help in the Error alert box in Figure 124 on page 171, the application opens a window with additional information on the cause of the error.

When users click the Help button, open an additional window that displays the help information. Avoid removing or obscuring information in the window where users clicked Help.

Place the Help button at the trailing edge of a group of command buttons. For languages that read from left to right, the Help button should be the rightmost button.

Default Command Buttons The default command button is the button that the application activates when users press Enter (or Return). The JFC gives the default command button a heavier border than other command buttons. In most cases, you should make the action that users are most likely to perform the default button, as shown with the OK button in the following figure. The default button does not need to have keyboard focus when users press Enter.

FIGURE 114 Dialog Box With a Default Command Button

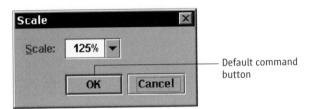

Default command button

When keyboard focus is on a component that accepts the Enter key, such as a multiline text area, the default button is not activated when users press the key. Instead, the insertion point moves to the beginning of a new line. To operate the default button, users must move focus to a component that does not accept Enter or press Ctrl-Enter.

☕ If a dialog box has a default button, make it the first command button in the group. For example, in languages that read from left to right, the default button is the leftmost button.

☕ Since the Enter (and Return) key is already supplied by the JFC for keyboard access, do not add a mnemonic for the default command button.

You are not required to have a default command button in every dialog box and alert box. A command that might cause users to lose data should never be the default button, even if it is the action that users are most likely to perform. The alert box in Figure 115 asks users if they want to replace an existing file. The alert box has Replace and Cancel buttons, neither of which is the default command button. Even though the Replace button has focus, it cannot be activated with the Enter key; it must be activated with the spacebar. This approach gives the user time to reconsider a hasty, automatic confirmation.

⊙ The corresponding code for Figure 115 appears on the companion CD-ROM.

FIGURE 115 Alert Box Without a Default Button

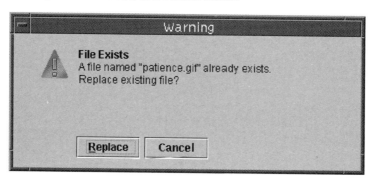

Common Dialog Boxes

The find, login, preferences, and progress dialog boxes are common in many applications. These dialog boxes are not supplied by the JFC. The following sections show simple versions of these dialog boxes that are consistent with the Java look and feel. You can adapt the designs for these dialog boxes to suit your needs.

Find Dialog Boxes

A find dialog box is a multiple-use window that enables users to search for a specified text string. In most cases, you should make this dialog box modeless so users can perform multiple searches in succession. An example is shown in Figure 116.

⊙ The corresponding code for Figure 116 appears on the companion CD-ROM.

FIGURE 116 Sample Find Dialog Box

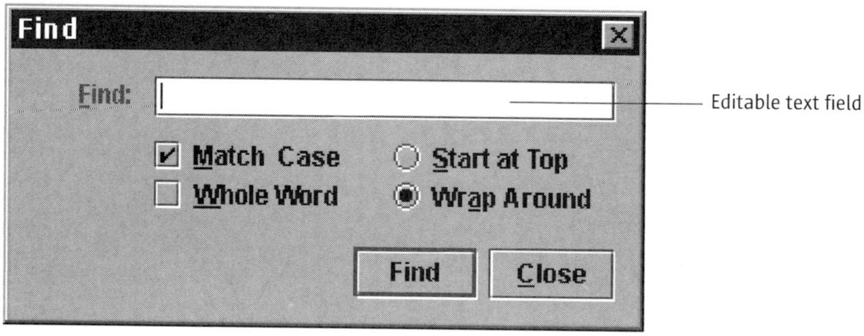

Editable text field

Login Dialog Boxes   A login dialog box (shown in Figure 117) enables users to identify themselves and enter a password. Depending on where you use this single-use dialog box in your application, you can make it modal or modeless.

⊙ The corresponding code for Figure 117 is available on the companion CD-ROM.

FIGURE 117 Sample Login Dialog Box

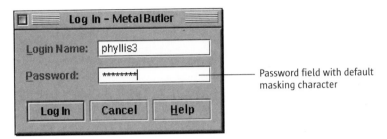

Password field with default masking character

For a discussion of effective interaction in login dialog boxes, see "Design for Smooth Interaction" on page 124.

Preferences Dialog Boxes   A preferences dialog box (as shown in Figure 118) enables users to view and modify the characteristics of an application.

As a general rule, you should make this single-use dialog box modeless.

⊙ The corresponding code for Figure 118 is available on the companion CD-ROM.

FIGURE 118 Sample Preferences Dialog Box

If your preferences dialog box is very complex, you can simplify it by using a tabbed pane to organize the options, as shown in Figure 111 on page 160.

Progress Dialog Boxes

A progress dialog box provides feedback for long operations and lets users know that the system is working on the previous command.

The progress dialog box in Figure 119 monitors the progress of a file copy operation. The dialog box includes the JFC progress bar, a command button that users can click to stop the process, and labels to further explain the progress of the operation. If users can perform other tasks while the operation is in progress, you should make a progress dialog box modeless.

⊙ The corresponding code for Figure 119 is available on the companion CD-ROM.

FIGURE 119 Sample Progress Dialog Box

☕ Display a progress dialog box (or supply a progress bar elsewhere in your application) if an operation takes longer than 6 seconds.

☕ If a progress bar dialog box includes a button to stop the process, place it after the progress bar. (In languages that read from left to right, the button appears to the right of the progress bar.) If the state will remain as it was before the process started, use a Cancel button. If the process might alter the state as it progresses (for example, deleted records will not be restored), use a Stop button. If stopping the process could lead to data loss, give users a chance to confirm the Stop command by displaying a Warning alert box.

☕ Close a progress dialog box automatically when the operation is complete.

☕ If delays are a common occurrence in your application (for example, a web browser), build a progress bar into the primary window so that you don't have to keep displaying a progress dialog box.

⊕ Because translation of the word "Stop" can result in words with subtly different meanings, point out to your translators the specialized meaning of the Stop button in a progress dialog box. Stop indicates that the process might leave the system in an altered state, whereas Cancel means that no change in the system state will occur.

Color Choosers

A **color chooser** provides one or more content panes from which users can select colors and a preview mechanism by which users can view the selected colors in context. You can display a color chooser in a dialog box, as shown in the following figure. The three command buttons (OK, Cancel, and Help) are part of the dialog box, not the color chooser. (A color chooser can also be implemented in a multiple-use dialog box.)

FIGURE 120 JFC-Supplied Color Chooser

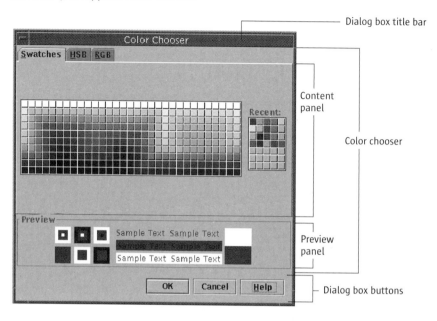

As supplied by the JFC, the color chooser offers users three methods for selecting a color:

- **Swatches.** Users can select a color from a palette (as shown in the preceding figure).

- **HSB.** Users can choose the hue, saturation, and brightness values for a color.

- **RGB.** Users can choose the red, green, and blue values for a color.

In addition, the color chooser offers a preview panel within the dialog box.

If your application requires a different method for choosing colors, you can add a content pane with that feature. You can also remove existing content panes. If you use only one content pane, the tabs disappear. In addition, you can specify your own preview panel or alter the supplied one.

The color chooser is a panel. The color panel can be inserted in a dialog box by using the JDialog container. This operation is accomplished with the static method CreateDialog on the JColorChooser container. Alternately, this can be done with the ShowDialog method, which creates, displays, and dismisses the dialog box.

Alert Boxes

An alert box, which conveys a message or warning to users, provides an easy way for you to create a secondary window. The JFC provides four types of alert boxes: Info, Warning, Error, and Question. Each alert box is provided with a symbol that indicates its type. You provide the title, the message, and the command buttons and their labels.

The layout of an alert box is provided in the JFC, so you don't have to worry about the spacing and alignment of the message, symbol, and command buttons. If you provide additional components, such as a text field, follow the guidelines in "Between-Component Spacing Guidelines" on page 68. You can make an alert box modal or modeless.

FIGURE 121 Standard Components in an Alert Box

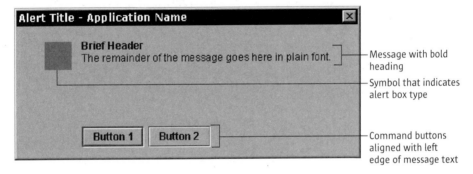

ᵕ In an alert box, begin your message with a brief heading in boldface. Start the body of the message on a separate line.

ᵕ If appropriate, provide a Help button in an alert box that opens an additional window with more information. Do not close the alert box when users click the Help button.

▤ In the message for an alert box, the `<B>...</B>` tags can be used to render a heading in boldface. The `<BR>` tag can be used to create a line break between the heading and the message body.

▤ An alert box is created using the `JOptionPane` component.

For guidance on window title text for alert boxes, see "Title Text in Secondary Windows" on page 153.

Info Alert Boxes   An Info alert box presents general information to users. The symbol in the Info alert box is a blue circle with the letter i. The following dialog box, which contains a schedule reminder, provides information about a meeting.

FIGURE 122   Info Alert Box

☕ Provide a Close button to dismiss an Info alert box. Provide additional command buttons, such as a Help button, if needed.

Warning Alert Boxes   A Warning alert box warns users about the possible consequences of an action and asks users for a response. The symbol in the Warning alert box is a yellow triangle with an exclamation point. The alert box in Figure 123 warns users that a file save operation will replace an existing file.

⊙ The corresponding code for Figure 123 appears on the companion CD-ROM.

FIGURE 123   Warning Alert Box

☕ Keep the message in a Warning alert box brief, and use terms that are familiar to users.

☕ Include at least two buttons in a Warning alert box: one button to perform the action and the other to cancel the action. Provide the command buttons with labels that describe the action they perform.

☕ Do not make a command button whose action might cause loss of data the default button. Users might press the Enter (or Return) key without reading the message. If the action that could result in data loss is the most common action, do not provide a default button. (For an example of a dialog box with this situation, see Figure 115 on page 164.)

Error Alert Boxes   An Error alert box reports system and application errors to users. The symbol in the Error alert box is a red octagon with a rectangle. The following Error alert box reports that a printer is out of paper and provides users with three options. Clicking the Continue button resumes printing and dismisses the alert box. Clicking the Cancel button terminates the print job and dismisses the alert box. Clicking the Help button opens a secondary window that gives background information about the error.

FIGURE 124 Error Alert Box

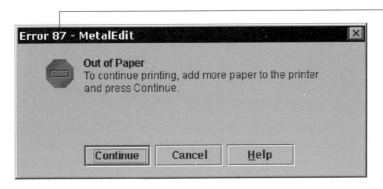

Error number
in title

☕ Include an error number in the title bar of an Error alert box. The error number is helpful for users in obtaining technical assistance, especially if the error message is localized in a language not spoken by the technical support personnel.

☕ In the message of an Error alert box, explain what happened, the cause of the problem, and what the user can do about it. Keep the message brief and use terms that are familiar to users.

☕ If appropriate, provide a Help button in an Error alert box to open a separate window that gives background information about the error. Do not close the alert box when users click the Help button.

☕ If possible, provide buttons or other controls to resolve the error noted in the Error alert box. Label the buttons according to the action they perform. If users cannot resolve the error from the alert box, provide a Close button.

Question Alert Boxes   A Question alert box requests information from users. You can add components to this alert box (for example, a text field, list box, or combo box) in which users can type a value or make a selection. The layout of the standard components (the symbol, message, and command buttons) is provided by the JFC. If you add components, follow the guidelines in "Between-Component Spacing Guidelines" on page 68. The symbol in the Question alert box is a green rectangle with a question mark.

The following Question alert box includes a label and text field in addition to the standard components.

FIGURE 125 Question Alert Box

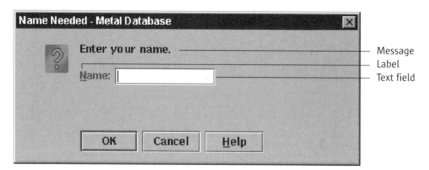

☕ When you add components to a Question alert box, align them with the leading edge of the message. For languages that read from left to right, the leading edge is the left edge.

9: MENUS AND TOOLBARS

A **menu** displays a list of options (menu items) for users to choose or browse through. Typically, menus are logically grouped and displayed by an application so that a user need not memorize all available commands. Menus in the Java look and feel can appear "sticky"—that is, they remain posted on screen after users click the menu title. Usually the primary means to access your application's features, menus also provide a quick way for users to see what those features are.

In Java look and feel applications, you can provide three kinds of menus: drop-down menus, submenus, and contextual menus. A **drop-down menu** is a menu whose titles appear in the menu bar. A **submenu** appears adjacent to a menu item in a drop-down menu; its presence is indicated by an arrow next to the item. A **contextual menu** displays lists of commands, settings, or attributes that apply to the selected item or items under the pointer. Contextual menus can also have submenus.

FIGURE 126 Drop-down Menu, Submenu, Contextual Menu, and Toolbar

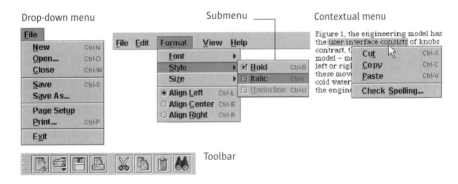

A **toolbar** is a collection of frequently used commands or options that appear as a row of toolbar buttons. Toolbars normally appear horizontally beneath a primary window's menu bar, but they can be dragged anywhere in the window or into their own window. Toolbars typically contain buttons, but you can provide other components (such as text fields and combo boxes) as well. Toolbar buttons can contain menu indicators, which denote the presence of a menu. Toolbars are provided as shortcuts to features available elsewhere in the application, often in the menus.

Menu Elements

Figure 127 shows an example of a drop-down menu that is activated and displayed. Within the Format menu, the Style item is activated; a submenu appears that includes the Bold, Italic, and Underline checkbox menu items. (The Italic checkbox menu item is highlighted as if the pointer is positioned over it.) In the Java look and feel, menus use a highlight color (primary 2) for the background of activated menu titles and menu items.

A separator divides the menu items for specifying font, style, and size from the alignment radio button items. Keyboard shortcuts appear to the right of the frequently used menu items, and mnemonics are included for each menu title and menu item.

⊙ The corresponding code for Figure 127 is available on the companion CD-ROM.

FIGURE 127 Menu Elements

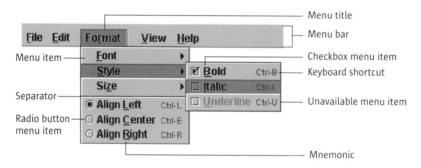

Menu Bars

The **menu bar** appears at the top of a primary window and contains menu titles, which describe the content of each menu. Menu titles usually appear as text; however, it is possible to use a graphic or a graphic with text as a menu title. Each menu title needs a mnemonic. See "Mnemonics" on page 118 for details.

A drop-down menu appears when users choose a menu title in the menu bar.

☕ Use a single word for each menu title.

☕ Use menu titles that make it easy for users to determine which menu contains the items of interest to them. For example, the Format menu typically contains commands that enable users to change the formatting of their documents or data.

☕ Be sure to include mnemonics for every menu title in your menu bar.

☕ Do not display menu bars in secondary windows.

☕ If you are writing an applet that runs in the user's current browser window (with the browser menu bar), do not display your own menu bar in the applet. Although applets displayed inside a browser window can have their own menu bars in the JFC, users are often confused when both the browser window and the applet have menu bars. If your applet requires a menu bar, display the applet in a separate browser window that does not have its own menu bar or navigation controls.

🖳🖵 Even on Macintosh systems, which ordinarily place a menu bar only at the top of the screen, menu bars are displayed in windows for a Java look and feel application. On the Macintosh, the screen-top menu bar remains, but, since all the application menus are in the windows, the only command in the screen-top menu bar is Quit in the File menu. (Exit also appears in the File menu of primary windows.)

Drop-down Menus

The menu bar contains all of the drop-down menus and submenus in your application. Each menu in the menu bar is represented by its menu title. The titles describe the content of each menu.

Users can display menus in two ways:

- To post a menu (that is, to display it and have it stay open until the next click), users click the menu title. Users can then move the pointer over other menu titles to view other menus.

- To pull down a menu, users press the mouse button when the pointer is over the menu title. The menu title is highlighted, and the menu drops down. When users choose a command and release the mouse button, the menu closes.

For details on keyboard operations in menus, see Table 20 on page 252.

Submenus

A submenu is a menu that users open by highlighting a menu item in a higher-level menu. The title for a submenu is its menu item in the higher level drop-down menu. Sometimes you can shorten a menu by moving related choices to a submenu. Submenus (such as the Style submenu shown in the following figure) appear adjacent to the submenu indicator. For instance, the Style item opens a submenu consisting of three items: Bold, Italic, and Underline. Note that the items in the Style submenu include both keyboard shortcuts and mnemonics.

Users display submenus by clicking or by dragging over the menu item in the higher-level menu item that is the submenu's title. In Figure 128, the first item in the submenu aligns with the submenu indicator, slightly overlapping the higher-level drop-down menu. Just as in other menus, items in the submenu are highlighted when the user moves the pointer over them.

⊙ The corresponding code for Figure 128 is available on the companion CD-ROM.

FIGURE 128 Menu Item With Its Submenu

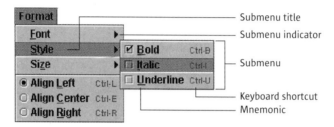

For a list of keyboard operations in submenus, see Table 20 on page 252.

☕ Because many people (especially novice users, children, and older people) find submenus difficult to use, minimize the use of submenus, especially with these populations. If at all possible, avoid using a second level of submenus. If you want to present a large or complex set of choices, display them in a dialog box.

▦➣ Submenus are created using the JMenu component.

Menu Items   A simple **menu item** consists of the command name, such as Undo.

When a menu item is available for use, its text is displayed in black, as shown in Figure 129.

⊙ The corresponding code for Figure 129 is available on the companion CD-ROM.

FIGURE 129 Typical Menu Items

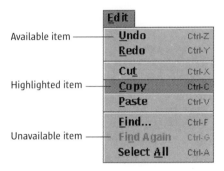

Available item ──────
Highlighted item ──────
Unavailable item ──────

When users position the pointer over an individual item within a menu, the menu item (if available) is highlighted.

Users can activate menu items in two ways:

■ In a posted menu, users click a menu item to activate it and close the menu.

■ In a pulled-down menu, users drag over a menu item to highlight it. Releasing the mouse button activates the command and closes the menu.

Keyboard shortcuts and mnemonics can also be used to activate menu items. For details, see "Keyboard Shortcuts" on page 115 and "Mnemonics" on page 118.

For a list of keyboard operations for menu items, see Table 20 on page 252.

Available and Unavailable Items   When menu items do not apply to the current context, they are dimmed and cannot be activated. Keyboard navigation skips over them. Here are some guidelines for handling available and unavailable menu items in your application.

☕ If an application feature is not currently applicable, make the corresponding menu item unavailable and dim its text. For example, the Undo command might not be available until the user has made a change in a document window.

☕ If all the items in a menu are unavailable, do not make the menu unavailable. If the menu itself is still available, users can display the menu and view all its (unavailable) items. Similarly, if all the items in a submenu are currently not available, do not make the original menu title unavailable.

Composition and Construction of Items   Here are some recommendations for the use of concise language, consistent capitalization, and keyboard operations in menu items.

☕ Make your menu items brief. Menu items can be verb phrases, such as Align Left. They can also be nouns, such as Font, particularly when they display a submenu or a dialog box.

☕ Never give a menu item the same name as its menu title. For example, an Edit menu should not contain an Edit menu item.

☕ Use headline capitalization for menu items.

☕ Include mnemonics for all menu items.

☕ Offer keyboard shortcuts for frequently used menu items.

☕ Use the same keyboard shortcut if a menu item appears in multiple menus—for instance, if a Cut item appears in a contextual menu as well as in a drop-down Edit menu, use Ctrl-X for both.

☕ Use the same mnemonic if a menu item appears in several menus—for instance, if a Copy item appears in a contextual menu as well as in a drop-down Edit menu, use Copy for both.

Commonly used keyboard shortcuts and mnemonics are described in Table 12 on page 246 and Table 13 on page 247.

Ellipses in Items   Ellipses (...) are punctuation marks that indicate the omission of one or more words that must be supplied in order to make a construction complete. In your menus, you can use ellipses in a similar way: to indicate that the command issued by a menu item needs more specification in order to make it complete.

☕ If a menu item does not fully specify a command and users need a dialog box to finish the specification, use an ellipsis after the menu item. For example, after choosing Save As..., users are presented with a file chooser to specify a file name and location.

☕ Do not use an ellipsis mark simply to indicate that a secondary or utility window will appear. For example, choosing Preferences displays a dialog box; because that display is the entire effect of the command, however, Preferences is not followed by an ellipsis.

Separators   A **separator** is a line graphic that is used to divide menu items into logical groupings.

Two separators are shown in Figure 130.

⊙ The corresponding code for Figure 130 is available on the companion CD-ROM.

FIGURE 130 Separators in a Menu

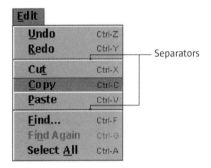

Users can never choose a separator.

You can use separators to make lengthy menus easier to read. For instance, in the typical File menu, shown in Figure 134 on page 182, the commands that affect saving are separated from those that are relevant to printing.

☕ Use separators to group similar menu items in a way that helps users find items and better understand their range of choices.

☕ While separators serve important functions on menus, avoid using them elsewhere in your application. Instead, use blank space or an occasional titled border to delineate areas in dialog boxes or other components.

☕ If a menu is or has the potential to become very long (for instance, in menus that present lists of bookmarks or email recipients), display the menu choices in multiple columns.

Menu Item Graphics   You can add application graphics before the leading edge of menu items in your application, as shown in the following figure. Such graphics should correspond to toolbar button graphics in your application.

FIGURE 131 Menu Item Graphics in a Menu

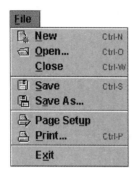

☕ Provide menu item graphics when there are corresponding toolbar button graphics in your application. The graphics help users associate the toolbar button with the corresponding menu command.

Checkbox Menu Items   A **checkbox menu item** is a menu item that appears with a checkbox next to it to represent an on or off setting. A check mark in the adjacent checkbox graphic indicates that the attribute associated with that menu item is turned on. A dimmed checkbox menu item shows a gray box (checked or unchecked) that indicates that the setting cannot be changed. The following figure shows checked, unchecked, and unavailable menu items.

FIGURE 132 Checkbox Menu Items

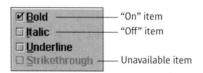

You can use checkbox menu items to present users with a nonexclusive choice.

For a list of keyboard operations for checkbox menu items, see Table 20 on page 252.

☕ Use the standard checkbox graphic for checkbox menu items.

☕ Use checkbox menu items with restraint. As with all menu items, after users choose a checkbox menu item, the menu is dismissed. To choose another item, users must reopen the menu. If users must set more than one or two related attributes, place the checkboxes in a dialog box (or provide a utility window or toolbar buttons for the attributes).

💻 Use checkbox menu items instead of the toggle menu items often used on other platforms to indicate choices you can turn on or off. These toggle menu items (for instance, commands like Italics On and Italics Off) confuse users. It is unclear if the commands are telling users the current state of the selected object or the state they can change the object to by choosing the menu item.

Radio Button Menu Items

A **radio button menu item** is a menu item that appears with a radio button next to it to represent an off or on setting. Each radio button menu item offers users a single choice within a set of radio button menu items, as illustrated in the following set of alignment options.

FIGURE 133 Radio Button Menu Items

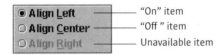

For a list of keyboard operations for radio button menu items, see Table 20 on page 252.

☕ To indicate that the radio button items are part of a set, group them and use separators to separate them from other menu items.

Common Menus

Several drop-down menus, such as File, Edit, Format, View, and Help, occur in many applications. These menus are not supplied by the JFC. The following sections show simple versions of these menus that are consistent with the Java look and feel. You can adapt these menus to suit your needs.

☕ If your application needs the commonly used menus, place the menu titles in this order: File, Edit, Format, View, and Help. If needed, insert other menus between the View and Help menus (and sometimes between Edit and View).

Typical File Menu   The first menu in the menu bar displays commands that apply to an entire document or the application as a whole. (The first menu it the leftmost in locales with left-to-right reading order.) Typically, this is called the File menu, but in some cases another title might be more appropriate. Figure 134 illustrates common File menu items in order, with mnemonics and keyboard shortcuts.

You can add or remove menu items as needed.

⊙ The corresponding code for Figure 134 is available on the companion CD-ROM.

FIGURE 134 Typical File Menu

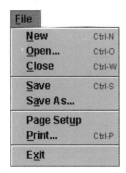

👆 Place commands that apply to the document or the main object (or the application as a whole) in the File menu.

👆 If your application manipulates objects that your users might not think of as "files," give the File menu another name. Ensure that the name corresponds to the type of object or procedure represented by an entire window in your application. For example, a project management application could have Project as its first menu, or a mail application could have a Mailbox menu.

👆 When the Close item dismisses the active window, close any dependent windows at the same time.

👆 Provide an Exit item, which closes all associated windows and terminates the application. (Be sure to use Exit, not Quit.)

Typical Edit Menu   The Edit menu displays items that enable users to change or edit the contents of their documents or other data. These items give users typical editing features that apply to multiple data types, like graphics and text.

Figure 135 shows common Edit menu items in order, with mnemonics and keyboard shortcuts.

FIGURE 135 Typical Edit Menu

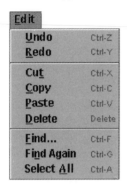

☕ Place commands that modify the contents of documents or other data in the Edit menu, including Undo, Redo, Cut, Copy, Paste, and Find.

▦🖾 The Swing Undo package can be used to provide Undo and Redo features.

Typical Format Menu   The Format menu displays items that enable users to change such elements in their documents as font, size, styles, and other attributes.

Figure 136 shows some common Format menu items with their mnemonics.

⊙ The corresponding code for Figure 136 is available on the companion CD-ROM.

FIGURE 136 Typical Format Menu

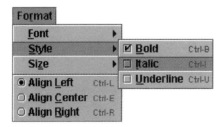

Typical View Menu   The View menu provides ways for users to adjust the presentation of data in the active window. For instance, the View menu in a network management application might have items that enable users to view large or small icons for network objects. Other applications might offer list views and details views. The possibilities for view names depend on the objects in your application.

FIGURE 137 Typical View Menu

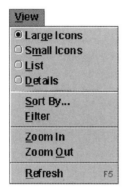

☕ Because the View menu enables users to change only the view of the data (and not the content) in the current primary window, ensure that the commands in the View menu alter the presentation of the underlying data without changing it.

Typical Help Menu   The Help menu provides access to online information about the features of your application. This menu also provides access to the application's About box, which displays basic information about the application. For details, see "Designing About Boxes" on page 104.

Help menu items vary according to the needs of the application. If the help system you are using includes a built-in search feature, you might want to include an Index or a Search item. Additional items might include a tutorial, bookmarks for your product's home page, a bug database, release notes, a Send Comments item, and so forth.

Figure 138 shows common Help menu items (in the typical order) with their mnemonics.

⊙ The corresponding code for Figure 138 is available on the companion CD-ROM.

FIGURE 138 Typical Help Menu

☕ In your Help menu, allow access to online information about the features of the application.

☕ Place a separator before an About Application item that displays a window with the product name, version number, company logo, product logo, legal notices, and names of contributors to the product.

🗗 JavaHelp™, a standard extension to the Java 2 SDK, can be used to build a help system for your applications.

Contextual Menus

Contextual menus, sometimes called "pop-up menus," offer only menu items that are applicable or relevant to the object or region at the location of the pointer. The appearance of contextual menus in the Java look and feel is similar to that of drop-down menus, including the display of mnemonics, keyboard shortcuts, and submenus. Contextual menus do not have a menu title.

◉ The corresponding code for Figure 139 is available on the companion CD-ROM.

Figure 139 shows a contextual menu offering editing commands.

FIGURE 139 Contextual Menu

Users can display a contextual menu by clicking or pressing mouse button 2 while the pointer is over an object or area that is associated with that menu. (On the Macintosh platform, users click or press the mouse button while holding down the Control key.)

For keyboard operations appropriate to contextual menus, see Table 20 on page 252.

☕ Ensure that any features you present in contextual menus are also available in more visible and accessible places, such as drop-down menus. Users might not know contextual menus are available, especially if you do not use contextual menus consistently throughout your application.

☕ Display keyboard shortcuts and mnemonics in contextual menus that are consistent with their usage in any corresponding drop-down menus.

☕ If no object is selected when a contextual menu is displayed, select the object under the pointer and display the contextual menu appropriate to that object. For instance, if the object under the pointer is text, display the contextual menu with editing commands.

☕ If the pointer is over an existing selection at the time the user opens the contextual menu, display the menu that is associated with that selection.

☕ If the pointer is not over the currently selected object when the user opens the contextual menu, create a new selection at the point where the user pressed the mouse button. Display the contextual menu that is appropriate to the object that is beneath the pointer.

☕ If the user opens a contextual menu when the pointer is over an area that cannot be selected, such as the background of a container, remove any existing selection and display the contextual menu for the container.

▤⊃ Contextual menus are created using the `JPopupMenu` component.

Toolbars

A toolbar provides quick and convenient access to a set of frequently used commands or options. Toolbars typically contain buttons, but other components (such as text fields and combo boxes) can be placed in the toolbar as well. An optional, textured "drag area" on the toolbar indicates that users can drag the toolbar anywhere in the window or into a separate window. The drag area is on the leading edge when the toolbar is horizontal and on the top when it is vertical.

Figure 140 shows a toolbar with a drag area on the leading edge. For another example, see Figure 8 on page 23.

⊙ The corresponding code for Figure 140 is available on the companion CD-ROM.

FIGURE 140 Horizontal Toolbar

Drag area ——

Users typically access the components in the toolbar by clicking. For information on the keyboard operations that are appropriate for toolbars, see Table 32 on page 261.

☕ Include commonly used menu items as buttons (or other components) in your toolbar.

☕ Even if your window has a toolbar, make all toolbar commands accessible from menus.

☕ Be sure to provide tool tips for all toolbar buttons.

☕ Consider providing text on toolbar buttons as a user option. This feature makes the meaning of the button clear to new users. It also enables low-vision users to utilize large fonts.

☕ Because toolbars can be difficult for users with motor impairments and are not always regarded as a good use of space, provide a way to hide each toolbar in your application.

☕ Provide large and small graphics (such as 24 x 24 and 16 x 16 pixels) in your application and enable users to select the large graphics in all parts of the application, including the toolbars.

Toolbar Placement   In general, a toolbar is located at the edge of the window or area on which it operates.

☕ If your window has a menu bar, place the toolbar horizontally immediately under the menu bar.

☕ If you use multiple toolbars, provide a way for users to control their display and organize their contents within logical groupings of features.

Draggable Toolbars   You can specify that your toolbar be draggable. Users can then move the toolbar or display it in a separate window. Users drag the toolbar by holding down the mouse button while the pointer is over the drag area. An outline of the toolbar moves as the user moves the pointer. The outline provides an indication of where the toolbar will appear if the user releases the mouse button.

When the pointer is over a "hot spot," the outline has a dark border, indicating the toolbar will anchor to an edge of the container, as shown in Figure 141. The toolbar automatically changes its orientation between horizontal and vertical depending on the edge of the window where it anchors.

⊙ The corresponding code for Figure 141 is available on the companion CD-ROM.

FIGURE 141 Outline of a Toolbar Being Dragged

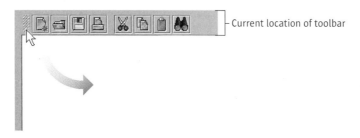
— Current location of toolbar

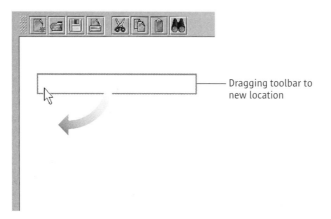
— Dragging toolbar to new location

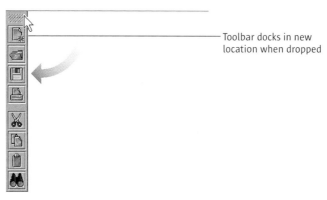
— Toolbar docks in new location when dropped

If the pointer is outside a hot spot, the outline has a light border, indicating that the toolbar will be displayed in a separate window. The following figure shows the toolbar in a separate window. When the user closes the toolbar window, the toolbar returns to its original location in the primary window.

FIGURE 142 Toolbar in a Separate Window

▦▷ A toolbar can dock (attach) along the interior top, bottom, left, or right edge of a container. (The relocated toolbar does not obscure the container contents; rather, the contents of the container are repositioned to compensate for the new placement of the toolbar.)

Toolbar Buttons   A **toolbar button** is a command button or toggle button that appears in a toolbar, typically as part of a set of such buttons. Toolbar buttons can also act as titles to display menus. In other contexts, command buttons typically use text to specify the operation or state they represent, but toolbar buttons typically use graphics.

Toolbar graphics can be difficult for users to understand. Weigh the comprehensibility of your graphics against the space taken up by button text before deciding whether to use button text in addition to the button graphics. Consider giving users the choice of whether to display button text.

☕ Use button graphics that are either 16 x 16 or 24 x 24 pixels (but not both in the same toolbar), depending on the space available in your application.

☕ Provide optional text-only toolbar buttons to enable viewing by low-vision users.

☕ If you use text on the toolbar buttons, provide a user setting to display only the graphics. Using graphics only, you can conserve space and display more commands and settings in the toolbar.

☕ To create functional groupings of toolbar buttons in your application, provide a separate toolbar for each. Using this technique, the drag area serves as both a visual separator and a way to move the toolbar button groups to convenient locations.

For guidelines on the vertical and horizontal measurements for toolbar buttons in toolbars, see "Toolbar Button Spacing" on page 70.

For more information on command buttons, see "Command Buttons" on page 196. For details on toggle buttons, see "Toggle Buttons" on page 200.

Mouse-over Borders   To conserve space, you can use mouse-over borders (also called "rollover borders") on toolbar buttons. This border appears around a button when users move the pointer over it; otherwise, the border is invisible.

The following figure shows a toolbar button with a mouse-over border activated for the Open button.

FIGURE 143 Mouse-over Border on a Toolbar Button

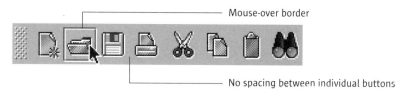

For specifications on spacing between toolbar buttons with mouse-over borders, see "Toolbar Button Spacing" on page 70.

The `JToolBar.isRollover` client property is set to true to enable mouse-over borders.

Drop-down Menus in Toolbar Buttons   You can attach a drop-down menu to a toolbar button. The menu appears when the user clicks (or presses and holds the mouse button over) the toolbar button.

Figure 144 shows the drop-down menu indicated by a **drop-down arrow** on the Open button. The menu shows a list of recently used files that users can open. The mnemonics use numbers because the menu items are likely to change often.

FIGURE 144 Toolbar Button With a Drop-down Menu

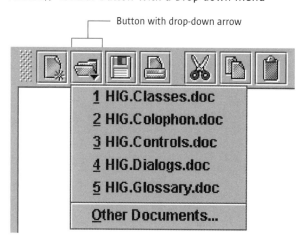

For a discussion of how to use drop-down arrows as menu indicators, see "Using Badges in Button Graphics" on page 95.

☕ Provide a menu indicator (the drop-down arrow) in the graphic for any toolbar button that has a drop-down menu.

🖥🖳 The behavior of drop-down arrows in toolbar buttons is unlike that of some applications that do not use the Java look and feel. In the toolbar buttons of these other applications, a click activates a default command, whereas a press displays a menu.

Tool Tips for Toolbar Buttons   You can provide tool tips for the toolbar components. The tool tip displays information about the component whenever the user rests the pointer over that component. If you specify a keyboard shortcut for a toolbar component, the JFC displays the shortcut in the tool tip. Figure 145 shows a tool tip that describes the Cut button.

⊙ The corresponding code for Figure 145 is available on the companion CD-ROM.

FIGURE 145 Tool Tip for a Toolbar Button

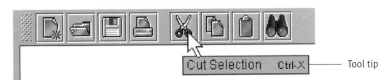

☕ Ensure that the keyboard shortcuts for toolbar buttons match the keyboard shortcuts for the corresponding menu items.

☕ Attach tool tips to all toolbar components that do not include text identifiers.

☕ If your application does not have menus, attach tool tips to the toolbar buttons in order to display keyboard shortcuts.

Tool Tips   A **tool tip** provides information about a component or area whenever the user moves the pointer to that area (and does not press a mouse button). These small rectangles of text can be used anywhere in your application.

A tool tip is commonly associated with an interface element, where it provides a short description of the component's function. If a component has a keyboard shortcut, the shortcut is automatically displayed in the tool tip.

Figure 146 shows a tool tip that describes a slider.

FIGURE 146 Tool Tip for a Slider

You can also use tool tips with application graphics. A chart might have one tool tip that provides the name and size of the graphic or several tool tips that describe different areas of the graphic.

Figure 147 shows a tool tip on an area of the bar chart in the sample applet, Retirement Savings Calculator.

FIGURE 147 Tool Tip on an Area Within a Chart

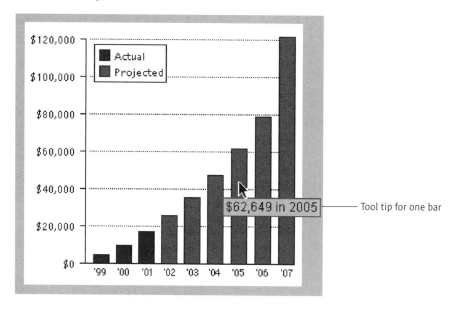

You can adjust the timing of the tool tips in your application. By default, a tool tip appears after the user rests the pointer on the component or area for 750 milliseconds. It disappears after 4 seconds or when the user activates the component or moves the pointer away from the component.

For keyboard operations in tool tips, see Table 31 on page 261.

Allow for the possibility that tool tips might become lengthy in some locales. Always use an onset of 250 milliseconds for tool tips and leave them displayed for 15 seconds.

☕ Make tool tips active by default, but provide users a way to turn them off for the entire application. For example, you might provide a checkbox either in the View menu or in a preferences dialog box.

☕ Use headline capitalization for short tool tips and sentence capitalization for longer ones. Try to be consistent within your application.

⊟⊃ A tool tip is specified in its associated component (and not by calling the `JToolTip` class directly).

⊟⊃ If a component has a tool tip, the `AccessibleDescription` for that component is automatically set to the tool tip text.

For details on the Java 2 Accessibility API, see "Support for Accessibility" on page 30.

10: BASIC CONTROLS

Buttons, combo boxes, and sliders are examples of controls—interface elements users can manipulate to perform an action, select an option, or set a value. A **button** is a **control** that users click to perform an action, set or toggle a state, or set an option. In the Java look and feel, buttons include command and toggle buttons, toolbar buttons, checkboxes, and radio buttons. A **combo box** is a control that enables users to select one option from an associated list; users can also type an option into an editable combo box. A **list box** is a control that presents a set of choices from which a user can select one or more items; items in a list box can be text, graphics, or both. (A related list component, called a selectable list, is described in Chapter 12.) A **slider** is a control that enables users to set a value in a range.

FIGURE 148 Buttons, Combo Box, List Box, and Slider

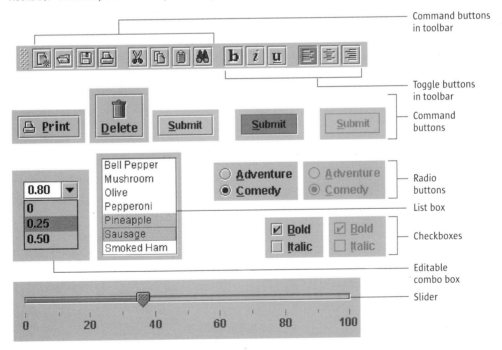

For text in buttons, sliders, and combo boxes, use headline capitalization.

⊕ Make sure you use layout managers to lay out your controls so they allow for the longer text strings frequently associated with localization.

Command Buttons

A **command button** is a button with a rectangular border that contains text, a graphic, or both. These buttons typically use button text, often a single word, to identify the action or setting that the button represents. See "Command Buttons in Dialog Boxes" on page 159 for a list of commonly used command button names and their recommended usage.

Command buttons in a dialog box can stand alone or appear in a row, as shown in Figure 149.

⊙ The corresponding code for Figure 149 is available on the companion CD-ROM.

FIGURE 149 Command Buttons in a Dialog Box

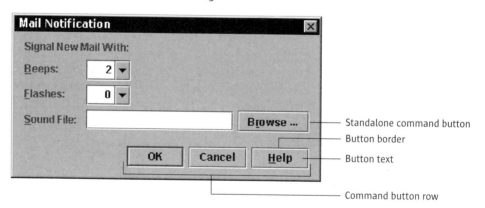

— Standalone command button
— Button border
— Button text
— Command button row

Command buttons that appear in toolbars are called "toolbar buttons." Typically, they use button graphics instead of button text.

Figure 150 shows toolbar buttons for a text-editing application.

⊙ The corresponding code for Figure 150 is available on the companion CD-ROM.

FIGURE 150 Toolbar Buttons

See "Toolbar Buttons" on page 189 for details on toolbar buttons. For a discussion of badges in toolbar buttons, see "Using Badges in Button Graphics" on page 95.

When a command button is unavailable, the dimmed appearance indicates that it cannot be used. The following figure shows the appearance of available, pressed, and unavailable command buttons.

FIGURE 151 Available, Pressed, and Unavailable Command Buttons

Users can click command buttons to specify a command or initiate an action, such as Save, Cancel, or Submit Changes.

For a list of keyboard operations for the activation of command buttons, see Table 17 on page 250.

☕ Display mnemonics in button text, with the exception of default command buttons and the Cancel button in dialog boxes.

☕ To make command buttons without text more accessible, create tool tips that describe or name the functions of the buttons.

⊕ Make your button text easier to localize by using resource bundles. A resource bundle stores text separately so that localizers don't have to change the application's source code to accommodate translation.

For more on resource bundles in the localization process, see "Resource Bundles" on page 50.

For general details on keyboard operations and mnemonics, see "Keyboard Operations" on page 111 and "Mnemonics" on page 118. For details on displaying a command button's tool tip, see Table 31 on page 261.

For details on the layout and spacing of command buttons, see "Command Button Spacing and Padding" on page 71.

Default Command Buttons

One of the buttons in a window can be the **default command button**. The JFC gives default command buttons a heavier border.

Default command buttons typically appear in dialog boxes. The default command button is activated when users press Enter (or Return).

A default command button (such as Save in Figure 152) should represent the action most often performed (if that action does not lead to loss of user data).

⊙ The corresponding code for Figure 152 is available on the companion
CD-ROM.

FIGURE 152 Default and Nondefault Command Buttons

The Enter and Return equivalents activate the default command button
unless keyboard focus is currently on a component that accepts the Enter or
Return key. For instance, if the insertion point is in a multiline text area and
the user presses Enter, the insertion point moves to the beginning of a new
line rather than activating a default button. In this case, users can press Ctrl-
Enter to activate the default button. Alternatively, they can press Ctrl-Tab to
move the focus out of the current component and then press Enter.

Since you are not required to have a default button in every circumstance,
you can use discretion about including them in your interface elements.

☕ In most situations, make OK the default button.

☕ Never make an unsafe choice the default button. For instance, a button
that would result in the loss of unsaved changes should not be the default
command button.

▤⌐ The JFC does not automatically implement the Escape key as the
keyboard equivalent for the Cancel button, so this behavior must be
implemented. As with the Enter and Return keys for the default command
button, the Cancel button should not require keyboard focus to be activated
by the Escape key.

Combining Graphics With Text in Command Buttons   In some circumstances, you
might use a graphic along with text to identify the action or setting
represented by a command button.

Figure 153 shows a Print button with a graphic on the leading edge of the
text and a Delete button with a graphic above the button text.

⊙ The corresponding code for Figure 153 is available on the companion
CD-ROM.

FIGURE 153 Command Buttons Containing Both Text and Graphics

☕ In command buttons containing both text and graphics, place the text after or below the image.

☕ When adding graphics to buttons that typically use text, such as dialog box command buttons, place the graphic on the leading edge of the button text (that is, to the left of the text in left-to-right locales). Include the graphic in such contexts, for instance, if the graphic serves as a reminder of the toolbar button that initially displayed the dialog box.

☕ In contexts that typically use graphical buttons, such as toolbars, place button text beneath the graphic or on the trailing edge (right in left-to-right locales) of the button. Consider giving users the choice of what to display and where to display it.

☕ Use mnemonics in your command buttons—with the exception of the default and Cancel buttons.

☕ Provide a way to display text in command buttons as an aid to low-vision users.

For a list of commonly used mnemonics organized by menus, see Table 9 on page 120. For an alphabetical list of commonly used mnemonics, see Table 13 on page 247. Try to use these mnemonics if possible. Do not duplicate mnemonics.

Using Ellipses in Command Buttons

When a command button does not fully specify an operation but instead that operation is completed by a dialog box, notify the user by placing an ellipsis mark after the button text. (Note that this applies only to text in buttons. No ellipsis is used in graphics-only buttons.) For example, after clicking a Print… button, users are presented with a dialog box in which to specify printer location, how many copies to print, and so forth. By contrast, a Print command that prints one copy to the default printer without displaying a dialog box would not require an ellipsis mark.

☕ When users must interact with a dialog box to finish the specification of a command initiated in a command button, use an ellipsis mark (…) after the button text. (Do not use an ellipsis with graphics-only buttons.) When a full specification of the command is made in the button text, do not use ellipses.

⊟⊃ The button text added to a command button that uses ellipses must contain three periods.

Toggle Buttons

A **toggle button** is a button that represents a setting with two states—on and off. Toggle buttons look similar to command buttons and display a graphic or text (or both) to identify the button. The graphic or button text should remain the same whether the button is in the on or off state. The state is indicated by highlighting the background of the buttons.

Users can click toggle buttons to turn a setting on or off—for instance, to switch between italic and plain style in selected text.

You can use toggle buttons to represent an independent choice, like checkboxes (see page 202), or an exclusive choice within a set, like radio buttons (see page 203).

⊞▭ Toggle buttons can be placed in a button group to get radio button behavior.

Independent Choice

An independent toggle button behaves like a checkbox. Whether it appears alone or with other buttons, its setting is independent of other controls. An example of an independent toggle button is a Bold button on a toolbar, as shown in the following illustration.

FIGURE 154 Independent Toggle Buttons in a Toolbar

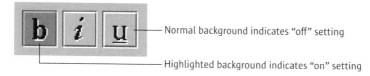

Normal background indicates "off" setting

Highlighted background indicates "on" setting

When users click the Bold button, it is highlighted to indicate that the bold style has been applied to the selection or that text to be entered will be bold. If the button is clicked again, it reverts to the normal button appearance and the bold style is removed from the selection.

☕ Although checkboxes and independent toggle buttons have the same function, as a general rule, use checkboxes in dialog boxes and menus and use toggle buttons with a graphic in toolbars.

☕ Use toggle buttons (instead of checkboxes) in dialog boxes if you need consistency with a toolbar.

For recommendations on the spacing of toggle buttons, see "Toggle Button Spacing" on page 71.

Exclusive Choice   A toggle button can work as part of a group to represent an exclusive choice within the set. A common example is a set of toolbar toggle buttons representing left, centered, and right text alignment, as shown in the following figure.

FIGURE 155 Exclusive Toggle Buttons

If users click the button representing left alignment, the button is highlighted to indicate that text is aligned flush with the left border of the document. If users then click the button representing centered alignment, the appearance of the Align Left button reverts to the normal button appearance and the Center button is highlighted to indicate centered alignment of the selected text.

You can use grouped toggle buttons with labels equally well in toolbars or dialog boxes. In the example in Figure 156, the label identifies the abbreviations in the button text within a dialog box.

⊙ The corresponding code for Figure 156 is available on the companion CD-ROM.

FIGURE 156 Grouped Toggle Buttons With a Label

└─ Label

For spacing guidelines for exclusive toggle buttons, see "Checkbox and Radio Button Layout and Spacing" on page 73.

Checkboxes

A **checkbox** is a control that represents a setting or value with an on or off choice. The setting of an individual checkbox is independent of other checkboxes—that is, more than one checkbox in a set can be checked at any given time.

A check mark within the checkbox indicates that the setting is selected. The following figure shows both available and unavailable checkboxes in selected and unselected states.

FIGURE 157 Checkboxes

The user clicks a checkbox to switch its setting from off to on, or on to off. When a checkbox is unavailable, the user cannot change its setting.

For a list of keyboard operations for checkboxes, see Table 15 on page 250.

☕ Use the checkbox graphic that is supplied with the component (the square box with or without the check mark inside).

☕ Although checkboxes and independent toggle buttons have the same function, as a general rule, use checkboxes in dialog boxes and menus, and use toggle buttons with a graphic in toolbars.

🌐 Display checkbox text to the right of the graphic unless the application is designed for locales with right-to-left writing systems, such as Arabic and Hebrew. In this case, display the text to the left of the graphic.

⊟⟫ The setMnemonic method can be used to specify mnemonics in checkboxes.

In addition to standard checkboxes, the JFC includes a component that is the functional equivalent of the checkbox for use in menus. See "Checkbox Menu Items" on page 180 for more information.

See "Checkbox and Radio Button Layout and Spacing" on page 73 for specific measurement guidelines.

Radio Buttons

A **radio button** represents an exclusive choice within a set of related options. Within a set of radio buttons, only one button can be on at any given time. The following figure shows active radio buttons and inactive radio buttons in both on and off states.

FIGURE 158 Radio Buttons

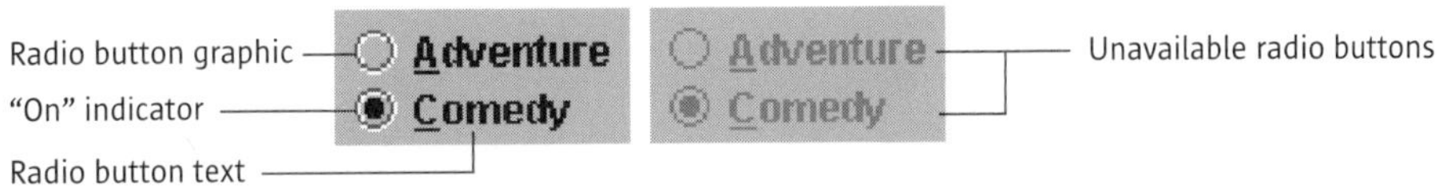

Radio button graphic —— ○ **Adventure**   ○ Adventure —— Unavailable radio buttons
"On" indicator —— ◉ **Comedy**   ◉ Comedy
Radio button text ——

When users click a radio button, its setting is always set to on. An inner filled circle within the round button graphic indicates that the setting is selected. If another button in the set has previously been selected, its state changes to off. When a radio button is unavailable, users cannot change its setting.

For a list of keyboard operations for radio buttons, see Table 21 on page 253.

☕ Use the supplied radio button graphics (the open buttons with inner filled and unfilled circles).

☕ Provide mnemonics for each radio button choice, or place a mnemonic on the label for the radio button group. In the latter case, the user navigates among the individual radio buttons with Tab and Shift-Tab. Putting the mnemonics on each radio button choice is preferable, since that makes navigation easier for users.

☕ Although radio buttons and toggle buttons in a radio button group have the same function, use radio buttons in dialog boxes and use grouped toggle buttons with graphics in toolbars. Grouped toggle buttons with text identifiers work well in either situation.

⊕ Display radio button text to the right of the graphic unless the application is designed for locales with right-to-left writing systems, such as Arabic and Hebrew. In those locales, place the text to the left of the graphic.

The JFC includes a component that is the functional equivalent of the radio button for use in menus. See "Radio Button Menu Items" on page 181 for more information.

See "Checkbox and Radio Button Layout and Spacing" on page 73 for specifications on spacing between radio button choices.

List Boxes

A list box is a one-column arrangement of items (text, graphics, or both) that enables users to set a variable or a property somewhere in the application. List boxes can be used as an alternative to combo boxes, radio buttons, and checkboxes. A similar control, also implemented with the `JList` component, is the selectable list. For details, see "Selectable Lists" on page 226.

You can use a list box to present users with a set of exclusive or nonexclusive choices. For example, you might use a list box to present the days of the week, from which users could select one day on which to start their calendars, as shown in the following figure.

FIGURE 159 Exclusive List Box

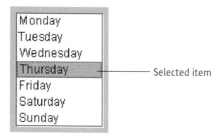
— Selected item

Or, you might use a list box to display pizza toppings, from which users could make several choices, as shown in the following figure.

FIGURE 160 Nonexclusive List Box

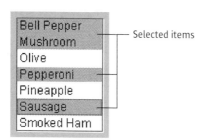
— Selected items

NOTE – Throughout this section, list boxes and selectable lists are referred to as **list components** when their behavior and appearance is the same.

Use headline capitalization in list components.

Provide a label with a mnemonic to enable keyboard navigation into list components.

☕ When resizing a list component, be sure that it always displays a whole number of lines.

Scrolling
You can provide vertical and horizontal scrolling of the items in list components by placing the list inside a scroll pane. Users can then scroll the list as described in "Scroll Panes" on page 142.

☕ If you place a list component in a scroll pane, set the vertical and horizontal scrollbars to appear only when needed. This behavior is the default behavior of scroll panes. If at all possible, display the list component with a width that makes horizontal scrolling unnecessary.

Selection Models for List Components
The JFC provides three selection models that you can use to enable users to select list items: single item, single range, and multiple ranges. Single-item selection provides users with an exclusive choice. Single-range and multiple-range selection provide users with nonexclusive choices.

When the user clicks an item in the list box, that item is chosen: the choice persists even when the user has moved on to the next component. When a user clicks an item in a selectable list, it is selected. If the user later selects another object, this selection disappears.

Despite the different selection models for the two kinds of list components, the methods for making those choices are the same. For simplicity, in the rest of this section, the word "selection" is used to encompass both behaviors.

For the keyboard operations appropriate for list boxes and selectable lists, see Table 19 on page 251.

Single Item
You can enable users to select a single item by clicking it. The item gets keyboard focus. The prior selection, if any, is deselected. In the following figure, the user has selected Thursday.

FIGURE 161 Single-Item Selection in a List Component

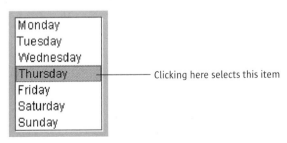

Clicking here selects this item

Single Range of Items   You can enable users to select a single item or a range of items. Users select an item by clicking it. The item gets keyboard focus and becomes the anchor point of the selection. Users extend the selection by dragging or by moving the pointer to another item and Shift-clicking.

In Figure 162, the user first clicked Pineapple and then Shift-clicked Sausage.

⊙ The corresponding code for Figure 162 is available on the companion CD-ROM.

FIGURE 162 Range of Selected Items in a List Component

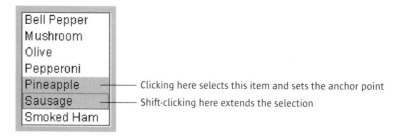

Multiple Ranges of Items   You can enable users to select a single item, a range of items, or multiple ranges of items (also known as "discontinuous," "discontiguous," or "disjoint" ranges). Users select a single item by clicking it and extend the selection by Shift-clicking. To start another range, users Control-click an item. That item then gets keyboard focus and becomes the anchor point of the new range. In addition, the selection of the item is toggled—if the item was initially selected, it is deselected, and vice versa. Shift-clicking extends the new range.

In the following figure, the user chose the first range by clicking Bell Pepper and then Shift-clicking Mushroom. The user chose additional ranges by Control-clicking Pepperoni and extending to Sausage with a Shift-click. Finally, the user deselected an item in the range by Control-clicking Pineapple.

FIGURE 163 Multiple Ranges of Selected Items in a List Component

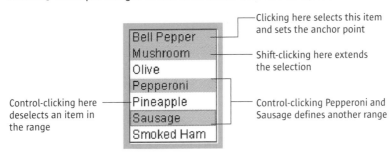

Combo Boxes   A combo box is a component with a drop-down arrow that users click to display an associated list of choices. If the list is too long to display fully, a vertical scrollbar appears. The current selection appears in an editable or noneditable text field next to the drop-down arrow. The user displays the list by clicking or dragging the drop-down arrow.

The currently selected item appears in the pulled-down combo box. As a user moves the pointer over the list, each option under the pointer is highlighted. If the user selects an option from the list, that option replaces the current selection. In the following figure, the currently selected item is Vanilla, and the Guanabana option will replace Vanilla when the mouse button is lifted or the spacebar is pressed.

FIGURE 164 Combo Box Display

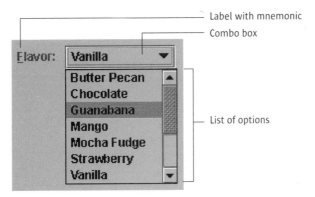

Users can close editable or noneditable combo boxes by clicking the drop-down arrow in the combo box again, selecting an item from the list, or clicking anywhere outside the combo box.

For a list of keyboard operations appropriate for combo boxes, see Table 16 on page 250.

You can use combo boxes to provide a way for users to indicate a choice from a set of mutually exclusive options. Noneditable combo boxes enable users to select one item from a limited set of items. Editable combo boxes provide users the additional option of typing in an item that might or might not be on the list.

☕ Use headline capitalization for the text in the combo box list.

☕ To facilitate keyboard access, provide labels with mnemonics for combo boxes.

☕ You can specify the maximum number of items to be displayed in a combo box before a scrollbar appears. The default is 8; however, if you know that your list contains 9 or 10 items, it is good practice to display all the items so users don't have to scroll to see just one or two additional items.

🖳🖳 In the JFC, the term "combo box" includes both of what Microsoft Windows applications call "list boxes" and "combo boxes."

Noneditable Combo Boxes   Noneditable combo boxes (sometimes called "list boxes" or "pop-up menus") display a list from which users can select one item.

The following figure shows a noneditable combo box with a drop-down arrow to the right of the currently selected item. (Note the gray background in the default Java look and feel theme, indicating that users cannot edit text.)

FIGURE 165 Noneditable Combo Box

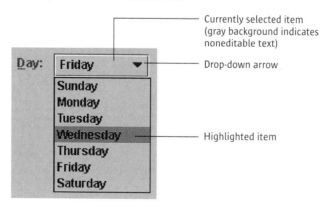

To make a selection, users have two options:

- They can click the combo box to post the list, position the pointer over the desired option to highlight it, and click.

- They can press the mouse button in the combo box (which posts the list), drag through the list to the desired choice and release the mouse button.

In either case, the currently selected item changes to reflects the choice.

☕ Use a noneditable combo box instead of a group of radio buttons or a list box if space is limited in your application.

Editable Combo Boxes   Editable combo boxes combine an editable text field with a drop-down arrow that users click to display an associated list of options.

As shown in Figure 166, editable combo boxes initially appear as editable text fields with a drop-down arrow. The white background of the editable combo box indicates that users can type, select, and edit text.

⊙ The corresponding code for Figure 166 is available on the companion CD-ROM.

FIGURE 166 Editable Combo Box

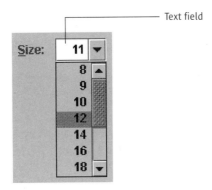

To make a selection, users have three options:

- They can click the drop-down arrow to display the list, position the pointer over the desired option to highlight it, and click.

- They can drag from the drop-down arrow to the desired selection and release the mouse button.

- To make a customized selection, they can type text in the field and press Enter (or move focus to another component). If the list is open, it will close.

You can use an editable combo box to save users time by making the most likely menu choices available while still enabling users to type other values in the text field. An example might be the specification of a font size. The combo box might initially display a current size of 11. Users could select from a list of standard sizes (8, 9. 10, 12, 14, 16, or 18 points) or type in their own values—for instance, 22 points.

☕ Whenever possible, interpret user input into an editable combo box in a case-insensitive way. For example, it should not matter whether the user types Blue, blue, or BLUE.

Sliders
A slider is a control that is used to select a value from a continuous or discontinuous range. The position of the indicator reflects the current value. Major tick marks indicate large divisions along the range of values (for instance, every ten units); minor tick marks indicate smaller divisions (for instance, every five units).

The default slider in the Java look and feel is a nonfilling slider. An example is a slider that adjusts left-right balance in a stereo speaker system, as shown in the following figure.

FIGURE 167 Nonfilling Slider

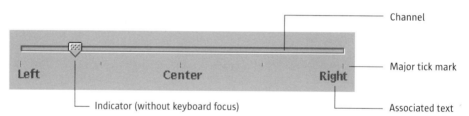

A filling slider is also available. The filled portion of the channel, shown in the following figure, represents the range of values below the current value—in this case, the percentage of a paycheck allotted to a retirement savings plan.

FIGURE 168 Filling Slider

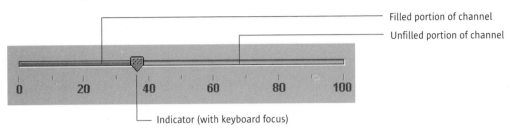

Filled portion of channel

Unfilled portion of channel

Indicator (with keyboard focus)

Users can drag the indicator to set a specific value or click the channel to move back and forth by one unit. Sliders can represent a series of discrete values, in which case the indicator snaps to the value closest to the end point of the drag operation.

For a list of keyboard operations for sliders, see Table 24 on page 255.

☕ If the slider represents a continuous range or a large number of discrete values and the exact value that is chosen is important, provide a text field where the chosen value can be displayed. For instance, a user might want to specify an annual retirement savings contribution of 2.35%. In such a situation, consider making the text field editable to give users the option of typing in the value directly. Be sure to link the slider and the text field so that each is automatically updated when the user alters the other.

▤⊃ The `JSlider.isFilled` client property can be used to enable the optional filling slider.

11: TEXT COMPONENTS

Text components enable users to view and edit text in an application. The simplest text component you can provide is a **label**, which presents read-only information. A label is usually associated with another component and describes its function. A **text field** is a rectangular area that displays a single line of text, which can be editable or noneditable. A **password field** is an editable text field that displays masking characters in place of the characters that the user types.

Other text components display multiple lines of text. A **text area** displays text in a single font, size, and style. You can configure an **editor pane** to display different types of text through the use of a plug-in editor. The JFC editors include a plain text editor, a styled text editor, an RTF (rich text format) editor, and an HTML (Hypertext Markup Language) editor.

FIGURE 169 Text Components

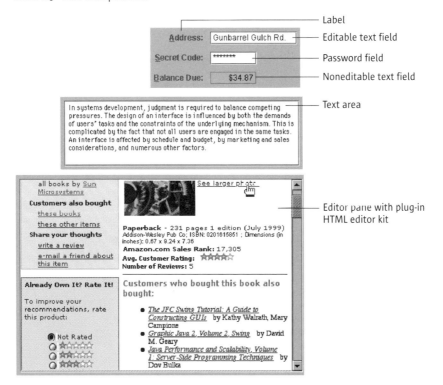

⊕ Make your text easier to localize by using resource bundles. A resource bundle stores text separately so that localizers don't have to change the application's source code to accommodate translation.

For guidelines on translating text, see "Planning for Internationalization and Localization" on page 48.

Labels

A label consists of read-only text, graphics, or both. Labels serve two functions in an application:

- To identify components and enable navigation to components that don't have their own text strings

- To communicate status and other information

Users cannot select a label or any of its parts.

Labels That Identify Controls   You can associate a label with a component (such as a text field, slider, or checkbox) to describe the use of the component.

In Figure 170, the Salary Contribution label lets users know they can use the slider to adjust their salary contribution.

⊙ The corresponding code for Figure 170 is available on the companion CD-ROM.

FIGURE 170 Label That Describes the Use of a Slider

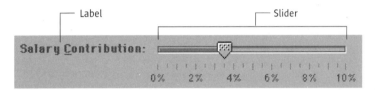

You can also use a label to describe a group of components.

In Figure 171, the Color label describes a group of three radio buttons. The other text (Red, Yellow, and Blue) is part of the radio buttons and not a separate component. The Color label is not a separate component for the purpose of navigation.

⊙ The corresponding code for Figure 171 is available on the companion CD-ROM.

FIGURE 171 Label That Describes a Radio Button Group

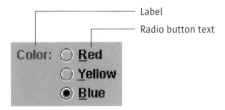

☕ Keep label text brief, and use terminology that is familiar to users.

☕ Use headline capitalization in the label text and place a colon at the end of the text.

Available and Unavailable Labels   You can make a label available or unavailable so that its state is the same as that of the component it describes. Available labels are drawn in the primary 1 color defined in the application's color theme.

Unavailable labels are drawn in the secondary 2 color defined in the application's color theme. The following figure shows an available and unavailable label.

FIGURE 172 Available and Unavailable Labels

Size: ——— Available

Size: ——— Unavailable

☕ Make a label unavailable when the component it describes is unavailable.

Mnemonics in Labels   You can specify a mnemonic for a label. When the mnemonic is activated, it gives focus to the component that the label describes. This technique is often used with a label that accompanies an editable text field. In the following figure, the text field gets focus when users press Alt-N.

FIGURE 173 Label With a Mnemonic

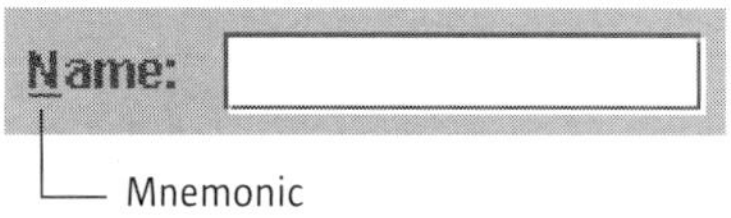

Name: [   ]

└── Mnemonic

☕ If you can't add a mnemonic directly to the component that requires one, as in the case of an editable text field, place the mnemonic in the component's label.

▤ The `displayedMnemonic` property can be used to specify the mnemonic in a label.

▤ The `labelFor` property can be used to associate a label with another component so that the component gains focus when the label's mnemonic is activated. This practice automatically sets the target's accessible name. The `labelFor` property is most easily set by using the `JLabel.setLabelFor()` method.

For a description of the alignment of labels and the spacing between a label and its components, see "Label Alignment and Spacing" on page 67.

Labels That Communicate Status and Other Information   You can use a label to communicate status or give information to users. In addition, you can instruct your application to alter a label to show a change in state.

The progress bar in Figure 174 uses two labels that change as the operation progresses. The application changes the top label to reflect the file currently being copied, and it updates the bottom label as the progress bar fills.

⊙ The corresponding code for Figure 174 is available on the companion CD-ROM.

FIGURE 174 Labels That Clarify the Meaning of a Progress Bar

Use sentence capitalization in the text of a label that communicates status. Do not provide end punctuation unless the text is a complete sentence.

To ensure that the information in a status label is accessible to all users, the accessibleDescription property of the window containing the label should be set to the text of the label. Whenever the label changes, a VISIBLE_PROPERTY_CHANGE event should be generated to cue assistive technology to read the label again.

Text Fields
A text field is a rectangular area that displays a single line of text. A text field can be editable or noneditable.

Noneditable Text Fields
In a noneditable text field, users can select and copy text to paste elsewhere (something they cannot do with labels), but they cannot change the text in the fields. Only the application can change the contents of a noneditable text field. The background of a noneditable text field is the secondary 3 color defined in the application's color theme. In the default theme, the background color is gray, as shown in the following figure.

FIGURE 175 Noneditable Text Field

16.3%

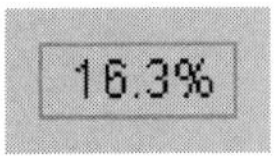

Editable Text Fields   In an editable text field, users can type or edit a single line of text. For example, a find dialog box has a text field in which users type a string for which they want to search.

When a text field has keyboard focus, it displays a blinking bar that indicates the insertion point. When users type in text that is too long to fit in the field, the text scrolls horizontally. By default, the background of an editable text field is white.

The following figure shows an editable text field with keyboard focus. The Language label is a separate component from the text field.

FIGURE 176 Editable Text Field With Blinking Bar

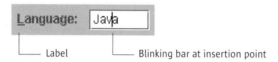

Language: [Java]

└── Label   └── Blinking bar at insertion point

In an editable text field, users can:

- Insert characters at the insertion point and replace selected text by typing

- Cut, copy, and paste text by using menu commands or keyboard shortcuts (Ctrl-X for Cut, Ctrl-C for Copy, and Ctrl-V for Paste)

- Set the insertion point by single-clicking

- Select a word by double-clicking

- Select the entire line of text by triple-clicking

- Select a range of characters by dragging

- Select everything by navigating to the text field using the Tab key or the label's mnemonic

The following figure shows a text field with the letters `Jeffer` selected. The insertion point is at the end of the selected text and indicates that the text field has keyboard focus. The selected text is overwritten when the user types or pastes new text.

FIGURE 177 Editable Text Field With Selected Text

[Thomas Jefferson]

When keyboard focus enters a text field by some means other than a user's mouse click, select the entire contents of the text field. (This situation might occur if the user navigated into the text field with a mnemonic or with the Tab key, or if the initial focus when a dialog box opens is in the text field. (Figure 84 on page 129 shows an example of such a situation.) Users can then start typing characters to replace the existing text, or they can press the Tab key to move to the next field, leaving the original text intact. When the text is selected, pressing the left or right arrow keys deselects the text and moves the insertion point (if possible), enabling users to correct the text using only the keyboard. Of course, if users click in a text field, place the insertion point as close to the click point as possible, without selecting text.

To associate a mnemonic with a text field, you must give the text field a label. You can then assign a mnemonic to the label, and make the mnemonic give focus to the text field. For details, see "Mnemonics in Labels" on page 216. For keyboard operations appropriate to text fields, see Table 29 on page 260.

☕ Depending on the type of data, you might be able to check individual characters for errors as they are typed—for example, if users try to type a letter into a text field that should contain only numbers. In this case, do not display the character in the field. Instead, sound the system beep. If the user types three illegal characters in a row, display an Error alert box that explains the legal entries for the text field.

☕ If you plan an action based on the string in the text field (such as searching for the string or performing a calculation), start the action when users signify that they have completed the entry by pressing Enter or by moving keyboard focus outside the text field. Do not start the action before the user has completed the text entry.

For keyboard operations for editable text fields, see Table 29 on page 260.

Password Fields

The password field is an editable text field that displays a masking character instead of the characters that users type. Asterisks are displayed in the password field by default. You can designate any Unicode character as the masking (also called "secure") character, but make sure the character is available in the current font.

The password field is commonly used in a login dialog box, as shown in Figure 178. The Password label is a separate component from the password field.

⊙ The corresponding code for Figure 178 is available on the companion CD-ROM.

FIGURE 178 Password Field

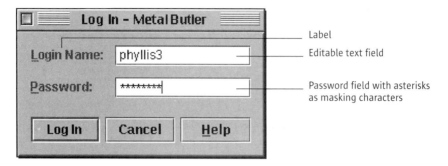

A password field provides users with some of the editing capabilities of an editable text field, but not the cut and copy operations. For keyboard operations appropriate to password fields, see Table 29 on page 260.

The setEchoChar method can be used to change the masking character—for example, from asterisks to pound signs.

Text Areas

A text area provides a rectangular space in which users can view, type, and edit multiple lines of text. The JFC renders such text in a single font, size, and style, as shown in the following figure.

FIGURE 179 Text Area

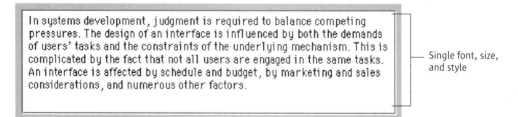

Users can type and replace text in a text area. See "Text Fields" on page 217 for a description of text-editing features supplied by the JFC. For keyboard operations appropriate to text areas, see Table 28 on page 258.

You can enable word wrap so that the text wraps to the next line when it reaches the edge of the text area, as shown in the preceding figure. You can enable scrolling by placing the text area inside a scroll pane. In this case, the text scrolls horizontally or vertically when it is too long to fit in the text area.

The following figure shows a text area inside a scroll pane. For information on scrolling, see "Scroll Panes" on page 142.

FIGURE 180 Text Area in a Scroll Pane

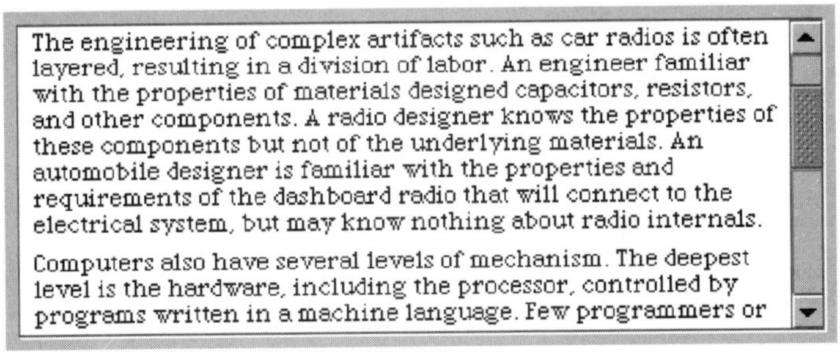

☕ If you place text in a scroll pane, ensure that the vertical scrollbar is always there and provide a horizontal scrollbar only as needed. This is not the default behavior of scroll panes.

☕ If the text area contains prose, enable word wrap. If the text area contains information for which exact line breaks are important, such as code or poetry, enable horizontal scrolling.

▤▭ The `lineWrap` and `wrapStyleWord` properties of the text area can be set to true to enable word wrap on word boundaries.

Editor Panes

An editor pane is a multiline text pane that uses a **plug-in editor kit** to display a specific type of text, such as RTF (rich text format) or HTML (Hypertext Markup Language). An editor kit is capable of displaying all fonts included with the AWT. The JFC provides four kits that you can plug into an editor pane:

- Default editor kit
- Styled text editor kit
- RTF editor kit
- HTML editor kit

You can also create your own editor kit or use a third-party editor kit. For an example of how to create an editor kit, see *Java Swing*, described in "Java" on page 9.

▤▭ The `setEditable` method can be used to turn text editing on or off in an editor kit.

Default Editor Kit   You can use the default editor kit to edit and display text in a single font, size, and style. This kit is functionally equivalent to a text area.

Styled Text Editor Kit   You can embed images and components (such as tables) in a styled text editor kit.

You can use a styled text editor kit to edit and display multiple fonts, sizes, and styles, as shown in Figure 181.

⊙ The corresponding code for Figure 181 is available on the companion CD-ROM.

FIGURE 181 Styled Text Editor Kit

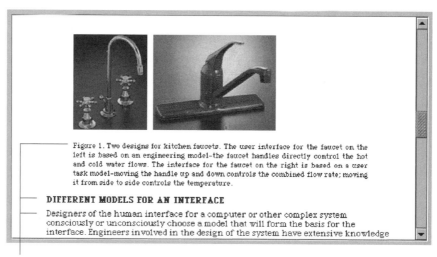

Multiple font sizes and styles

RTF Editor Kit   You can use an RTF editor kit to read, write, and display RTF text, as shown in the following figure. The RTF editor kit offers all the capabilities provided by the styled editor kit, and more.

FIGURE 182 RTF Editor Kit

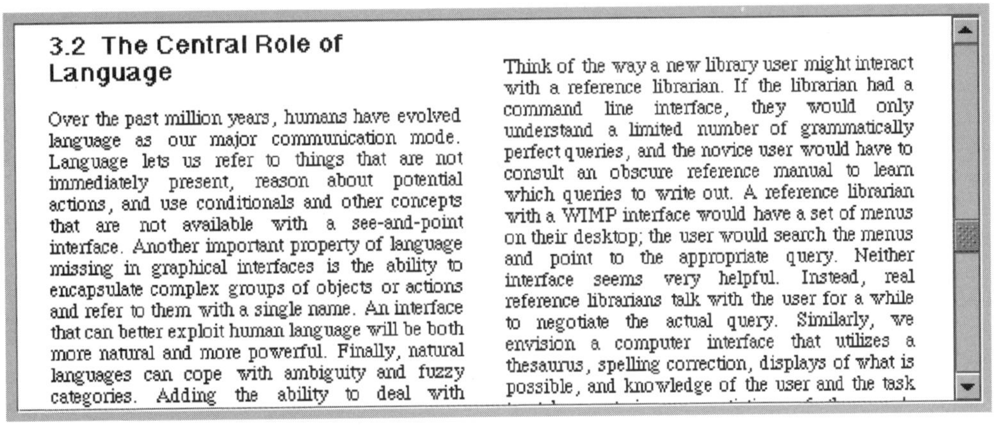

3.2 The Central Role of Language
Over the past million years, humans have evolved language as our major communication mode. Language lets us refer to things that are not immediately present, reason about potential actions, and use conditionals and other concepts that are not available with a see-and-point interface. Another important property of language missing in graphical interfaces is the ability to encapsulate complex groups of objects or actions and refer to them with a single name. An interface that can better exploit human language will be both more natural and more powerful. Finally, natural languages can cope with ambiguity and fuzzy categories. Adding the ability to deal with
Think of the way a new library user might interact with a reference librarian. If the librarian had a command line interface, they would only understand a limited number of grammatically perfect queries, and the novice user would have to consult an obscure reference manual to learn which queries to write out. A reference librarian with a WIMP interface would have a set of menus on their desktop; the user would search the menus and point to the appropriate query. Neither interface seems very helpful. Instead, real reference librarians talk with the user for a while to negotiate the actual query. Similarly, we envision a computer interface that utilizes a thesaurus, spelling correction, displays of what is possible, and knowledge of the user and the task

HTML Editor Kit You can use an HTML editor kit to display text in HTML 3.2. Users can click a link on the HTML page to generate an event, which you can use to replace the contents in the pane.

FIGURE 183 HTML Editor Kit

all books by Sun Microsystems
Customers also bought
these books
these other items
Share your thoughts
write a review
e-mail a friend about this item
Already Own It? Rate It!
To improve your recommendations, rate this product:
Not Rated
See larger photo
Paperback - 231 pages 1 edition (July 1999)
Addison-Wesley Pub Co; ISBN: 0201615851 ; Dimensions (in inches): 0.67 x 9.24 x 7.36
Amazon.com Sales Rank: 17,305
Avg. Customer Rating:
Number of Reviews: 5
Customers who bought this book also bought:
The JFC Swing Tutorial: A Guide to Constructing GUIs by Kathy Walrath, Mary Campione
Graphic Java 2, Volume 2, Swing by David M. Geary
Java Performance and Scalability, Volume 1: Server-Side Programming Techniques by Dov Bulka
Links

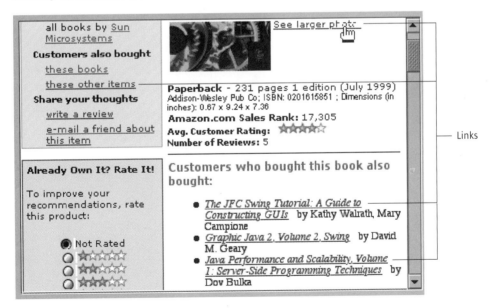

12: SELECTABLE LISTS, TABLES, AND TREE COMPONENTS

A **selectable list** is a one-column arrangement of items in which the items users select are designated for a subsequent action, usually in an associated component such as a table or a text field. Tables and trees provide a way to organize related information so that users can easily compare the data. A **table** is a two-dimensional arrangement of data. A **tree component** is an outline of hierarchical relationships.

FIGURE 184 Selectable List, Table, and Tree Component

Selectable list (with associated table)

Table

First Name	Last Name	Employee ID	Project
Jakob	Lehn	532	Butler
Peter	Winter	27	FireDog
Sophia	Amann	377	Krakatoa
Samuel	Stewart	452	Butler
Eva	Kidney	1273	Moonbeam
Mary	Dole	811	FireDog
Roscoe	Arrowsmith	28	FireDog
Mira	Brooks	192	Moonbeam

Tree component

Selectable Lists

Selectable lists are one-column collections of data in which selected items are designated for a subsequent action. Command buttons can operate on this selection. When users make another selection, any previous selection is deselected. This is the same way selection works for many other objects, including text. List boxes, which are also implemented with the `JList` component, have a different selection model. In list boxes, the choices that the user makes are persistent.)

In selectable lists, as in list boxes, a single item, a single range, or multiple ranges can be selected. See "Selection Models for List Components" on page 205 for details.

☕ Provide users with as much flexibility in making selections as makes sense for your application.

🍴 Selectable lists are created using the `JList` component.

Selectable Lists and Associated Tables

Selectable lists are appropriate when you want a user to select a few items from a long list so that your application can then display details of the selected items in a table. The user selects an item in the list on the left (in left-to-right locales) and presses the Add button. The selected item is removed from the list on the left and appears (with additional detail) in the table on the right. The most recently moved item appears selected in the table, as shown in the following figure.

FIGURE 185 Selectable List and Associated Table

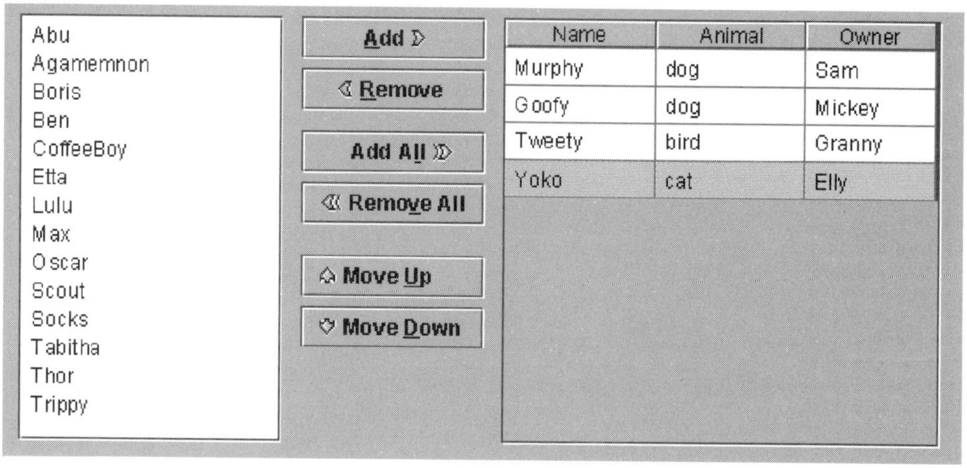

Selectable Lists and Associated Text Fields   Selectable lists are also typically used in file choosers. Users select an item from a list of files, and an editable text field reflects the choice, as shown in the following figure.

FIGURE 186 Selectable List in File Chooser at Time of Selection

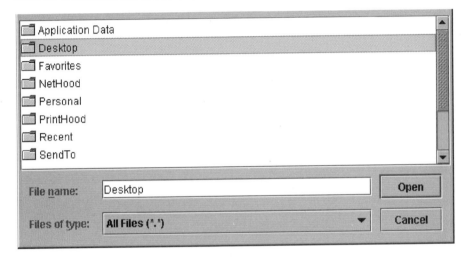

When keyboard focus moves to the editable text field, the selected item remains in the list, but the highlighting is removed, as shown in the following figure.

FIGURE 187 Selectable List in File Chooser After Change in Keyboard Focus

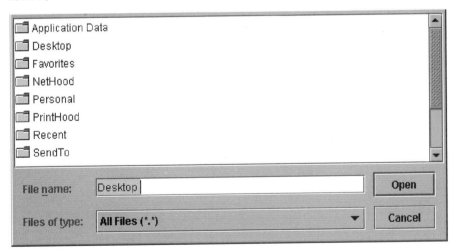

NOTE – Typically, double-clicking in a selectable list activates a dialog box's default command. You must program this behavior explicitly; the JFC does not provide it automatically.

Except for selection behavior, selectable lists are the same as list boxes, described in "List Boxes" on page 204.

☕ Be sure to put your selectable list in a scroll pane if it contains too many items to display all at once.

☕ Always display a whole number of lines in scrolling lists.

Tables

A table organizes related information into a series of rows and columns. Each field in the table is called a "cell." By default, a cell contains a text field, but you can replace it with graphics and other components, such as a checkbox or combo box. The cell with keyboard focus has an inner border, which is drawn in the primary 1 color in the application's color theme.

The following figure illustrates the use of a table to display the records of employees in a company database. The cell with the value 377 is selected and has keyboard focus, but cannot be edited. The table lets you change an employee's project, but not the first or last name or employee ID.

FIGURE 188 Table in a Scroll Pane

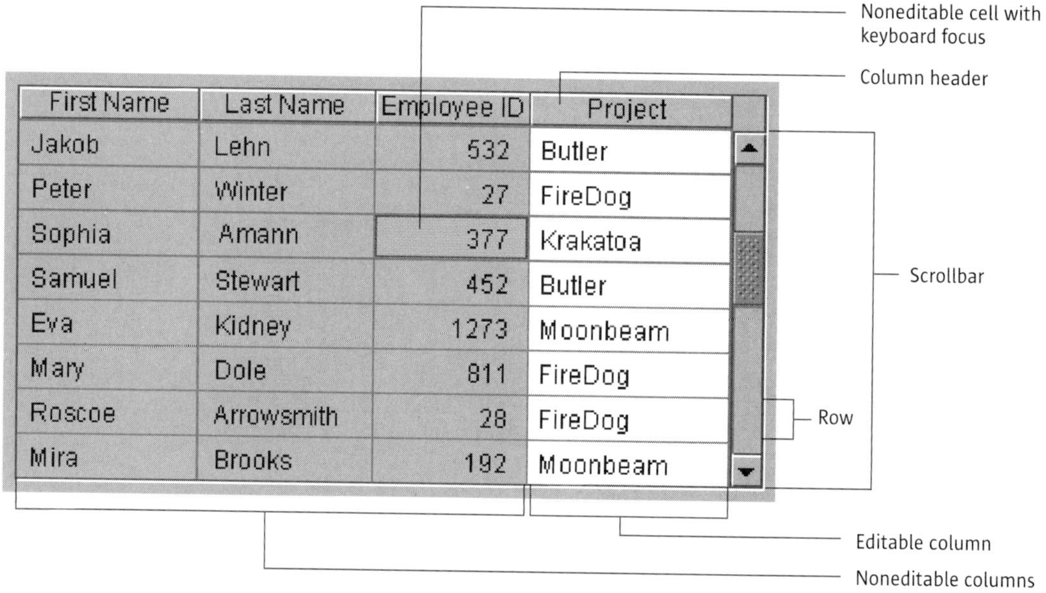

First Name	Last Name	Employee ID	Project
Jakob	Lehn	532	Butler
Peter	Winter	27	FireDog
Sophia	Amann	377	Krakatoa
Samuel	Stewart	452	Butler
Eva	Kidney	1273	Moonbeam
Mary	Dole	811	FireDog
Roscoe	Arrowsmith	28	FireDog
Mira	Brooks	192	Moonbeam

Noneditable cell with keyboard focus

Column header

Scrollbar

Row

Editable column

Noneditable columns

The background color of a cell depends on:

- Whether the cell is selected
- Whether the cell is editable or noneditable
- The background color of the table

The following table shows how a cell gets its background color.

TABLE 10 Background Color of Table Cells

Type of Cell	Background Color	Example
An unselected cell (editable)	The background color of the table, which is white by default.	Kidney
An unselected cell (noneditable)	The secondary 3 color, which is gray in the default color scheme.	Lena
A selected cell that is editable and currently has keyboard focus	White. The inner border is drawn in the primary 1 color to indicate that the cell has keyboard focus. (For information on color themes in the Java look and feel, see "Colors" on page 55.)	Mary
A selected cell that is noneditable and currently has keyboard focus	The primary 3 color, which is light blue in the default color theme. The inner border is primary 1.	Sophia
Any other selected cell	The primary 3 color, which is light blue in the default color theme.	Atticus

Users can select a cell and edit its contents if the component in that cell supports editing. For example, if a cell contains a text field, users can type, cut, copy, and paste text. For more information on editing text in a table, see "Editable Text Fields" on page 218.

Users can press Tab to advance to the next cell and select its contents. For the keyboard operations that are appropriate for tables, see Table 27 on page 256.

⊞⊃ The gray background of noneditable cells is not a default JFC behavior, but it is a recommended practice. You must explicitly specify the color.

Table Appearance   The JFC provides several options that enable you to define the appearance of your table. You can turn on the display of horizontal and vertical lines that define the table cells, as shown in Figure 188 on page 228. You can set the horizontal and vertical padding around the content of a cell. You can also set the width of the columns.

☕ When resizing a table vertically, make sure that it always displays a whole number of rows.

Table Scrolling   You can provide scrolling of your table by placing the table inside a scroll pane. A table has column headers only when it is in a scroll pane. For information on scrolling, see "Scroll Panes" on page 142.

Column Reordering   You can enable users to rearrange the columns in the table. When users drag the column header to the right or left, the entire column moves. Releasing the mouse button places the column at the new location.

The following figure shows the Last Name column being dragged to the right. In this case, the column is selected (although users can also drag an unselected column).

FIGURE 189   Reordering Columns by Dragging a Column Header

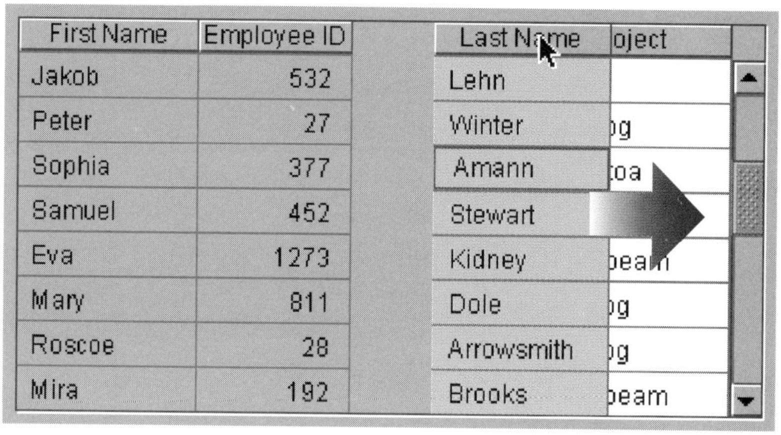

Column Resizing   You can enable users to resize the columns in a table. Users drag the border of the column header to the right to make the column wider and to the left to make the column narrower. When users resize a column, you must decide whether to change the width of the entire table or adjust the other columns so that the overall width is preserved. The JFC-supplied resize options are described in the following table. (Numbers represent relative widths.)

TABLE 11   Table Resize Options

The original table. The double arrow shows the east resize pointer before the columns are resized.	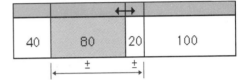
Resize next Resizes the columns on either side of the border being moved. One column becomes bigger, while the other becomes smaller.	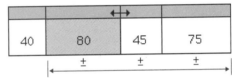
Resize subsequent Resizes the column whose border was moved and all columns to its right. This option is the default option.	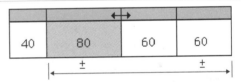
Resize last Resizes the column whose border was moved and the last (rightmost) column.	
Resize all Resizes all other columns, distributing the remaining space proportionately.	
Resize off Resizes the column whose border was moved and makes the table wider or narrower to adjust the space added or removed from the column. This is the only option that changes the overall width of the table.	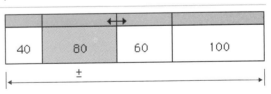

Use either the Resize Next or Resize Off options (described in Table 11) to avoid unexpected results in your tables.

Row Sorting   You can give users the ability to sort the rows in a table by clicking the column headers. An email application, which displays a list of messages in a table, is well suited for row sorting. As shown in the following figure, users can sort the messages by date, sender, or subject. The header of the From column appears in bold to indicate that the messages are currently sorted alphabetically by sender.

FIGURE 190 Row Sorting in an Email Application

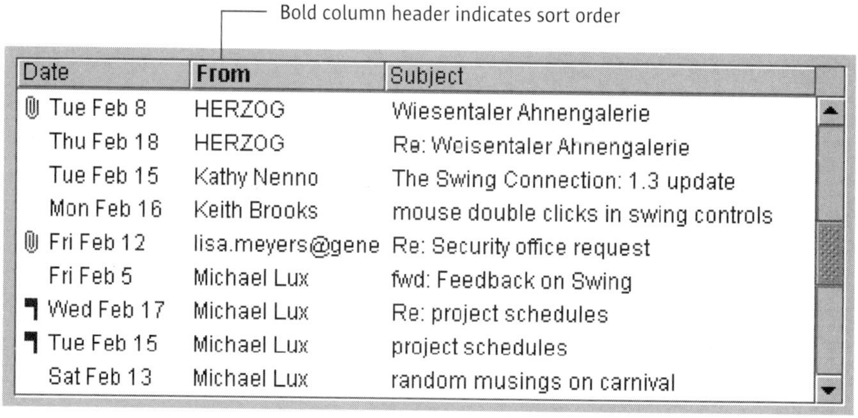

Bold column header indicates sort order

Date	**From**	Subject
📎 Tue Feb 8	HERZOG	Wiesentaler Ahnengalerie
Thu Feb 18	HERZOG	Re: Weisentaler Ahnengalerie
Tue Feb 15	Kathy Nenno	The Swing Connection: 1.3 update
Mon Feb 16	Keith Brooks	mouse double clicks in swing controls
📎 Fri Feb 12	lisa.meyers@gene	Re: Security office request
Fri Feb 5	Michael Lux	fwd: Feedback on Swing
⤷ Wed Feb 17	Michael Lux	Re: project schedules
⤷ Tue Feb 15	Michael Lux	project schedules
Sat Feb 13	Michael Lux	random musings on carnival

☕ Put column header text in bold to indicate the table column that currently determines the sort order. If something happens to invalidate the sort order, remove the visual indicator.

☕ If your application has a menu bar, provide row sorting as a set of menu items as well (for example, include "Sort by Sender" in the View menu). This practice makes sorting available through the keyboard.

▦⇨ Row sorting is not included with the table component. However, the JFC contains sample code that can be used to implement row sorting. See *The Java Tutorial* (described in "Java" on page 9) for more information.

Selection Models for Tables   When designing a table, you must decide which objects (cells, rows, or columns) users can select. The JFC provides 24 models for selecting objects in tables, but they are not all distinct.

☕ The following nine selection models are recommended for use in the Java look and feel:

- No selection
- Single cell
- Single range of cells
- Single row
- Single range of rows
- Multiple ranges of rows
- Single column
- Single range of columns
- Multiple ranges of columns

No Selection   You can turn off selection in a table. Nothing is selected when users click in a cell.

Single Cell   You can enable users to select a cell by clicking it. The cell gets keyboard focus, which is indicated by an inner border. Any previous selection is deselected.

In the following figure, the cell containing 377 is selected and has keyboard focus. The cell cannot be edited, as indicated by the primary 3 background color.

FIGURE 191   Single-Cell Selection

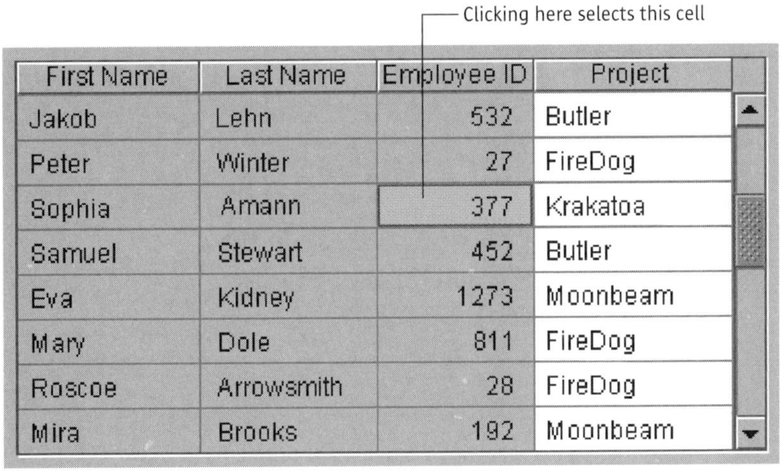

Clicking here selects this cell

First Name	Last Name	Employee ID	Project
Jakob	Lehn	532	Butler
Peter	Winter	27	FireDog
Sophia	Amann	377	Krakatoa
Samuel	Stewart	452	Butler
Eva	Kidney	1273	Moonbeam
Mary	Dole	811	FireDog
Roscoe	Arrowsmith	28	FireDog
Mira	Brooks	192	Moonbeam

Range of Cells   You can enable users to select a single cell or a rectangular range of cells. Users select a cell by clicking it. That cell gets keyboard focus and becomes the anchor point of the selection. Users extend the selection by moving the pointer to a new cell and Shift-clicking. Users can also select a range of cells by dragging through the range.

In the following figure, the user has selected the range by clicking Sophia and then Shift-clicking 1273. The cell containing Sophia is noneditable, as indicated by its blue background.

FIGURE 192   Range of Selected Cells

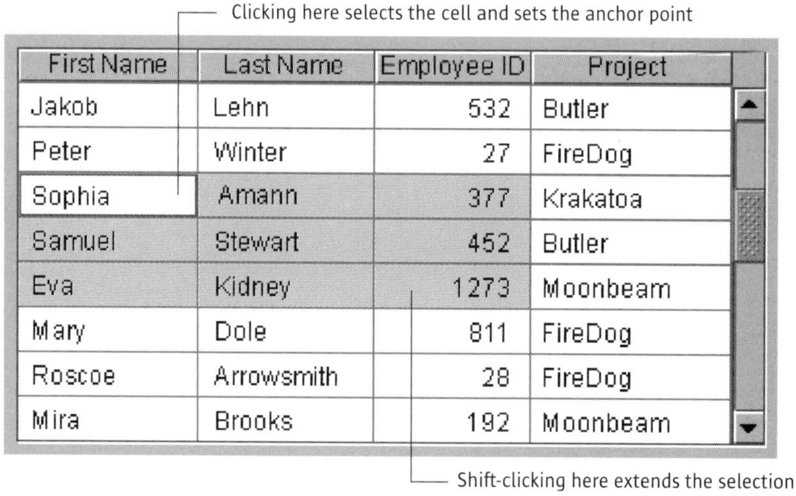

In range selection, the selection always extends from the cell with the anchor point to the cell where the user Shift-clicked. If users move the pointer within the selection and Shift-click, the selection becomes smaller. For example, if the user Shift-clicks Stewart in the preceding figure, the selection is reduced to four cells (Sophia, Amann, Samuel, and Stewart).

Single Row   You can enable users to select an entire row by clicking any cell in the row. The clicked cell gets keyboard focus, which is indicated by an inner border. Any previous selection is deselected.

In the following figure, the user has clicked the cell containing 811. This cell is not editable, as indicated by its background color.

FIGURE 193 Single-Row Selection

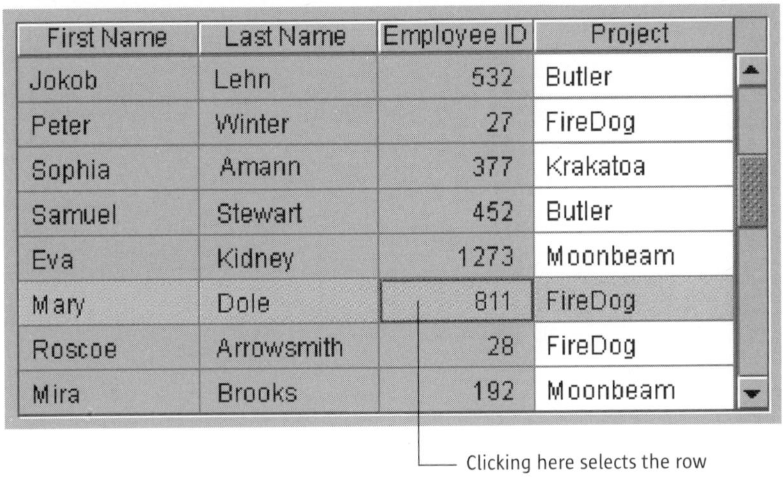

First Name	Last Name	Employee ID	Project
Jokob	Lehn	532	Butler
Peter	Winter	27	FireDog
Sophia	Amann	377	Krakatoa
Samuel	Stewart	452	Butler
Eva	Kidney	1273	Moonbeam
Mary	Dole	811	FireDog
Roscoe	Arrowsmith	28	FireDog
Mira	Brooks	192	Moonbeam

Clicking here selects the row

Single Range of Rows   You can enable users to select one row or a range of rows. Users select a row by clicking any cell in the row. The cell that has been clicked gets keyboard focus and becomes the anchor point of the selection. Users extend the selection by moving the pointer to a new row and Shift-clicking. Users can also select a range of rows by dragging through the range.

In the following figure, the user has clicked Krakatoa and then Shift-clicked the FireDog in Mary Dole's row. The cell containing Amann is editable, as indicated by its white background.

FIGURE 194 Range of Selected Rows

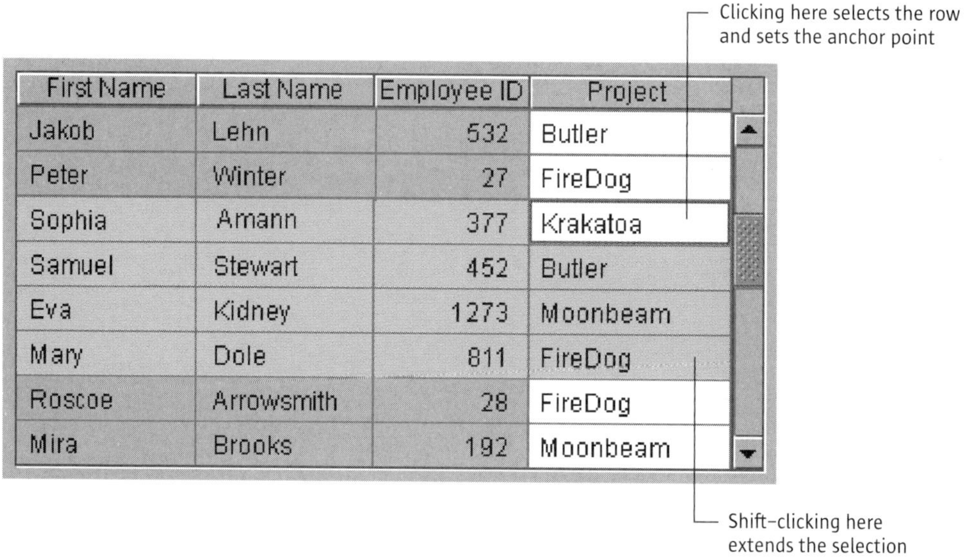

Clicking here selects the row
and sets the anchor point

First Name	Last Name	Employee ID	Project
Jakob	Lehn	532	Butler
Peter	Winter	27	FireDog
Sophia	Amann	377	Krakatoa
Samuel	Stewart	452	Butler
Eva	Kidney	1273	Moonbeam
Mary	Dole	811	FireDog
Roscoe	Arrowsmith	28	FireDog
Mira	Brooks	192	Moonbeam

Shift–clicking here
extends the selection

In range selection, the selection always extends from the row with the anchor point to the row where the user has Shift-clicked. If users Shift-click within an existing selection, the selection becomes smaller. For example, if the user Shift-clicks Butler in the preceding figure, the selection is reduced to the two rows containing Krakatoa and Butler.

Multiple Ranges of Rows   You can enable users to select a single row, a range of rows, or multiple row ranges (also known as "discontinuous," "discontiguous," or "disjoint" ranges). Users select a single row by clicking any cell in the row and extend the selection by Shift-clicking. To start another range, users Control-click any cell in a row. The cell gets keyboard focus and becomes the anchor point of the new range. The selection of the row toggles as follows:

- If the row is not already selected, it is selected. A subsequent Shift-click selects all rows from the anchor point to the row where the user has Shift-clicked.

- If the row is within an existing selection, the row is deselected. A subsequent Shift-click deselects all rows from the anchor point to the row where the user has Shift-clicked.

Users can also select another range by dragging through the range while holding down the Control key.

In Figure 195, the user has selected the first range by clicking Winter and then Shift-clicking Amann. The user has created another range by Control-clicking Mary and then Shift-clicking Roscoe. The cell containing Mary has keyboard focus and is noneditable.

⊙ The corresponding code for Figure 195 is available on the companion CD-ROM.

FIGURE 195 Multiple Ranges of Selected Rows

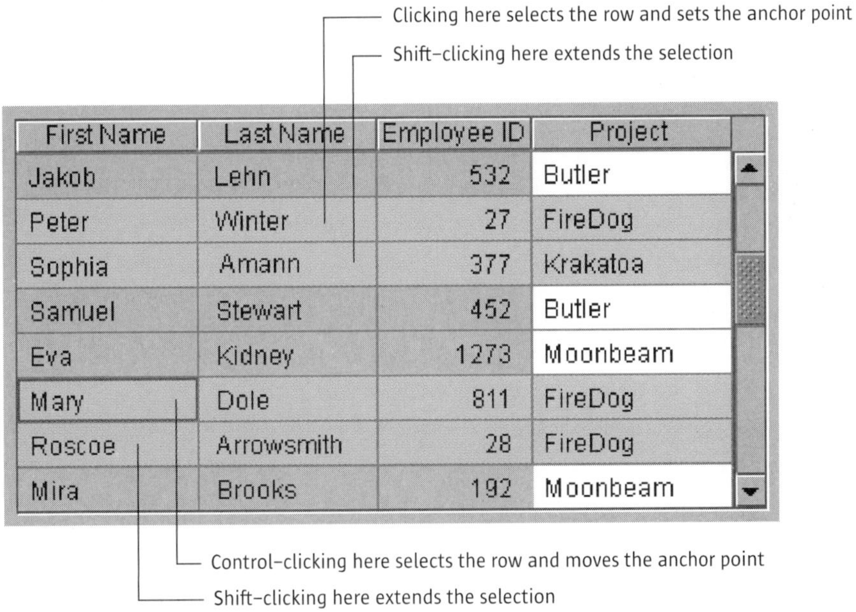

Clicking here selects the row and sets the anchor point

Shift–clicking here extends the selection

First Name	Last Name	Employee ID	Project
Jakob	Lehn	532	Butler
Peter	Winter	27	FireDog
Sophia	Amann	377	Krakatoa
Samuel	Stewart	452	Butler
Eva	Kidney	1273	Moonbeam
Mary	Dole	811	FireDog
Roscoe	Arrowsmith	28	FireDog
Mira	Brooks	192	Moonbeam

Control–clicking here selects the row and moves the anchor point

Shift–clicking here extends the selection

Multiple-range selection is well suited for an email application that uses a table to display message headers, as shown in Figure 190 on page 232. Users can select one or more message headers (especially useful for deleting, moving, or forwarding messages).

Single Column You can enable users to select an entire column by clicking any cell in the column. The cell that was clicked gets keyboard focus, which is indicated by an inner border. Any previous selection is deselected.

In the following figure, the user has clicked Krakatoa in the Project column. The white background indicates that the cell can be edited.

FIGURE 196 Single-Column Selection

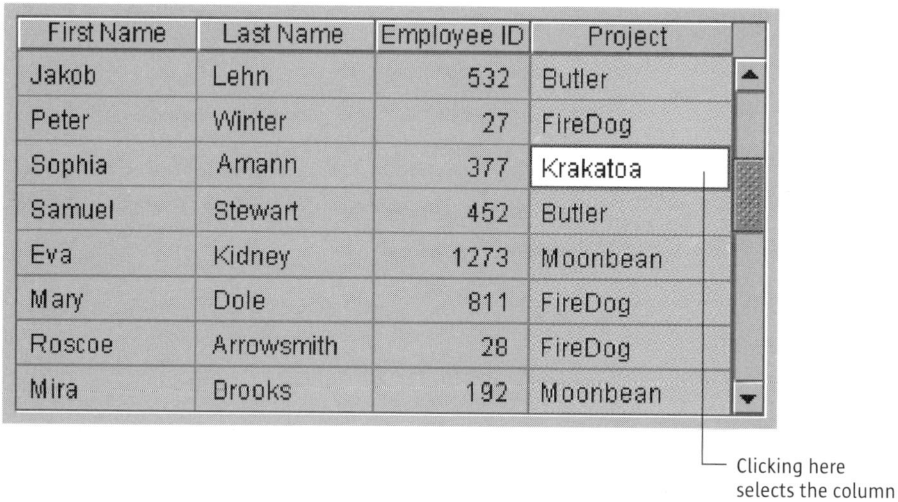

First Name	Last Name	Employee ID	Project
Jakob	Lehn	532	Butler
Peter	Winter	27	FireDog
Sophia	Amann	377	Krakatoa
Samuel	Stewart	452	Butler
Eva	Kidney	1273	Moonbean
Mary	Dole	811	FireDog
Roscoe	Arrowsmith	28	FireDog
Mira	Drooks	192	Moonbean

Clicking here
selects the column

Single Range of Columns   You can enable users to select one column or a range of columns. Users select a column by clicking any cell in the column. The cell that was clicked gets keyboard focus and becomes the anchor point of the selection. Users extend the selection by moving the pointer to a new column and Shift-clicking. Users can also select a range of columns by dragging through the range.

In the following figure, the user has clicked 1273 and then Shift-clicked Amann. The cell containing 1273 cannot be edited, as indicated by its background color.

FIGURE 197 Range of Selected Columns

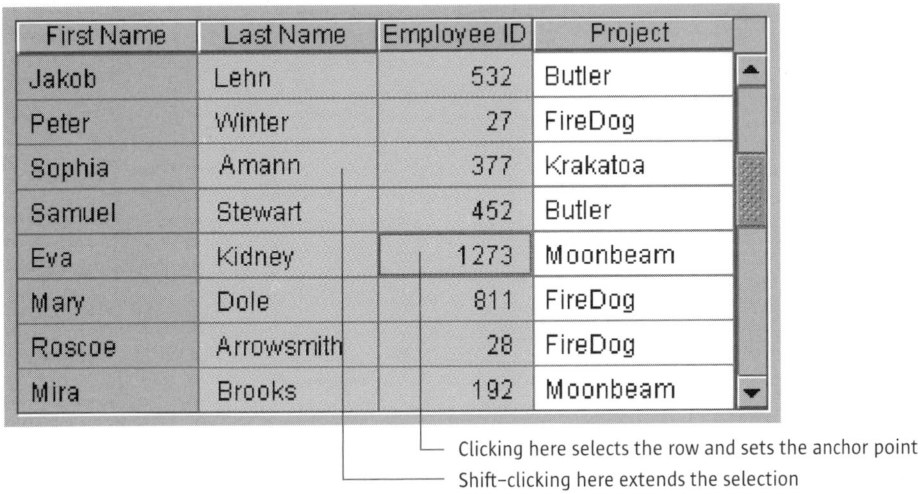

First Name	Last Name	Employee ID	Project
Jakob	Lehn	532	Butler
Peter	Winter	27	FireDog
Sophia	Amann	377	Krakatoa
Samuel	Stewart	452	Butler
Eva	Kidney	1273	Moonbeam
Mary	Dole	811	FireDog
Roscoe	Arrowsmith	28	FireDog
Mira	Brooks	192	Moonbeam

— Clicking here selects the row and sets the anchor point
— Shift–clicking here extends the selection

In range selection, the selection always extends from the column with the anchor point to the column where the user has Shift-clicked. If users Shift-click within an existing selection, the selection becomes smaller.

Multiple Ranges of Columns You can enable users to select a single column, a range of columns, or multiple-column ranges (also known as "discontinuous," "discontiguous," or "disjoint" ranges). Users select a single column by clicking any cell in the column and extend the selection by Shift-clicking. To start another range, users Control-click any cell in the column. The cell gets keyboard focus and becomes the anchor point of the range. The selection of the column toggles as follows:

- If the column is not already selected, it is selected. A subsequent Shift-click selects all columns from the anchor point to the column where the user Shift-clicked.

- If the column is within an existing selection, the column is deselected. A subsequent Shift-click deselects all columns from the anchor point to the column where the user Shift-clicked.

Users can also select or deselect another range by dragging through the range while holding down the Control key.

In the following figure, the user has clicked Peter and then Shift-clicked Amann. The user has selected another range by Control-clicking Krakatoa, which has keyboard focus and can be edited, as indicated by its white background.

FIGURE 198 Multiple Ranges of Selected Columns

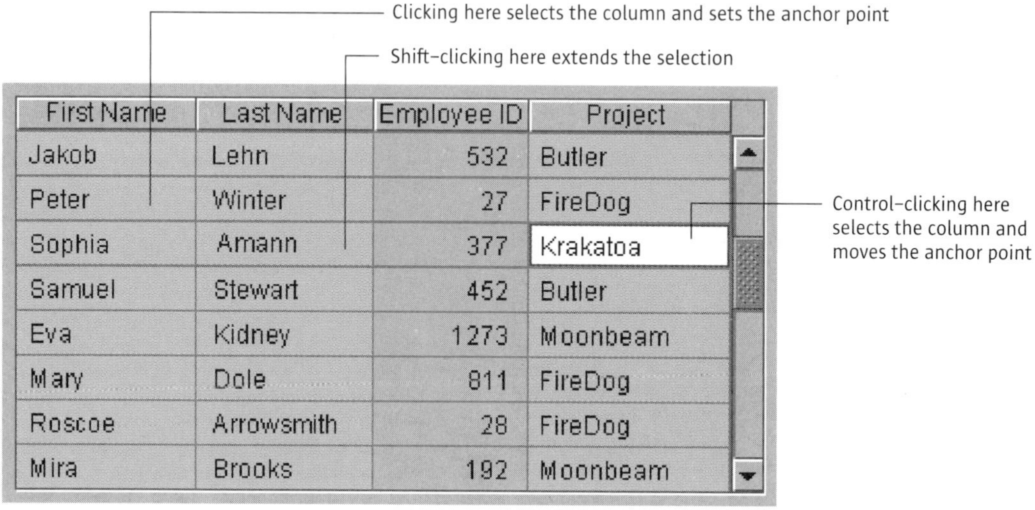

Clicking here selects the column and sets the anchor point

Shift–clicking here extends the selection

Control–clicking here selects the column and moves the anchor point

Give your users as much flexibility in your selection scheme as makes sense for your application. Enable selection of a range or multiple ranges if you can.

Tree Components

A tree component represents a set of hierarchical data in the form of an indented outline, which users can expand and collapse. Tree components are useful for displaying data such as the folders and files in a file system or the table of contents in a help system.

A tree component consists of nodes. The top-level node, from which all other nodes branch, is the root node. Nodes that might have subnodes are called "containers." All other nodes are called "leaves." The default icon for a container is a folder, and the default icon for a leaf is a file. Each node is accompanied by text.

Turners appear next to each container in the tree component. The **turner** points right when the container is collapsed and down when the container is expanded.

In the following figure, the Projects, Fire station, First floor, and Landscaping nodes are expanded containers; all the other containers are collapsed. Landscaping is a container without subnodes. Communications, Garage, and Shop are leaves.

The turner, container, and leaf graphics shown in Figure 199 are the default graphics provided by the JFC.

⊙ The corresponding code for Figure 199 is available on the companion CD-ROM.

FIGURE 199 Tree Component With Top-Level Lines

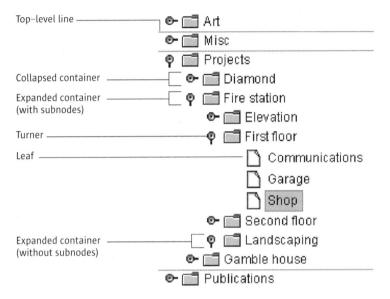

Users can click a right-pointing turner to expand its container so that the contents are visible in the tree component. The turner rotates to point downward. Clicking a downward-pointing turner collapses its container so that the contents are no longer visible. For the keyboard operations that are appropriate for tree components, see Table 33 on page 261.

☕ In most tree components, display the second level of the hierarchy as your highest level. Your outline will be easier to use if you do not display the root node.

☕ Display turners for all containers in the tree component, including the containers at the highest level. Turners remind users that they can expand and collapse the node.

▤▷ Setting the rootVisible property of the tree component to false turns off the display of the root node.

▤▷ Setting the showsRootHandles of the tree component to true turns on the display of turners for the highest-level containers.

Lines in Tree Components   The JFC provides three options for including lines in a tree component. The first option is not to include any lines. The second option is to draw lines that separate the top-level nodes, as shown in Figure 199 on page 241. The third option is to draw lines that define the hierarchical relationships of the nodes, as shown in the following figure.

FIGURE 200   Tree Component With Hierarchy Lines

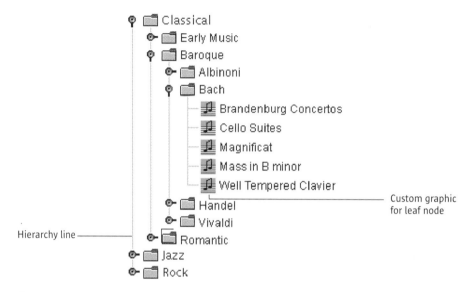

If your tree component contains three or more levels, use lines to delineate the hierarchical relationships of the nodes.

The client property `JTree.lineStyle` can be set to None to display no lines, to Horizontal to display top-level lines, and to Angled to display hierarchy lines.

Graphics in Tree Components   You can substitute your own graphics for the JFC-supplied container and leaf node graphics. For example, if your hierarchy represents the clients and servers in a network, you might include graphic representations of the clients and servers. In Figure 200, a custom music graphic is used for the leaf nodes. You might also use separate graphics to show when a container is expanded and when it is collapsed.

Editing in Tree Components   You can enable users to edit the text in a tree component. When editing is enabled, users can change text using the same editing commands that they use for text fields. These commands are described in "Editable Text Fields" on page 218.

To start editing a node in a tree component, users can:

- Click, pause, click, and wait 1200 milliseconds
- Triple-click
- Press F2 when a node is selected

☞ Setting the editable property to true enables editing of all nodes in the tree.

A: KEYBOARD SHORTCUTS, MNEMONICS, AND OTHER KEYBOARD OPERATIONS

This appendix presents common keyboard shortcuts and mnemonics in alphabetical order and summarizes JFC-supplied keyboard navigation, activation, and selection operations in a series of tables (arranged alphabetically by component). The left column describes a keyboard operation (for example, left arrow key) and the right column of each table describes the corresponding action (for example, moving focus to the left).

Navigating means to move the input focus from one user interface component to another; activating refers to operating the component; selecting means to choose one or more user objects such as text or icons, typically for a subsequent action. For an overview of these concepts, see "Keyboard Navigation and Activation" on page 113.

In general, navigating between components uses these keys:

- **Tab.** Moves keyboard focus to the next component or to the first member of the next group of components (the upper-left component in left-to-right reading order).

- **Ctrl-Tab.** Moves keyboard focus to the next component or to the first member of the next group of components when the current component accepts a tab (as in text fields, tables, text areas, and tabbed panes).

- **Shift-Tab.** Moves keyboard focus to the previous component or to the last component in the previous group of components in precisely the reverse order of the navigation specified by pressing Tab.

- **Ctrl-Shift-Tab.** Moves keyboard focus to the previous component or to the last component in the previous group of components in precisely the reverse order of the navigation specified by pressing Tab. Ctrl-Shift-Tab works when the current component accepts tabs.

- **Arrow keys.** Move keyboard focus between the individual components within a group of components—for example, between menu items in a menu, between tabs in a tabbed pane, or from character to character in a text field or text component.

Some actions in the table list several possible keyboard operations, separated by a comma. For example, both Home and Ctrl-Home move focus to the beginning of a list.

☕ Ensure that you provide multiple operations that take into account the differences between operating environments if your application runs on several.

🖶 Some of the keyboard operations described in the following tables might be temporarily incomplete or not implemented. However, these key sequences should be reserved for future versions of the JFC and the Java 2 platform.

🖶 The arrow keys are insensitive to the component orientation feature in the Java 2 SDK. (Component orientation is the automatic positioning of components to reflect the writing system of a locale—for instance, left to right, or right to left.) For example, the right arrow moves the action right regardless of the orientation of the locale.

Common Keyboard Shortcuts

The following table provides an alphabetically sorted list of common keyboard shortcuts. Use this table to see which keyboard shortcuts are used and which are available. (You can use these shortcuts for other purposes if your application does not provide the associated function and will not add that function in the foreseeable future.) For a table of keyboard shortcuts organized according to menus, see Table 8 on page 117.

TABLE 12   Alphabetical List of Common Keyboard Shortcuts

Sequence	Equivalent
Ctrl-A	Select All (Edit menu)
Ctrl-B	Bold (Format menu)
Ctrl-C	Copy (Edit menu)
Ctrl-E	Align Center (Format menu)
Ctrl-F	Find (Edit menu)
Ctrl-G	Find Again (Edit menu)
Ctrl-H	Replace (Edit menu)
Ctrl-I	Italic (Format menu)
Ctrl-L	Align Left (Format menu)

TABLE 12   Alphabetical List of Common Keyboard Shortcuts *(Continued)*

Sequence	Equivalent
Ctrl-N	New (File menu)
Ctrl-O	Open (File menu)
Ctrl-P	Print (File menu)
Ctrl-R	Align Right (Format menu)
Ctrl-S	Save (File menu)
Ctrl-U	Underline (Format menu)
Ctrl-V	Paste (Edit menu)
Ctrl-W	Close (File menu)
Ctrl-X	Cut (Edit menu)
Ctrl-Y	Redo (Edit menu)
Ctrl-Z	Undo (Edit menu)
Delete	Delete (Edit menu)
F1	Help
F5	Refresh
Shift-F1	Contextual help

Common Mnemonics

The following table provides an alphabetically sorted list of common mnemonics for menu items within the common menus. Use this table to determine which mnemonics are used and which are available. For a list of common mnemonics organized by the common order in menus, see Table 9 on page 120.

TABLE 13   Alphabetical List of Common Mnemonics

Letter	Menu Items
A	Select All (Edit menu), Save As (File menu), About Application (Help menu)
B	Bold (Format menu)
C	Copy (Edit menu), Close (File menu), Align Center (Format menu), Contents (Help menu)
D	Delete (Edit menu), Details (View menu)

TABLE 13   Alphabetical List of Common Mnemonics *(Continued)*

Letter	Menu Items
E	Edit menu
F	File menu, Find (Edit menu), Filter (View menu)
G	Large Icons (View menu)
H	Help menu
I	Index (Help menu), Italic (Format menu)
L	Align Left (Format menu), List (View menu)
M	Small Icons (View menu)
N	Find Again (Edit menu), New (File menu)
O	Open (File menu), Zoom Out (View menu)
P	Paste (Edit menu), Print (File menu)
R	Format menu, Redo (Edit menu), Align Right (Format menu), Refresh (View menu)
S	Save (File menu), Search (Help menu), Sort By (View menu)
T	Cut (Edit menu), Tutorial (Help menu)
U	Undo (Edit menu), Page Setup (File menu), Underline (Format menu)
V	View menu
X	Exit (File menu)
Z	Zoom In (View menu)

Backing Windows and Internal Windows   The following
table lists the keyboard operations for backing windows and internal
windows. For details on internal windows and backing windows, see
"Working With Multiple Document Interfaces" on page 149.

TABLE 14   Keyboard Operations for Backing Windows and Internal Windows

Keyboard Operation	Action
Ctrl-F4	Closes internal window that has keyboard focus
Ctrl-F7	Moves internal window (that is, switches to internal window mode, in which users press arrow keys to move windows around)
Ctrl-F8	Resizes internal window (that is, switches to internal window mode, in which users then press arrow keys to resize window)
Ctrl-F9	Minimizes internal window
Ctrl-Esc, Ctrl-Tab, Shift-Esc, Shift-Tab	Navigates first between open internal windows, then among minimized internal windows (See page 245 for a description of the directions associated with these keyboard operations. The Control and Shift keys work the same way with the Escape key here as they do with the Tab key in the explanation.)
Ctrl-F5, Enter, Return	Opens minimized internal window that has keyboard focus
Ctrl-F6, Ctrl-Shift-F6	Navigates among associated internal windows on the backing window and between an internal window and an associated secondary window (See page 245 for a description of the directions associated with these keyboard operations. The Control and Shift keys work the same way with the Escape key here as they do with the Tab key in the explanation.)
Ctrl-spacebar	Displays contextual menu in MDI

Checkboxes

The following table lists the keyboard operation for checkboxes. For more information on this component, see "Checkboxes" on page 202.

TABLE 15   Keyboard Operation for Checkboxes

Keyboard Operation	Action
Spacebar	Switches the setting of the checkbox

Combo Boxes

The following table lists the keyboard operations for combo boxes. For details on this component, see "Combo Boxes" on page 207.

TABLE 16   Keyboard Operations for Combo Boxes

Keyboard Operation	Action
Spacebar, down arrow, Alt-down arrow	Posts associated list
Up arrow, down arrow	When menu is posted, moves highlight up or down within list, selecting highlighted item
Enter, Return, spacebar	Closes list, maintaining latest selection
Escape	Closes list, returning to prior selection

Command Buttons

The following table lists the keyboard operations for command buttons. For more information on this component, see "Command Buttons" on page 196.

TABLE 17   Keyboard Operations for Command Buttons

Keyboard Operation	Action
Spacebar	Activates command button that has keyboard focus
Enter, Return	Activates default button (does not require keyboard focus)
Escape	Activates Cancel button (does not require keyboard focus)

HTML Editor Kits

HTML editor kits use the navigation, selection, and activation sequences described in Table 28 on page 258, plus the two listed here. For details on the appearance and behavior of this component, see "HTML Editor Kit" on page 223.

TABLE 18   Keyboard Operations for HTML Panes

Keyboard Operation	Action
Tab, Ctrl-Tab, Shift-Tab, Ctrl-Shift-Tab	Navigates to link and other focusable elements (see page 245 for a description of the directions associated with these keyboard operations)
Enter, Return, spacebar	Activates link

List Components

The actions listed in the following table assume multiple selection in list boxes and selectable lists. For more information on the appearance, behavior, and selection of these components, see "List Boxes" on page 204 and "Selectable Lists" on page 226.

TABLE 19   Keyboard Operations for Lists

Keyboard Operation	Action
Up arrow	Moves focus up one row or line and selects the item
Down arrow	Moves focus down one row or line and selects the item
Page Up	Moves focus up one information pane minus one line, selecting the first line in the information pane
Page Down	Moves focus down one information pane minus one line, selecting the last line in the information pane
Home, Ctrl-Home	Moves focus to beginning of list
End, Ctrl-End	Moves focus to end of list
Ctrl-A, Ctrl-/	Selects all items in list
Ctrl-\	Deselects all items in list

TABLE 19   Keyboard Operations for Lists *(Continued)*

Keyboard Operation	Action
Spacebar	Makes a selection and deselects any previous selection
Ctrl-spacebar	Switches selection without affecting previous selections
Shift-spacebar	Extends selection
Shift-down arrow	Extends selection down one item
Shift-up arrow	Extends selection up one item
Shift-Home	Extends selection to beginning of list
Shift-End	Extends selection to end of list
Shift-PgUp	Extends selection up one information pane
Shift-PgDn	Extends selection down one information pane

Menus

The keyboard operations in this table apply to menu bars, drop-down menus, submenus, contextual menus, menu items, radio button menu items, and checkbox menu items. For a discussion of menus, see Chapter 9.

⌨▷   In the Java 2 SDK, contextual menus cannot be posted from the keyboard.

TABLE 20   Keyboard Operations for Menus

Keyboard Operation	Action
F10	Moves focus to menu bar and posts first menu
Shift-F10	Displays contextual menu
Right arrow and left arrow	Navigates right or left among titles in menu bar, posting current menu, displaying submenus (right arrow), and navigating back from submenu to higher-level menu
Up arrow	Navigates within menus, displaying submenus

TABLE 20   Keyboard Operations for Menus *(Continued)*

Keyboard Operation	Action
Down arrow	Navigates within menus, moving to the next item without displaying a submenu
Enter, Return, spacebar	Activates menu item, dismisses menu, and goes to last window item that had focus
Escape	Dismisses menu without taking action and returns focus to last component that had focus; when in submenu, dismisses submenu and returns to higher-level drop-down or contextual menu

Radio Buttons
The following table lists the keyboard operation for radio buttons. For a discussion of the appearance and behavior of this component, see "Radio Buttons" on page 203.

TABLE 21   Keyboard Operation for Radio Buttons

Keyboard Operation	Action
Spacebar	Turns on radio button

Scrollbars
Users can operate scrollbars from the keyboard when keyboard focus is anywhere in the scroll pane. If there are scroll panes within scroll panes, the keyboard operates the innermost scrollbar. For a discussion of the appearance and behavior of this component, see "Scrollbars" on page 143.

TABLE 22   Keyboard Operations for Scrollbars

Keyboard Operation	Action
Up arrow	Moves information pane up one line
Down arrow	Moves information pane down one line
Page Up	Moves up one information pane minus one line
Page Down	Moves down one information pane minus one line
Ctrl-Home	Moves to beginning of data

TABLE 22   Keyboard Operations for Scrollbars *(Continued)*

Keyboard Operation	Action
Ctrl-End	Moves to end of data
Ctrl-PgDn	Moves right one information pane minus one column
Ctrl-Pg Up	Moves left one information pane minus one line or column

Secondary Windows and Utility Windows   The following

table lists the keyboard operations for secondary windows (dialog boxes and
alert boxes). Utility windows use the same operations. For comprehensive
treatment of dialog boxes and alert boxes, see Chapter 8. For a discussion of
utility windows, see "Utility Windows" on page 140.

    Keyboard navigation support for the `JDialogPane` component is not
fully operational in the Java 2 SDK. The action specified for the Escape key
must be programmed by the developer.

TABLE 23   Keyboard Operations for Dialog Boxes

Keyboard Operation	Action
Alt-F6	Navigates into secondary window; when in secondary window, navigates to the associated higher-level window
Escape	Activates Cancel button (no need for keyboard focus)
Enter, Return	Activates default command button (no need for keyboard focus)

Sliders

The following table lists the keyboard operations for sliders. Sliders can be either vertical or horizontal, so keyboard operations are provided for each case. For details on this component, see "Sliders" on page 210.

TABLE 24   Keyboard Operations for Sliders

Keyboard Operation	Action
Arrow keys	Changes value of slider
Home	Moves to leading-edge value (in left-to-right reading order, the value at the left edge or bottom)
End	Moves to the trailing-edge value (in left-to-right reading order, the value at the right edge or top of the slider)
Page Up, Ctrl-PgUp	Jumps towards right or top (approximately 20% of the scale)
Page Down, Ctrl-PgDn	Jumps towards left or bottom direction (approximately 20% of the scale)

Split Panes

The following table lists the keyboard operations for split panes. After users enter a split pane, pressing Tab cycles the focus to the components within the split pane. For a description of the appearance and behavior of this component, see "Split Panes" on page 147.

TABLE 25   Keyboard Operations for Split Panes

Keyboard Operation	Action
Tab, F6	Navigates between split panes and gives focus to last element that had focus
F8	Gives focus to splitter bar
Arrow keys, Home, End	Changes location of splitter bar in splitter pane

Tabbed Panes

The following table lists the keyboard operations for tabbed panes. For a description of the appearance and behavior of this component, see "Tabbed Panes" on page 145. When a tabbed pane initially gets focus, the focus goes to one of the tabs, not to one of the content panes.

TABLE 26   Keyboard Operations for Tabbed Panes

Keyboard Operation	Action
Arrow keys	Navigates through tabs
Ctrl-down arrow	Moves from tab to its associated content pane
Ctrl-up arrow	Moves from content pane to its associated tab
Ctrl-PgDn	Moves to next content pane (changing the corresponding tab)
Ctrl-PgUp	Moves to previous content pane (changing the corresponding tab)

Tables

The following table lists the keyboard operations for tables. For a description of the appearance and behavior of this component, see "Tables" on page 228.

TABLE 27   Keyboard Operations for Tables

Keyboard Operations	Action
Enter (or Return)	Deselects current selection and moves focus down one cell
Shift-Enter (or Shift-Return)	Deselects current selection and moves focus up one cell
Tab	Deselects current selection and moves focus right one cell
Shift-Tab	Deselects current selection and moves focus left one cell
Down arrow	Deselects current selection and moves focus down one cell
Up arrow	Deselects current selection and moves focus up one cell

TABLE 27 Keyboard Operations for Tables *(Continued)*

Keyboard Operations	Action
Page Down	Deselects current selection, scrolls down one information pane, and selects the last visible cell in the current column
Page Up	Deselects current selection, scrolls up one information pane, and gives focus to first visible cell in the current column
Ctrl-PgUp	Deselects current selection, scrolls left one information pane, and gives focus to first visible cell in the current row
Ctrl-PgDn	Deselects current selection, scrolls right one information pane, and selects the last visible cell in the current row
Home	Moves focus and information pane to first cell in the current row
End	Moves focus and information pane to last cell in the current row
Ctrl-Home	Moves focus and information pane to first cell in the current column
Ctrl-End	Moves focus and information pane to last cell in the current column
F2	Enables editing in a cell
Escape	Resets cell to the state it was in before it was edited
Ctrl-A	Selects entire table
Shift-down arrow	Extends selection down one row
Shift-up arrow	Extends selection up one row
Shift-left arrow	Extends selection left one column
Shift-right arrow	Extends selection right one column
Shift-Home	Extends selection to beginning of row
Shift-End	Extends selection to end of row
Ctrl-up arrow	Navigates up one row without affecting the selection

TABLE 27   Keyboard Operations for Tables *(Continued)*

Keyboard Operations	Action
Ctrl-down arrow	Navigates down one row without affecting the selection
Ctrl-Shift-up arrow	Navigate up one row and select the new item without deselecting any current selections
Ctrl-Shift-down arrow	Navigate down one row and select the new item without deselecting any current selections
Ctrl-Shift-Home	Extends selection to beginning of column
Ctrl-Shift-End	Extends selection to end of column
Shift-PgDn	Extends selection down one information pane
Shift-PgUp	Extends selection up one information pane
Ctrl-Shift-PgDn	Extends selection right one information pane
Ctrl-Shift-PgUp	Extends selection left one information pane

Text Areas and Default and Styled Text Editor Kits

The following table lists the keyboard operations for text areas and the default and styled text editor kits. For details on the appearance and behavior of these components, see "Text Areas" on page 220, "Default Editor Kit" on page 222, and "Styled Text Editor Kit" on page 222.

TABLE 28   Keyboard Operations for Text Areas and Default and Styled Text Editor Kits

Keyboard Operation	Action
Up arrow	Moves insertion point up one line
Down arrow	Moves insertion point down one line
Left arrow	Moves insertion point to the left one component or character
Right arrow	Moves insertion point to the right one component or character

TABLE 28   Keyboard Operations for Text Areas and Default and Styled Text Editor
Kits *(Continued)*

Keyboard Operation	Action
Page Up	Moves up one information pane
Page Down	Moves down one information pane
Ctrl-PgUp	Moves left one information pane
Ctrl-PgDn	Moves right one information pane
Home	Moves to beginning of line
End	Moves to end of row or line
Ctrl-Home	Moves to beginning of data
Ctrl-End	Moves to end of data
Ctrl-left arrow	Moves to beginning of previous word
Ctrl-right arrow	Moves to beginning of next word
Ctrl-A, Ctrl-/	Selects all
Ctrl-\	Deselects all
Shift-up arrow	Extends selection up one line
Shift-down arrow	Extends selection down one line
Shift-left arrow	Extends selection left one character
Shift-right arrow	Extends selection right one character
Shift-PgUp	Extends selection up one information pane
Shift-PgDn	Extends selection down one information pane
Ctrl-Shift-PgUp	Extends selection to the left one information pane
Ctrl-Shift-PgDn	Extends selection to the right one information pane
Shift-Home	Extends selection to beginning of line
Shift-End	Extends selection to end of line
Ctrl-Shift-Home	Extends selection to beginning of data
Ctrl-Shift-End	Extends selection to end of data
Ctrl-Shift-right arrow	Extends selection to next word
Ctrl-Shift-left arrow	Extends selection to previous word

Text Fields

The following table lists the keyboard operations for text fields. For details on this component, see "Text Fields" on page 217.

TABLE 29   Keyboard Operations for Text Fields

Keyboard Operation	Action
Right arrow	Moves insertion point one character to the right
Left arrow	Moves insertion point one character to the left
Ctrl-right arrow	Moves insertion point to beginning of next word
Ctrl-left arrow	Moves insertion point to beginning of current word, or, if insertion point is already at the beginning of the current word, moves it to the beginning of the previous word
Home	Moves insertion point to beginning of text field
End	Moves insertion point to end of text field
Shift-Home	Extends selection to beginning of line
Shift-End	Extends selection to end of line
Shift-left arrow	Extends selection one character to the left
Shift-right arrow	Extends selection one character to the right
Ctrl-Shift--left arrow	Extends selection to previous word
Ctrl-Shift--right arrow	Extends selection to next word
Ctrl-A	Selects all characters in the text field

Toggle Buttons

The following table lists the keyboard operation for toggle buttons. For details on this component, see "Toggle Buttons" on page 200.

TABLE 30   Keyboard Operation for Toggle Buttons

Keyboard Operation	Action
Spacebar	Switches button on or off

Tool Tips

The following table lists the keyboard operations for tool tips. For details on this component, see "Tool Tips" on page 191.

TABLE 31   Keyboard Operations for Tool Tips

Keyboard Operation	Action
Ctrl-F1	Displays or dismisses tool tip
Escape	Dismisses tool tip

Toolbars

The following table lists the keyboard operations for toolbars. For details on the appearance and behavior of this component, see "Toolbars" on page 186.

TABLE 32   Keyboard Operations for Toolbars

Keyboard Operation	Action
Arrow keys	Navigates within toolbar
Spacebar	Activates toolbar button

Tree Components

The following table lists the keyboard operations for tree components. For details on the appearance and behavior of this component, see "Tree Components" on page 240.

TABLE 33   Keyboard Operations for Tree Components

Keyboard Operation	Action
Right arrow	Expands current node
Left arrow	Collapses current node
Up arrow	Moves selection up one node
Down arrow	Moves selection down one node
Home	Moves selection to first node in tree
End	Moves selection to last node in tree
Page Up	Scrolls up one information pane
Page Down	Scrolls down one information pane

TABLE 33   Keyboard Operations for Tree Components *(Continued)*

Keyboard Operation	Action
Ctrl-PgUp	Moves left one information pane, if not everything is visible in a horizontal orientation
Ctrl-PgDn	Moves right one information pane, if not everything is visible in a horizontal orientation
Ctrl-A, Ctrl-/	Selects all nodes in tree
Ctrl-\	Deselects all
Shift-up arrow	Extends selection up
Shift-down arrow	Extends selection down
Shift-Home	Extends selection to beginning of tree
Shift-End	Extends selection to end of tree
Shift-PgUp	Extends selection up one information pane
Shift-PgDn	Extends selection down one information pane
Ctrl-Shift-PgDn	Extends selection right one information pane
Ctrl-Shift-PgUp	Extends selection left one information pane

GRAPHICS REPOSITORY

This appendix presents toolbar button and menu item graphics designed specifically for use in Java look and feel applications. The information is based on the Java Look and Feel Graphics Repository, which is available at `http://java.sun.com/products/jfc/tsc`.

⊙ The contents of this appendix are available on the companion CD-ROM.

☕ As a general rule, use 16 x 16 pixel graphics for menu items and 24 x 24 pixel graphics for toolbar buttons.

These professional-quality graphics can save valuable development time and ensure consistent graphics and terminology across Java look and feel applications.

The graphics are organized into six functional groups:

- General
- Navigation
- Text
- Tables
- Media
- Development tools

The repository provides:

- **Small and large graphics.** The 16 x 16 and 24 x 24 pixel graphics.

- **Description.** Explanation of the concept underlying each pair of graphics. Use this information to help you decide whether these graphics are appropriate to represent a specific feature of your application. You might use a modified, context-driven version of this explanation to describe the feature in your status bar.

- **Name.** Title to be used in corresponding menu items or button text. Variables, set off by curly braces, appear in some name fields. If the runtime value of this parameter is available, provide it for users.

- **Tool tip.** Brief phrase appearing next to the pointer when the pointer is over one of these graphics. Variables, set off by curly braces, appear in some of the tool tip fields. If the runtime value of this parameter is available, provide it for users.

- **Keyboard shortcut.** Keystroke combination (usually a modifier key and a character key) that activates the related menu item. Attach shortcuts to simple and constantly used features (like Ctrl-X for Cut). Ensure that each shortcut is unique within your application. For more information and guidelines on shortcuts, see "Keyboard Shortcuts" on page 115. For a summary of shortcuts, see Table 8 on page 117.

- **Mnemonic.** A mnemonic shows users which key to press (in conjunction with the Alt key) to activate a command or another GUI component. This section suggests appropriate letters to underline (in order of preference) in the related menu item or button. Choose from among the suggested mnemonics to aid consistency. For rules on choosing mnemonics for your toolbar buttons and menu items, see "Mnemonics" on page 118.

- **File name.** The relative path name for the specified graphic in the Java Archive. The online file name follows this format:

  `.../toolbarButtonGraphics/`*groupName*`/`*NameSize*`.gif`

  All of the graphics reside in the `toolbarButtonGraphics` folder of the Java Archive. Therefore, the file-name information includes only the *groupName* subdirectory and *NameSize*`.gif` file name.

  Because the graphics are located in subdirectories, the path information is necessary. For instance, the repository contains two graphics for Stop—one for media transport and one for general use.

- **Other notes.** Miscellaneous information about the graphics, including cross-references to related graphics or concepts.

Provide both graphics and text in a toolbar when you deem it appropriate—for instance, to accommodate novice or occasional users and those with poor vision. If you decide to display both button text and graphics, provide a way for end users to indicate their preferences for button text only, graphics only, or button text and graphics.

You can use the information in this appendix to create Swing actions. For more on Swing actions, see the *Java 2 Platform, Standard Edition, v 1.3 API Specification* by visiting `http://java.sun.com/j2se/1.3/docs/api/javax/swing/Action.html`.

General Graphics
This section provides general-purpose graphics that represent:

- Adding objects
- Saving edits or checkpoints
- Stopping tasks or processes
- Adjusting the screen display
- Changing magnification levels
- Specifying preferences and properties
- Printing
- Displaying and retrieving previously visited locations
- Creating and sending electronic mail
- Aligning and justifying objects
- Searching
- Editing objects and data
- Importing and exporting objects
- Providing help and information

Adding Objects
This section contains graphics that represent the addition of an object to an existing set of objects.

Add

Graphics	
Description	Adds an object to an existing set of objects
Name	Add {*Object Name*}
Tool Tip	Add {*Object Name*}
Mnemonic	A, D
File Name	.../general/Add16.gif .../general/Add24.gif
Other Notes	For more information on the plus symbol in the lower- right corner of the document graphic, see "Add Object Indicators" on page 98.

New

Graphics	
Description	Creates a new object
Name	New {*Object Name*}
Tool Tip	New {*Object Name*}
Shortcut	Ctrl-N
Mnemonic	N, W
File Name	.../general/New16.gif .../general/New24.gif
Other Notes	For more information on the twinkle symbol on the lower-right corner of the document graphic, see "New Object Indicators" on page 97.

Open

Graphics	
Description	Opens the specified object
Name	Open {*Object Name*}
Tool Tip	Open {*Object Name*}
Shortcut	Ctrl-O
Mnemonic	O, P, N
File Name	.../general/Open16.gif .../general/Open24.gif

Saving Edits or Checkpoints

The graphics in this section provide representations for saving edits or checkpoints for a specified object or group of objects.

Save

Graphics	
Description	Commits all interim edits or checkpoints for an object to a permanent storage area
Name	Save
Tool Tip	Save
Shortcut	Ctrl-S
Mnemonic	S, V
File Name	.../general/Save16.gif .../general/Save24.gif

Save All

Graphics	
Description	Commits all interim changes of a group of objects to a permanent storage area
Name	Save All
Tool Tip	Save All
Mnemonic	A, S, V, L
File Name	.../general/SaveAll16.gif .../general/SaveAll24.gif

Save As

Graphics	
Description	Saves the object being edited to a different, permanent storage area
Name	Save As
Tool Tip	Save As
Mnemonic	A, S, V
File Name	.../general/SaveAs16.gif .../general/SaveAs24.gif

Stopping a Task

The graphic in this section represents stopping an action or a process. Compare this section to "Stop" on page 297, which is for media transport processes.

Stop

Graphics	
Description	Halts the execution of a task
Name	Stop {*Action* or *Process*}
Tool Tip	Stop {*Action* or *Process*}
Mnemonic	S, T, P
File Name	.../general/Stop16.gif .../general/Stop24.gif
Other Notes	The Stop feature should be available only when there is an activity to halt.

Updating the Screen Display
This section provides graphics to represent updating the screen display with new data.

Refresh

Graphics	
Description	Updates screen display with new data
Name	Refresh {*Object Name*}
Tool Tip	Refresh {*Object Name*}
Mnemonic	R, F, S, H
File Name	.../general/Refresh16.gif .../general/Refresh24.gif

Changing Magnification Levels
This section provides graphics to represent changing the magnification level used to view an object.

Zoom

Graphics	
Description	Changes the magnification level used to view an object
Name	Zoom
Tool Tip	Zoom
Mnemonic	Z, M
File Name	.../general/Zoom16.gif .../general/Zoom24.gif

Zoom In

Graphics	
Description	Increases the magnification level used (to view the details of an object)
Name	Zoom In
Tool Tip	Zoom In
Mnemonic	I, Z, N, M
File Name	`.../general/ZoomIn16.gif` `.../general/ZoomIn24.gif`

Zoom Out

Graphics	
Description	Decreases the magnification level used (to view more of an object)
Name	Zoom Out
Tool Tip	Zoom Out
Mnemonic	O, Z, T, M
File Name	`.../general/ZoomOut16.gif` `.../general/ZoomOut24.gif`

Specifying Preferences and Properties

This section provides graphics to represent the display of:

- Global attributes of the current application that might be set by users (preferences)
- Local characteristics of a selected object that might be specified by users (properties)

Preferences

Graphics	
Description	Displays global attributes of the current application that might be set by users
Name	Preferences
Tool Tip	Preferences
Mnemonic	P, R, F
File Name	.../general/Preferences16.gif .../general/Preferences24.gif
Other Notes	See "Properties Indicators" on page 99.

Properties

Graphics	
Description	Displays local characteristics of a selected object that might be edited by users
Name	Properties
Tool Tip	Properties
Mnemonic	P, R, T, S
File Name	.../general/Properties16.gif .../general/Properties24.gif
Other Notes	See "Properties Indicators" on page 99.

Printing
This section provides graphics that represent operations such as page setup, printing, and print previews.

Page Setup

Graphics	
Description	Enables users to specify properties for the current print job
Name	Page Setup
Tool Tip	Page Setup
Mnemonic	G, S, P
File Name	.../general/PageSetup16.gif .../general/PageSetup24.gif
Other Notes	See "Properties Indicators" on page 99. Page setup properties might include printer selection, paper orientation, size, and so forth.

Print

Graphics	
Description	Sends an object or set of objects to be printed
Name	Print
Tool Tip	Print
Shortcut	Ctrl-P
Mnemonic	P, R, N
File Name	.../general/Print16.gif .../general/Print24.gif

Print Preview

Graphics	
Description	Provides a preliminary representation of the output that would be generated by the Print menu item
Name	Print Preview
Tool Tip	Print Preview
Mnemonic	R, P, V, W
File Name	.../general/PrintPreview16.gif .../general/PrintPreview24.gif

Displaying and Retrieving Previously Visited Locations This section provides graphics that represent bookmarks and history files.

A **bookmark** is a saved URL (uniform resource locator) for a web page that has been added to a list of saved URLs. When users view a particular web site and want to return to it subsequently, they can create a bookmark for the site.

On the other hand, a history file displays a list of previously visited locations (or opened files).

Bookmarks

Graphics	
Description	Displays a list of documents marked for later retrieval
Name	Bookmarks
Tool Tip	Bookmarks
Mnemonic	B, K, M, R
File Name	.../general/Bookmarks16.gif .../general/Bookmarks24.gif

History

Graphics	
Description	Displays a list of previously visited locations (or opened files)
Name	History
Tool Tip	History
Mnemonic	H, S, T, Y
File Name	.../general/History16.gif .../general/History24.gif

Creating and Sending Electronic Mail

This section provides graphics that represent the creation and sending of electronic mail messages.

Compose Mail

Graphics	
Description	Creates a new electronic mail message
Name	Compose Mail
Tool Tip	Compose Mail
Mnemonic	M, L, C
File Name	.../general/ComposeMail16.gif .../general/ComposeMail24.gif

Send Mail

Graphics	
Description	Sends the specified electronic mail message
Name	Send Mail
Tool Tip	Send Mail
Mnemonic	S, M, L, N
File Name	.../general/SendMail16.gif .../general/SendMail24.gif

Aligning Objects   This section contains graphics that represent the alignment of objects. Compare these graphics with the graphics in "Justifying Objects" on page 277.

Do not use these graphics for textual objects. Instead use the graphics described in "Text Alignment and Justification" on page 291.

Align Bottom

Graphics	
Description	Positions an object so that it lines up with the lower horizontal edge of its container
Name	Align Bottom {*Object Name*}
Tool Tip	Align Bottom {*Object Name*}
Mnemonic	B, T, M
File Name	.../general/AlignBottom16.gif .../general/AlignBottom24.gif

Align Center

Graphics	
Description	Positions an object so that it is in the middle of its container along both horizontal and vertical axes
Name	Align Center {*Object Name*}
Tool Tip	Align Center {*Object Name*}
Shortcut	Ctrl-E
Mnemonic	C, N, T, R
File Name	.../general/AlignCenter16.gif .../general/AlignCenter24.gif
Other Notes	Do not use these graphics for textual objects; see "Align Center" on page 291.

Align Left

Graphics	
Description	Positions an object to line up with the leading vertical edge of its container
Name	Align Left {*Object Name*}
Tool Tip	Align Left {*Object Name*}
Shortcut	Ctrl-L
Mnemonic	L, F, T
File Name	`.../general/AlignLeft16.gif` `.../general/AlignLeft24.gif`
Other Notes	Do not use these graphics for textual objects; see "Align Left" on page 292.

Align Right

Graphics	
Description	Positions an object to line up with the trailing vertical edge of its container
Name	Align Right {*Object Name*}
Tool Tip	Align Right {*Object Name*}
Shortcut	Ctrl-R
Mnemonic	R, G, H, T
File Name	`.../general/AlignRight16.gif` `.../general/AlignRight24.gif`
Other Notes	Do not use these graphics for textual objects; see "Align Right" on page 292.

Align Top

Graphics	
Description	Positions an object to line up with the upper horizontal edge of its container
Name	Align Top {*Object Name*}
Tool Tip	Align Top {*Object Name*}
Mnemonic	T, P
File Name	`.../general/AlignTop16.gif` `.../general/AlignTop24.gif`

Justifying Objects   This section provides graphics to represent the justification of objects. Compare these graphics to those described in "Text Alignment and Justification" on page 291.

Horizontally Justify

Graphics	
Description	Positions an object so that it fills the middle of its container evenly all the way to either vertical edge
Name	Horizontally Justify {*Object Name*}
Tool Tip	Horizontally Justify {*Object Name*}
Mnemonic	H, R, Z
File Name	`.../general/AlignJustifyHorizontal16.gif` `.../general/AlignJustifyHorizontal24.gif`
Other Notes	Do not use these graphics for textual objects; see "Justify" on page 291.

Vertically Justify

Graphics	
Description	Positions an object to fill the middle of its container evenly all the way to either horizontal edge
Name	Vertically Justify {*Object Name*}
Tool Tip	Vertically Justify {*Object Name*}
Mnemonic	V, R, T
File Name	`.../general/AlignJustifyVertical16.gif` `.../general/AlignJustifyVertical24.gif`
Other Notes	Do not use these graphics for textual objects; see "Justify" on page 291.

Searching   This section provides graphics that represent search operations ranging from simple find-and-replace features within a document or a web page to a more comprehensive search feature with a scope as broad as one or more web sites or the entire World Wide Web.

Find In

Graphics	
Description	Displays a window that enables the user to specify criteria to search for a specified object
Name	Find In {*Scope*}
Tool Tip	Find In {*Scope*}
Shortcut	Ctrl-F
Mnemonic	F, N, D
File Name	`.../general/Find16.gif` `.../general/Find24.gif`
Other Notes	Compare to "Search" on page 279. Find is used within an object (such as a document), whereas Search is used for more extensive operations across objects (for instance, multiple documents within a folder).

Find Again

Graphics	
Description	Searches for the next instance of the object specified by the previous Find In command
Name	Find Again {*Object Name*}
Tool Tip	Find Again {*Object Name*}
Shortcut	Ctrl-G
Mnemonic	A, G, N
File Name	.../general/FindAgain16.gif .../general/FindAgain24.gif
Other Notes	Compare to "Find In" on page 278 and "Search" on page 279.

Replace

Graphics	
Description	Substitutes one object for another
Name	Replace
Tool Tip	Replace
Shortcut	Ctrl-H
Mnemonic	R, P, L, C
File Name	.../general/Replace16.gif .../general/Replace24.gif

Search

Graphics	
Description	Searches for a specified object
Name	Search {*Object Name*} {*in Scope*}
Tool Tip	Search {*Object Name*} {*in Scope*}
Mnemonic	S, R, C, H
File Name	.../general/Search16.gif .../general/Search24.gif
Other Notes	Compare to "Find In" on page 278.

Editing Objects and Data   The graphics in this section represent common editing features such as copying, cutting, pasting, undoing, and redoing.

Copy

Graphics	
Description	Duplicates the selected object and makes it available to be pasted elsewhere
Name	Copy
Tool Tip	Copy
Shortcut	Ctrl-C
Mnemonic	C, P, Y
File Name	.../general/Copy16.gif .../general/Copy24.gif

Cut

Graphics	
Description	Removes the selected object from its current location and makes it available to be pasted elsewhere
Name	Cut
Tool Tip	Cut
Shortcut	Ctrl-X
Mnemonic	T, C
File Name	.../general/Cut16.gif .../general/Cut24.gif
Other Notes	See also "Delete" and "Remove" on page 281.

Delete

Graphics	
Description	Removes the selected object from its current location
Name	Delete
Tool Tip	Delete
Shortcut	Delete
Mnemonic	D, L, T
File Name	.../general/Delete16.gif .../general/Delete24.gif
Other Notes	See also "Remove" on page 281 and "Cut" on page 280.

Remove

Graphics	
Description	Removes the selected item from its current context
Name	Remove
Tool Tip	Remove
Mnemonic	R, M, V
File Name	.../general/Remove16.gif .../general/Remove24.gif
Other Notes	See also "Delete" on page 281 and "Cut" on page 280.

Paste

Graphics	
Description	Inserts an object or data previously placed in a temporary holding area
Name	Paste
Tool Tip	Paste
Shortcut	Ctrl-V
Mnemonic	P, S, T
File Name	.../general/Paste16.gif .../general/Paste24.gif
Other Notes	The object or data is usually placed in the temporary holding area by the Cut or Copy command. Compare to "Copy" and "Cut" on page 280.

Edit

Graphics	
Description	Enables users to modify the selected object
Name	Edit
Tool Tip	Edit
Mnemonic	E, D, T
File Name	.../general/Edit16.gif .../general/Edit24.gif

Undo

Graphics	
Description	Reverses the last transaction
Name	Undo {*Action*}
Tool Tip	Undo {*Action*}
Shortcut	Ctrl-Z
Mnemonic	U, N, D
File Name	.../general/Undo16.gif .../general/Undo24.gif

Redo

Graphics	
Description	Reverses the effect of the last undone transaction
Name	Redo {*Action*}
Tool Tip	Redo {*Action*}
Shortcut	Ctrl-Y
Mnemonic	R, D
File Name	`.../general/Redo16.gif` `.../general/Redo24.gif.`

Importing and Exporting Objects

The graphics in this section represent the importing and exporting of objects. To **import** involves bringing objects or data (for example, documents created in another application, text files, and graphics files) into your application. To **export** means to save an object or data in a format other than your application's native format.

Import

Graphics	
Description	Opens an object or data that is in a format other than the application's native format
Name	Import
Tool Tip	Import
Mnemonic	I, M, P, T
File Name	`.../general/Import16.gif` `.../general/Import24.gif`

Export

Graphics	
Description	Saves an object or data in a format other than the application's native format
Name	Export
Tool Tip	Export
Mnemonic	X, E, P, T
File Name	.../general/Export16.gif .../general/Export24.gif

Providing Help and Information

This section contains graphics that represent standard and contextual help, information about an object or a task, About boxes, and tips of the day.

Help

Graphics	
Description	Provides instructions and information to aid users in completing tasks
Name	Help
Tool Tip	Help
Shortcut	F1
Mnemonic	H, L, P
File Name	.../general/Help16.gif .../general/Help24.gif
Other Notes	As a general rule, help provides a system for browsing, searching, viewing, and reading information. It has more options than contextual help but might require activity that is tangential to the user's task.

Contextual Help

Graphics	
Description	Displays information to users based on their working location in a piece of software
Name	Contextual Help
Tool Tip	Contextual Help
Shortcut	Shift-F1
Mnemonic	C, T, X, H
File Name	`.../general/ContextualHelp16.gif` `.../general/ContextualHelp24.gif`
Other Notes	Compare to the previous section.

Information

Graphics	
Description	Displays information about an object or task
Name	Information
Tool Tip	Information
Mnemonic	I, N, F, O
File Name	`.../general/Information16.gif` `.../general/Information24.gif`

About

Graphics	
Description	Provides information about the application as a whole
Name	About {*Application Name*}
Tool Tip	About {*Application Name*}
Mnemonic	A, B, T
File Name	`.../general/About16.gif` `.../general/About24.gif`
Other Notes	For more information on About boxes, see "Designing About Boxes" on page 104.

Tip of the Day

Graphics	
Description	Provides a short hint about a feature of the application
Name	Tip of the Day
Tool Tip	Tip of the Day
Mnemonic	T, D, P
File Name	.../general/TipOfTheDay16.gif
	.../general/TipOfTheDay24.gif

Navigation

This section contains graphics that represent vertical and horizontal traversal as well as traversal to an initial, well-known location.

Vertical Traversal

The graphics in this section apply to navigation through objects with a vertical orientation.

Down To

Graphics	
Description	Moves to the next location
Name	Down to {*Location*}
Tool Tip	Down to {*Location*}
Shortcut	Alt-down arrow
Mnemonic	D, W, N
File Name	.../navigation/Down16.gif
	.../navigation/Down24.gif
Other Notes	Use Down To when the orientation of the object being traversed is vertical. For horizontally oriented objects, use "Forward To" on page 288.

Up

Graphics	
Description	Moves to the previous location
Name	Up to {*Location*}
Tool Tip	Up to {*Location*}
Shortcut	Alt-up arrow
Mnemonic	U, P
File Name	.../navigation/Up16.gif .../navigation/Up24.gif
Other Notes	Use Up when the orientation of the object being traversed is vertical. For horizontally oriented objects, use "Back To" on page 287.

Horizontal Traversal   The graphics in this section apply to navigation through objects with a horizontal orientation, such as web pages in a web site.

Back To

Graphics	
Description	Moves to the previous location
Name	Back to {*Location*}
Tool Tip	Back to {*Location*}
Shortcut	Alt-left arrow
Mnemonic	B, C, K
File Name	.../navigation/Back16.gif .../navigation/Back24.gif
Other Notes	Use Back To when the orientation of the object being traversed is horizontal. For vertically oriented objects, see "Up" on page 287.

Forward To

Graphics	
Description	Moves to the next location
Name	Forward to {*Location*}
Tool Tip	Forward to {*Location*}
Shortcut	Alt-right arrow
Mnemonic	F, R, W, D
File Name	.../navigation/Forward16.gif .../navigation/Forward24.gif
Other Notes	Use Forward To when the orientation of the object being traversed is horizontal. For vertically oriented objects, use "Down To" on page 286.

Returning to an Initial Location
This graphic represents movement to an initial location—for instance, the first page in a web site.

Home To

Graphics	
Description	Moves to an initial location
Name	Home To {*Location*}
Tool Tip	Home To {*Location*}
Shortcut	Home
Mnemonic	H, M, O
File Name	.../navigation/Home16.gif .../navigation/Home24.gif

Table Graphics

The graphics in this section represent frequently used table features, including operations on columns and tables.

Column Operations

This section contains graphics for operations on table columns.

Delete Column

Graphics	
Description	Removes the current column in a table
Name	Delete Column
Tool Tip	Delete Column
Mnemonic	C, D, L, T
File Name	.../table/ColumnDelete16.gif .../table/ColumnDelete24.gif

Insert Column After

Graphics	
Description	Adds a new column after the current column in a table
Name	Insert Column After
Tool Tip	Insert Column After
Mnemonic	C, I, A
File Name	.../table/ColumnInsertAfter16.gif .../table/ColumnInsertAfter24.gif

Insert Column Before

Graphics	
Description	Adds a new column before the current column in a table
Name	Insert Column Before
Tool Tip	Insert Column Before
Mnemonic	C, I, B
File Name	.../table/ColumnInsertBefore16.gif .../table/ColumnInsertBefore24.gif

Row Operations   This section contains graphics for operations on table rows.

Delete Row

Graphics	
Description	Removes the current row of a table
Name	Delete Row
Tool Tip	Delete Row
Mnemonic	R, D, W, L
File Name	`.../table/RowDelete16.gif` `.../table/RowDelete24.gif`

Insert Row After

Graphics	
Description	Adds a new row after the current row in a table
Name	Insert Row After
Tool Tip	Insert Row After
Mnemonic	R, I, A
File Name	`.../table/RowInsertAfter16.gif` `.../table/RowInsertAfter24.gif`

Insert Row Before

Graphics	
Description	Adds a new row before the current row in a table
Name	Insert Row Before
Tool Tip	Insert Row Before
Mnemonic	R, I, B
File Name	`.../table/RowInsertBefore16.gif` `.../table/RowInsertBefore24.gif`

Text

This section presents graphics for the alignment and justification of textual objects as well as the use of type styles for text.

Text Alignment and Justification

These graphics represent the alignment of text objects. For the alignment of graphical objects, see "Aligning Objects" on page 275.

Align Center

Graphics	
Description	Places the selected text in the middle of the specified unit
Name	Align Center
Tool Tip	Align Center
Shortcut	Ctrl-E
Mnemonic	C, N, T, R
File Name	.../text/AlignCenter16.gif .../text/AlignCenter24.gif
Other Notes	An example of the unit specified in the description is a line or paragraph. Use this graphic only for text. The generic Align Center graphic might be more appropriate for other uses. See "Align Center" on page 275 for details.

Justify

Graphics	
Description	Spaces selected lines of text to come out evenly at both margins, including the last line (called "forced justify")
Name	Justify
Tool Tip	Justify
Mnemonic	J, S, T, F
File Name	.../text/AlignJustify16.gif .../text/AlignJustify24.gif
Other Notes	Use these graphics only for text. The generic "Horizontally Justify" on page 277 and "Vertically Justify" on page 278 might be more appropriate for other uses.

Align Left

Graphics	
Description	Places the selected text along the left edge of the specified unit
Name	Align Left
Tool Tip	Align Left
Shortcut	Ctrl-L
Mnemonic	L, F, T
File Name	`.../text/AlignLeft16.gif` `.../text/AlignLeft24.gif`
Other Notes	An example of the unit specified in the description is a line or paragraph. Use the Align Left graphic only for text. See "Align Left" on page 276 for graphics that might be more appropriate for other needs.

Align Right

Graphics	
Description	Places the selected text along the right edge of the specified unit
Name	Align Right
Tool Tip	Align Right
Shortcut	Ctrl-R
Mnemonic	R, G, H, T
File Name	`.../text/AlignRight16.gif` `.../text/AlignRight24.gif`
Other Notes	An example of the unit specified in the description is a line or paragraph. Use this graphic only for text. See "Align Right" on page 276 for graphics that might be more appropriate for other needs.

Type Style Graphics

This section contains graphics that represent frequently used type styles for text.

Bold

Graphics	**b** **b**
Description	Displays text in boldface type style
Name	Bold
Tool Tip	Bold
Shortcut	Ctrl-B
Mnemonic	B, L, D
File Name	`.../text/Bold16.gif` `.../text/Bold24.gif`

Italic

Graphics	*i* *i*
Description	Displays text in an italic type style
Name	Italic
Tool Tip	Italic
Shortcut	Ctrl-I
Mnemonic	I, T, L, C
File Name	`.../text/Italic16.gif` `.../text/Italic24.gif`

Normal

Graphics	n n
Description	Displays text without any deviations from the regular style
Name	Normal
Tool Tip	Normal
Mnemonic	N, R, M, L
File Name	`.../text/Normal16.gif` `.../text/Normal24.gif`

Underline

Graphics	<u>u</u> <u>U</u>
Description	Displays text with a thin line underneath each character
Name	Underline
Tool Tip	Underline
Shortcut	Ctrl-U
Mnemonic	U, N, D, R
File Name	`.../text/Underline16.gif` `.../text/Underline24.gif`

Media

The graphics in this section represent:

- Creation, selection, or opening of a **movie** (that is, a full-motion video with sound that is formatted for inclusion in an application)

- Movement through time-sensitive data

Creating a Movie   The graphics in this section represent the creation, selection, or opening of a movie.

Movie

Graphics	
Description	Creates, selects, or opens a movie
Name	Movie
Tool Tip	Movie
Mnemonic	M, V, O
File Name	`.../media/Movie16.gif` `.../media/Movie24.gif`

Moving Through Time-Based Media   This section contains graphics that represent movement through **time-based media** including spoken audio, music, images, animation, and video.

Several of these graphics use the concept of the play head, which defines the location in the media stream where the time-based media recommences its presentation once an action is carried out. For instance, "Pause" on page 295 stops the media display temporarily without changing the position of the play head. On the other hand, "Stop" on page 297 halts the presentation of the time-based media and moves the play head to the beginning of the media object.

Fast Forward

Graphics	
Description	Advances rapidly through time-based media
Name	Fast Forward
Tool Tip	Fast Forward
Mnemonic	F, S, T
File Name	.../media/FastForward16.gif .../media/FastForward24.gif

Pause

Graphics	
Description	Stops the media display temporarily without changing the position of the play head
Name	Pause
Tool Tip	Pause
Mnemonic	P, S, A
File Name	.../media/Pause16.gif .../media/Pause24.gif
Other Notes	When play is continued, Pause does not return to the beginning of the media object, but resumes where it left off.

Play

Graphics	
Description	Renders time-based media
Name	Play
Tool Tip	Play
Mnemonic	P, L, Y
File Name	.../media/Play16.gif .../media/Play24.gif

Rewind

Graphics	◀◀ ◀◀
Description	Moves quickly backward through time-based media
Name	Rewind
Tool Tip	Rewind
Mnemonic	R, W, N, D
File Name	.../media/Rewind16.gif .../media/Rewind24.gif
Other Notes	Use these graphics only for media transport or other temporal events.

Step Back

Graphics	
Description	Moves the play head back one unit
Name	Step Back
Tool Tip	Step Back
Mnemonic	B, C, K, S
File Name	.../media/StepBack16.gif .../media/StepBack24.gif

Step Forward

Graphics	▕▶ ▕▶
Description	Moves the play head forward one unit
Name	Step Forward
Tool Tip	Step Forward
Mnemonic	F, R, W, D
File Name	.../media/StepForward16.gif .../media/StepForward24.gif
Other Notes	Use these graphics only for media transport or other temporal events.

Stop

Graphics	▪ ▪
Description	Halts the presentation and returns to the beginning of the media object
Name	Stop
Tool Tip	Stop
Mnemonic	S, T, P
File Name	.../media/Stop16.gif .../media/Stop24.gif
Other Notes	Use these graphics only for media transport or other temporal events. The generic graphic described in "Stop" on page 268 is more appropriate for other uses.

Volume

Graphics	
Description	Provides a way to adjust the sound volume
Name	Volume
Tool Tip	Volume
Mnemonic	V, L, M
File Name	`.../media/Volume16.gif` `.../media/Volume24.gif`
Other Notes	Use these graphics only for audio media.

Graphics for Development Tools
The development graphics represent objects or processes in the software development process.

Creating and Deploying Applications and Applets
The graphics in this section represent:

- The creation, selection, and opening of an application, an applet, a J2EE application, a J2EE application client, and a J2EE server

- The addition of a J2EE application client to a J2EE application

- The **deployment** (that is, installation in an operational environment) of an application

A **J2EE application** consists of J2EE components (application clients, applets, HTML pages, **JSP** pages (JavaServer Pages), **servlets**, and enterprise beans) that run on the J2EE platform. J2EE applications are typically designed for distribution across multiple computing tiers.

A **J2EE application client** is a first-tier client program that executes in its own Java virtual machine, but might access J2EE components in the web or business tier.

A **J2EE server** is a collection of runtime services provided by the J2EE platform. These include **HTTP** (Hypertext Transfer Protocol), **HTTPS** (Secure Hypertext Transfer Protocol), **JTA** (Java Transaction API), **RMI-IIOP** (Remote Method Invocation-Internet Inter-ORB Protocol), **Java IDL** (Java Interface Definition Language), **JDBC** (Java Database Connectivity), **JMS** (Java Message Service), **JNDI** (Java Naming and Directory Interface), **JavaMail**, and **JAF** (JavaBeans Activation Framework). Although J2EE servers usually come packaged with web and EJB containers, they are not required to. For example, an OS vendor could supply the runtime services while a separate vendor supplied the J2EE containers.

For deployment, a J2EE application is packaged in an **EAR** (Enterprise Archive) file.

NOTE – You can use a twinkle badge with these graphics to indicate a new applet, application, J2EE application, J2EE application client, J2EE server, bean, enterprise bean, host, and server. For details, see "New Object Indicators" on page 97.

Applet

Graphics	
Description	Creates, selects, or opens an applet
Name	Applet
Tool Tip	Applet
Mnemonic	A, P, L, T
File Name	.../development/Applet16.gif .../development/Applet24.gif

Application

Graphics	
Description	Creates, selects, or opens an application
Name	Application
Tool Tip	Application
Mnemonic	A, P, L, N
File Name	.../development/Application16.gif .../development/Application24.gif

J2EE Application

Graphics	
Description	Creates, selects, or opens a J2EE application
Name	J2EE Application
Tool Tip	J2EE Application
Mnemonic	E, A, P, L, C
File Name	.../development/J2EEApplication16.gif .../development/J2EEApplication24.gif

J2EE Application Client

Graphics	
Description	Creates, selects, or opens a J2EE application client
Name	J2EE Application Client
Tool Tip	J2EE Application Client
Mnemonic	C, L, N, T
File Name	.../development/J2EEApplicationClient16.gif .../development/J2EEApplicationClient24.gif

Add J2EE Application Client

Graphics	
Description	Adds a J2EE application client to a J2EE application
Name	Add J2EE Application Client
Tool Tip	Add J2EE Application Client
Mnemonic	C, L, N, T, A
File Name	.../development/J2EEApplicationClientAdd16.gif .../development/J2EEApplicationClientAdd24.gif

J2EE Server

Graphics	
Description	Creates, selects, or opens a J2EE server
Name	J2EE Server
Tool Tip	J2EE Server
Mnemonic	S, R, V
File Name	`.../development/J2EEServer16.gif` `.../development/J2EEServer24.gif`

Deploy Application

Graphics	
Description	Deploys a J2EE application to a J2EE server
Name	Deploy Application
Tool Tip	Deploy Application
Mnemonic	D, P, L, Y, A
File Name	`.../development/ApplicationDeploy16.gif` `.../development/ApplicationDeploy24.gif`

Creating and Adding Beans and Enterprise Beans

The graphics in this section represent the creation, selection, and opening of a **bean** (a component using the **JavaBeans** specification) and an enterprise bean (a component based on the **EJB** architecture for development and deployment of object-oriented, distributed, enterprise-level applications).

Bean

Graphics	
Description	Creates, selects, or opens a bean
Name	Bean
Tool Tip	Bean
Mnemonic	B, N, E
File Name	`.../development/Bean16.gif` `.../development/Bean24.gif`

Add Bean

Graphics	
Description	Adds a bean to an existing set of objects
Name	Add Bean
Tool Tip	Add Bean
Mnemonic	B, N, D
File Name	.../development/BeanAdd16.gif .../development/BeanAdd24.gif

Enterprise JavaBean

Graphics	
Description	Creates, selects, or opens an enterprise bean
Name	Enterprise JavaBean
Tool Tip	Enterprise Bean
Mnemonic	E, J, B, N, T, P
File Name	.../development/EnterpriseJavaBean16.gif .../development/EnterpriseJavaBean24.gif

Creating Hosts and Servers

The graphics in this section represent the creation, selection, or opening of a **host** (a computer system that is accessed by one or more computers and workstations at remote locations) and a **server** (a network device that manages resources and supplies services to a **client**).

Host

Graphics	
Description	Creates, selects, or opens a host
Name	Host
Tool Tip	Host
Mnemonic	H, S, T
File Name	.../development/Host16.gif .../development/Host24.gif

Server

Graphics	
Description	Creates, selects, or opens a server
Name	Server
Tool Tip	Server
Mnemonic	S, R, V
File Name	`.../development/Server16.gif` `.../development/Server24.gif`

Creating and Adding Java Archive Files

The graphics in this section represent the creation, selection, and opening of:

- **JAR** (Java Archive) files
- Enterprise JavaBeans JAR files (a Java Archive file for an enterprise bean)
- EAR (Enterprise Archive) files

It also provides graphics to represent the addition of a Java Archive file to an existing set of objects.

JAR

Graphics	
Description	Creates, selects, or opens a JAR file
Name	Java Archive
Tool Tip	Java Archive
Mnemonic	J, R, A
File Name	`.../development/Jar16.gif` `.../development/Jar24.gif`

Enterprise JavaBean JAR

Graphics	
Description	Creates, selects, or opens an Enterprise JavaBeans JAR
Name	Enterprise JavaBean JAR
Tool Tip	Enterprise JavaBean JAR
Mnemonic	E, J, B, N, T, P
File Name	`.../development/EnterpriseJavaBeanJar16.gif` `.../development/EnterpriseJavaBeanJar24.gif`

Add JAR

Graphics	
Description	Adds a JAR to an existing set of archives
Name	Add Java Archive
Tool Tip	Add Java Archive
Mnemonic	J, R, A, D
File Name	`.../development/JarAdd16.gif` `.../development/JarAdd24.gif`

Creating and Adding Web Archive Files and Web Components

The graphics in this section represent the:

- Creation, selection, and opening of a J2EE Web Archive file (**WAR**)

- Addition of a WAR to an existing set of objects

- Creation, selection, and opening of a **web component** (an executable file that is contained in a WAR file)

- Addition of a web component to a WAR file

WAR

Graphics	
Description	Creates, selects, or opens a J2EE WAR file
Name	J2EE Web Archive
Tool Tip	J2EE Web Archive
Mnemonic	W, R, A
File Name	.../development/War16.gif .../development/War24.gif

Add WAR

Graphics	
Description	Adds a WAR to an existing set of objects
Name	Add J2EE Web Archive
Tool Tip	Add J2EE Web Archive
Mnemonic	W, B, R, C
File Name	.../development/WarAdd16.gif .../development/WarAdd24.gif

Web Component

Graphics	
Description	Creates, selects, or opens a web component
Name	Web Component
Tool Tip	Web Component
Mnemonic	W, B, C, M
File Name	.../development/WebComponent16.gif .../development/WebComponent24.gif

Add Web Component

Graphics	
Description	Adds a web component to a WAR file
Name	Add J2EE Web Component
Tool Tip	Add J2EE Web Component
Mnemonic	W, B, C, A, D
File Name	`.../development/WebComponentAdd16.gif`
	`.../development/WebComponentAdd24.gif`

c: LOCALIZATION WORD LISTS

This appendix contains a list of words and phrases encountered in using or developing standard Java applications with the Java look and feel. The tables provide translations for interface elements and concepts in French, German, Spanish, Italian, Swedish, Japanese, Simplified Chinese, Traditional Chinese, and Korean. The terms appear in two tables—one for European and another for Asian languages. The tables follow these conventions:

- Terms that are intended for use as menu names, menu items, or button text are boldfaced.

- Parenthetical explanations of terms in English are not necessarily translated into other languages.

- Synonyms are separated by commas in some languages.

European Languages

TABLE 34   Word List for European Languages

	English	French	German
1	**About** *{Application}* (item in Help menu)	**A propos de l'application**	**Anwendungsinfo**
2	About boxes	Boîtes de dialogue A propos de	Feldinfo
3	Abstract Window Toolkit	Outils de fenêtre abstraite	Abstract Window Toolkit
4	accessibility	accessibilité	Eingabehilfe
5	active components	composants actifs	aktive Komponenten
6	active windows	fenêtres actives	aktive Fenster
7	alert boxes	boîtes d'alerte	Warnfelder
8	**Align Center** (item in Format menu)	**Centrer**	**Zentriert**
9	**Align Left** (item in Format menu)	**Aligner à gauche**	**Linksbündig**
10	**Align Right** (item in Format menu)	**Aligner à droite**	**Rechtsbündig**
11	alignment	alignement	Ausrichtung
12	anchor point	point d'ancrage	Ankerpunkt
13	animation	animation	Animation
14	applet	applet	Applet
15	application	application	Anwendung
16	**Apply** (button)	**Appliquer**	**Übernehmen**
17	arrow keys	touches de défilement	Pfeiltasten
18	assistive technologies	technologies d'assistance	Hilfstechnologien
19	background	arrière-plan	Hintergrund
20	backing windows	fenêtres auxiliaires	Notizblockfenster
21	Beeps (label in notification dialog box)	Bips (libellé dans la boîte de dialogue d'avertissement)	Signaltöne (Bezeichnung im Benachrichtigungsdialogfeld)
22	bit depth	profondeur de bits	Bit-Tiefe
23	**Bold** (item in Format menu)	**Gras**	**Fett**
24	bold text	texte gras	fettgedruckter Text
25	borders	bordures	Rahmen
26	**Browse** (button)	**Parcourir**	**Durchsuchen**

TABLE 34 Word List for European Languages *(Continued)*

	Spanish	Italian	Swedish
1	**Acerca de** (la aplicación)	**Informazioni sull'applicazione**	**Om prognamn**
2	Cuadros de diálogo Acerca de	finestre Informazioni su	Om-rutor
3	Caja de herramientas de ventanas abstractas	Abstract Window Toolkit	Abstract Window Toolkit
4	accesibilidad	accessibilità	åtkomlighet
5	componentes activos	componenti attivi	aktiva komponenter
6	ventanas activas	finestre attive	aktiva fönster
7	cuadros de diálogo de alerta	finestre di avviso	varningsrutor
8	**Centrar**	**Centra**	**Centrera**
9	**Alinear a la izquierda**	**Allinea a sinistra**	**Vänsterjustera**
10	**Alinear a la derecha**	**Allinea a destra**	**Högerjustera**
11	alineación	allineamento	justering, blankettinpassning
12	punto de anclaje	punto di ancoraggio	förankringspunkt
13	animación	animazione	animering
14	subprograma	applet	miniprogram
15	aplicación	applicazione	program, tillämpning
16	**Aplicar**	**Applica**	**Använd**
17	teclas de flecha	tasti freccia	piltangenter
18	tecnología de asistencia	tecnologie di assistenza	hjälpmeddelande
19	fondo	sfondo	bakgrund, arbeta i bakgrunden
20	ventanas de apoyo	finestre ausiliarie	underliggande fönster
21	Señales acústicas (etiqueta del cuadro de diálogo de notificaci ón)	Segnali acustici (etichetta nella finestra di dialogo di notifica)	ljudsignaler
22	profundidad de bit	profondità di bit	bitdjup
23	**Negrita**	**Grassetto**	**Fetstil**
24	texto en negrita	testo in grassetto	fetstil
25	bordes	bordi	konturlinjer
26	**Explorar**	**Sfoglia**	**Bläddra**

TABLE 34   Word List for European Languages *(Continued)*

	English	French	German
27	browser	navigateur	Browser
28	button border	bordure du bouton	Schaltflächenumrandung
29	button graphics	graphiques du bouton	Schaltflächengrafik
30	button text	texte du bouton	Schaltflächentext
31	**Cancel** (button)	**Annuler**	**Abbrechen**
32	capitalization	mise en majuscules	Großschreibung
33	caution symbol	symbole d'attention	Warnsymbol
34	CDE style look and feel	apparence de type CDE	Erscheinungsbild im CDE-Stil
35	cells (in tables)	cellules (d'un tableau)	Zellen (in Tabellen)
36	channels (in scrollbars)	canaux (dans les barres de défilement)	Kanäle (in Bildlaufleisten)
37	checkbox menu items	options de menu avec case à cocher	Kontrollkästchen-Menüelemente
38	checkboxes	cases à cocher	Kontrollkästchen
39	choosers	sélecteurs	Auswahl
40	clicking	cliquer	klicken
41	client properties	propriétés du client	Client-Eigenschaften
42	**Close** (button or item in File menu)	**Fermer**	**Schließen**
43	close control	commande de fermeture	Steuerelement schließen
44	color choosers	sélecteurs de couleurs	Farbauswahl
45	column (in tables)	colonne (d'un tableau)	Spalte (in Tabellen)
46	column header (in tables)	en-tête de colonne (d'un tableau)	Spaltenüberschrift (in Tabellen)
47	combo boxes	boîtes de dialogue mixtes	Kombinationsfelder
48	command button row	rangée de boutons de commande	Befehlsschaltflächen-Zeile
49	command buttons	boutons de commande	Befehlsschaltflächen
50	components	composants	Komponenten
51	containers	conteneurs	Container
52	content panel (in a color chooser)	panneau de contenu (dans un sélecteur de couleurs)	Inhaltbedienfeld (in einer Farbauswahl)
53	content panes	sous-fenêtres de contenu	Inhaltteilfenster

TABLE 34   Word List for European Languages *(Continued)*

	Spanish	Italian	Swedish
27	navegador	browser	(webb)läsare
28	borde de botón	bordo del pulsante	knappens kant
29	gráfico de botón	grafica del pulsante	bild för knapp
30	texto de botón	testo del pulsante	knappens text
31	**Cancelar**	**Annulla**	**Avbryt**
32	uso de mayúsculas	lettere maiuscole	versaler, gör till versaler
33	símbolo de precaución	simbolo di attenzione	varningssymbol
34	apariencia del estilo de CDE	aspetto stile CDE	CDE-känsla
35	celdas (en tablas)	celle (nelle tabelle)	celler
36	canales (en barras de desplazamiento)	canali (nelle barre di scorrimento)	kanaler
37	opciones de menú con casillas de verificación	voci di menu con casella di selezione	kryssrutealternativ
38	casillas de verificación	caselle di selezione	kryssrutor
39	selectores	selettori	väljare
40	hacer clic	clic del mouse	klicka
41	propiedades de cliente	proprietà client	klientegenskaper
42	**Cerrar**	**Chiudi**	**Stäng**
43	control de cierre	controllo di chiusura	stängningsknapp
44	selectores de color	selettori dei colori	färgväljare
45	columna (en tablas)	colonne (nelle tabelle)	kolumn
46	cabecera de columna (en tablas)	intestazione delle colonne (nelle tabelle)	kolumnrubrik
47	cuadros combinados	caselle combinate	kombinationsruta
48	fila de botones de comando	riga dei pulsanti di comando	knapprad
49	botones de comando	pulsanti di comando	kommandoknapp
50	componentes	componenti	komponent
51	contenedores	contenitori	behållare
52	panel de contenido (en un selector de color)	pannello del contenuto (in un selettore del colore)	innehållspanel
53	paneles de contenido	pannelli del contenuto	innehållsfönster

TABLE 34   Word List for European Languages *(Continued)*

English	French	German
54 **Contents** (item in Help menu)	**Contenu**	**Inhalt**
55 contextual menus	menus contextuels	Kontextmenüs
56 **Continue** (button in Error alert box)	**Continuer**	**Weiter**
57 control type style	caractères de type contrôle	Steuerelementtyp-Stil
58 Control-clicking	Ctrl + clic	Klicken bei gedrückter Umschalttaste
59 controls	contrôles	Steuerelemente
60 Control-Tab	Ctrl + Tab	STRG + Tab
61 **Copy** (item in Edit menu)	**Copier**	**Kopieren**
62 crosshair pointer	pointeur en croix	Kreuzzeiger
63 cross-platform color	couleur multi-plateforme	plattformübergreifende Farbe
64 cross-platform delivery	visualisation multi-plateforme	plattformübergreifende Übermittlung
65 currency formats	formats de devise	Währungsformat
66 **Cut** (item in Edit menu)	**Couper**	**Ausschneiden**
67 data structure	structure de données	Datenstruktur
68 Date Format (label in preferences dialog box)	Format de date (libellé dans la boîte de dialogue de préférences)	Datumsformat (Bezeichnung im Dialogfeld Einstellungen)
69 default	par défaut	Standardeinstellung
70 default command buttons	boutons de commande par défaut	Standardbefehlsschaltflächen
71 Default Font (label in preferences dialog box)	police par défaut (libellé dans la boîte de dialogue de préférences)	Standardschriftart (Bezeichnung in Dialogfeld Einstellungen)
72 default Java look and feel theme	apparence Java par défaut	Standard-Java-Erscheinungsbild
73 default pointer	pointeur par défaut	Standardzeiger
74 delay indication	indication de temporisation	Verzögerungsanzeige
75 destination feedback	réaction de destination	Ziel-Feedback
76 dialog boxes	boîtes de dialogue	Dialogfelder
77 dimmed text	texte en grisé	grau dargestellter Text
78 disabilities	invalidités	Behinderungen

TABLE 34   Word List for European Languages *(Continued)*

	Spanish	Italian	Swedish
54	**Contenido**	**Sommario**	**Innehåll**
55	menús contextuales	menu contestuali	sammanhangsberoende meny
56	**Continuar**	**Continua**	**Fortsätt**
57	estilo del tipo de control	stile di caratteri di controllo	teckensnitt för styrtecken
58	Control + clic	Ctrl + clic del mouse	Ctrl-klicka
59	controles	controlli	reglage
60	Control + Tab	Ctrl + Tab	Ctrl-Tabb
61	**Copiar**	**Copia**	**Kopiera**
62	puntero en forma de cruz	puntatore a croce	hårkorsmarkör
63	color para múltiples plataformas	colore multipiattaforma	plattformsoberoende färg
64	entrega en múltiples plataformas	utilizzo multipiattaforma	plattformsoberoende sändning
65	formatos de divisa	formati di valuta	valutaformat
66	**Cortar**	**Taglia**	**Klipp ut**
67	estructura de datos	struttura dei dati	datastruktur
68	Formato de fecha (etiqueta en cuadro de diálogo de preferencias)	Formato della data (etichetta nella finestra di dialogo delle preferenze)	Datumformat
69	predeterminado, de forma predeterminada	valore predefinito	standard
70	botones de comando predeterminados	pulsanti di comando predefiniti	standardkommandoknapp
71	Fuente predeterminada (etiqueta en cuadro de diálogo de preferencias)	Carattere predefinito (etichetta nella finestra di dialogo delle preferenze)	Standardteckensnitt
72	tema con apariencia Java predeterminada	tema predefinito dell'aspetto Java	standardtema för Java-känsla
73	puntero predeterminado	puntatore predefinito	standardmarkör
74	indicación de retraso	indicazione di ritardo	fördröjningsvarning
75	información de destino	feedback di destinazione	målåterkoppling
76	cuadros de diálogo	finestre di dialogo	dialogrutor
77	texto atenuado	testo non disponibile	nedtonad text
78	incapacidades, minusvalías	accesso facilitato	handikapp

TABLE 34   Word List for European Languages *(Continued)*

	English	French	German
79	disjoint selection	sélection disjointe	nichtzusammenhängende Auswahl
80	distribution	distribution	Verteilung
81	dithering	réduction	Rasterung
82	dockable toolbars	barres d'outils ancrables	verankerbare Symbolleisten
83	**Document** (item in Format menu)	**Document**	**Dokument** (Element im Menü "Format")
84	**Don't Save** (button in Warning alert boxes)	**Ne pas enregistrer**	**Nicht Speichern**
85	double-clicking	double-cliquer	doppelklicken
86	drag and drop	glisser-déposer	Ziehen und Ablegen
87	drag area	zone de déplacement	Ziehbereich
88	drag texture	texture de déplacement	Textur beim Ziehen
89	dragging	déplacement	Ziehen
90	drop-down arrows	flèches de défilement vers le bas	Dropdown-Pfeile
91	drop-down menus	menus déroulants	Dropdown-Menüs
92	**Edit** (menu)	**Editer**	**Bearbeiten**
93	editable combo boxes	boîtes de dialogue mixtes modifiables	bearbeitbare Kombinationsfelder
94	editable text fields	champs de texte modifiables	bearbeitbare Textfelder
95	editor panes	sous-fenêtres d'éditeur	Editorteilfenster
96	ellipsis marks	points de suspension	Auslassungszeichen
97	Error alert boxes	boîtes d'alerte d'erreur	Warnfelder mit Fehlermeldungen
98	error messages	messages d'erreur	Fehlermeldungen
99	exclusive choice (in toggle buttons)	choix exclusif (dans un bouton à bascule)	exklusive Auswahl (in Umschaltschaltflächen)
100	**Exit** (item in File menu)	**Quitter**	**Beenden**
101	extended selection	sélection étendue	erweiterte Auswahl
102	feedback	réaction	Feedback
103	fields	champs	Felder
104	**File** (menu)	**Fichier**	**Datei**
105	filling slider	curseur de remplissage	Füll-Schieberegler

TABLE 34   Word List for European Languages *(Continued)*

	Spanish	Italian	Swedish
79	selección discontinua	selezione discontinua	bruten markering
80	distribución	distribuzione	distribution
81	interpolación	dithering	nyansutjämning
82	barras de herramientas acoplables	barre degli strumenti ancorabili	dockningsbara verktygsfält
83	**Documento**	**Documento**	**Dokument**
84	**No guardar**	**Non salvare**	**Spara inte**
85	hacer doble clic	doppio clic del mouse	dubbelklicka
86	arrastrar y soltar	trascinare e rilasciare	dra och släpp
87	área de arrastre	area di trascinamento	dragruta
88	textura de arrastre	trascinamento trama	dra struktur
89	arrastre	trascinamento	dra
90	flechas de lista desplegable	frecce di selezione	nedrullningspil
91	menús desplegables	menu a discesa	nedrullningsbara menyer
92	**Editar**	**Modifica**	**Redigera**
93	cuadros combinados editables	caselle combinate modificabili	redigerbar kombinationsruta
94	campos de texto editables	campi di testo modificabili	redigerbara textfält
95	paneles del editor	riquadri dell'editor	redigeringsfönster
96	puntos suspensivos	puntini di sospensione	punkter, tre punkter
97	cuadros de alerta de error	finestre di avviso di errore	felrutor
98	mensajes de error	messaggi di errore	felmeddelanden
99	selección exclusiva (en botones de conmutación)	scelta esclusiva (negli interruttori)	envalsinställning
100	**Salir**	**Esci**	**Avsluta**
101	selección ampliada	selezione estesa	utökad markering
102	retroalimentación	feedback	bekräftelse
103	campos	campi	fält, rutor
104	**Archivo**	**File**	**Arkiv**
105	deslizador de relleno	cursore di riempimento	dragrelage för utfyllnad

TABLE 34   Word List for European Languages *(Continued)*

	English	French	German
106	**Find** (item in Edit menu)	**Rechercher**	**Suchen**
107	find dialog boxes	boîtes de dialogue de recherche	Dialogfelder "Suchen"
108	**Find Next** (item in Edit menu)	**Rechercher suivant**	**Weitersuchen**
109	Flashes (label in notification dialog box)	Clignotement (libellé dans la boîte de dialogue d'avertissement)	Blinksignal (Bezeichnung in Dialogfenster Benachrichtigung)
110	flush 3D effects	supprimer les effets 3D	3D-Effekte löschen
111	**Font** (menu or item in Format menu)	**Police**	**Zeichen**
112	fonts	polices	Schriftarten
113	**Format** (menu)	**Format**	**Format**
114	formatted text panes	sous-fenêtres de texte formaté	formatierte Textteilfenster
115	function keys	touches de fonction	Funktionstasten
116	GIF (Graphics Interchange Format)	GIF (abréviation de «Graphics Interchange Format»)	GIF (Graphics Interchange Format)
117	grids	grilles	Raster
118	hand pointers	pointeurs à main	Handzeiger
119	headline capitalization	mise en majuscule de la première lettre des mots dans les titres	Großschreibung in Überschriften
120	**Help** (button or menu)	**Aide**	**Hilfe**
121	Hidden Text (checkbox in preferences dialog box)	Texte masqué (case à cocher dans la boîte de dialogue préférences)	verborgener Text (Kontrollkästchen in Dialogfenster Einstellungen)
122	highlighting	mise en surbrillance	Hervorhebung
123	horizontal scrollbar	barre de défilement horizontale	horizontaler Rollbalken
124	hot spot	point de repère	Hotspot
125	HSB (tab for hue, saturation, and brightness in color choosers)	HSB (onglet de réglage de la teinte, de la saturation et de la luminosité dans un sélecteur de couleurs)	HSB (Register für Farbton, Sättigung und Helligkeit in Farbauswahl)
126	HTML editor kits	éditeurs HTML	HTML-Editor-Kits
127	I-beam pointer	pointeur en I	Einfügemarke, I-Zeiger
128	icons	icônes	Symbole
129	inactive components	composants inactifs	inaktive Komponenten
130	inactive menu items	options de menu inactives	inaktive Menüelemente

TABLE 34　Word List for European Languages *(Continued)*

	Spanish	Italian	Swedish
106	**Buscar**	**Trova**	**Sök**
107	cuadros de diálogo Buscar	finestre di dialogo di ricerca	sök-dialogrutor
108	**Buscar siguiente**	**Trova successivo**	**Sök nästa**
109	Parpadea (etiqueta del cuadro de diálogo de notificación)	Segnali luminosi (etichetta nella finestra di dialogo di notifica)	blinkar
110	vaciar efectos 3D	elimina effetti 3D	töm 3D-effekter
111	**Fuentes**	**Carattere**	**Teckensnitt**
112	fuentes	caratteri	teckensnitt
113	**Formato**	**Formato**	**Format**
114	paneles de texto con formato	riquadri di testo formattato	fönster med formaterad text
115	teclas de función	tasti funzione	funktionstangenter
116	GIF (Graphics Interchange Format)	GIF (Graphics Interchange Format)	GIF (Graphics Interchange Format)
117	rejillas	griglie	stödlinjer, rutnät
118	punteros de mano	puntatori a forma di mano	hand-markör
119	uso de mayúsculas en la primera letra de los títulos	titolo con iniziale maiuscola	versal rubrik
120	**Ayuda**	**Guida**	**Hjälp**
121	Texto oculto (casilla de verificación del cuadro de diálogo de preferencias)	Testo nascosto (casella di selezione nella finestra di dialogo delle preferenze)	dold text
122	resaltar	evidenziazione	markering
123	barra de desplazamiento horizontal	barra di scorrimento orizzontale	horisontell rullningslist
124	zona activa	punto focale	aktiv punkt
125	HSB (pestaña de tono, saturación y brillo en los selectores de color)	TSL (scheda per tonalità, saturazione e luminosità nei selettori del colore)	HSB
126	kits de edición de HTML	kit dell'editor HTML	HTML-redigeringsprogram
127	Puntero en forma de I	puntatore a forma di l	I-markör, insättningspunkt
128	iconos	icone	bilder
129	componentes inactivos	componenti non attivi	inaktiva komponenter
130	opciones de menú inactivas	voci di menu non attive	inaktiva menyalternativ

TABLE 34   Word List for European Languages *(Continued)*

	English	French	German
131	inactive windows	fenêtres inactives	inaktive Fenster
132	independent choice (in toggle buttons)	choix indépendant (dans un bouton à bascule)	unabhängige Auswahl (in Umschaltschaltflächen)
133	**Index** (item in Help menu)	**Index**	**Index**
134	indicators	indicateurs	Anzeigen
135	Info alert box	boîte d'alerte d'informations	Info-Warnfeld
136	information symbol	symbole d'information	Informationssymbol
137	initial keyboard focus	zone d'entrée clavier initiale	Anfangstastaturfokus
138	insertion point	point d'insertion	Einfügemarke
139	installation screens	écrans d'installation	Installationsbildschirme
140	internal utility windows	fenêtres d'utilitaires internes	internes Hilfsprogramm-Fenster
141	internal windows	fenêtres internes	interne Fenster
142	internationalization	internationalisation	Internationalisierung
143	**Italic** (item in Format menu)	**Italique**	**Kursiv**
144	italic text	texte en italique	kursiver Text
145	Java 2 SDK	Java 2 SDK	Java 2 SDK
146	Java 2D API	API Java 2D	Java 2D API
147	Java Accessibility API	API d'accessibilité Java	Java-Zugriffs-API
148	Java Accessibility Utilities	utilitaires d'accessibilité Java	Java-Zugriffs-Hilfsprogramme
149	Java Development Kit	environnement de développement Java	Java Development Kit
150	Java Foundation Classes	classes de base Java	Java Foundation Classes
151	JavaHelp	JavaHelp	JavaHelp
152	Java look and feel	apparence Java	Java-Erscheinungsbild
153	JFC application	application JFC	JFC-Anwendung
154	JPEG (Joint Photographic Experts Group)	JPEG (abréviation de «Joint Photographic Experts Group»)	JPEG (Joint Photographic Experts Group)

TABLE 34 Word List for European Languages *(Continued)*

	Spanish	Italian	Swedish
131	ventanas inactivas	finestre non attive	inaktiva fönster
132	selección independiente (en botones de conmutación)	scelta indipendente (negli interruttori)	oberoende val
133	**Índice**	**Indice**	**Innehåll**
134	indicadores	indicatori	indikatorer
135	cuadro de alerta de información	finestra di avviso di informazioni	informationsruta
136	símbolo de información	simbolo informazioni	informaitonssymbol
137	orientación inicial del teclado	immissione iniziale da tastiera	preliminär tangentbordsaktivering
138	punto de inserción	punto di inserimento	insättningspunkt
139	pantallas de instalación	schermate di installazione	installationsskärmbilder
140	ventanas de utilidad internas	finestre di utility interne	interna verktygsfönster
141	ventanas internas	finestre interne	interna fönster
142	internacionalización	internazionalizzazione	språkanpassa, internationalisera
143	**Cursiva**	**Corsivo**	**Kursiv**
144	texto en cursiva	testo in corsivo	kursiv text
145	Java 2 SDK	Java 2 SDK	Java 2 SDK
146	Java 2D API	Java 2D API	Java 2D API
147	Java Accessibility API (API de accesibilidad de Java)	API di Java Accessibility	Java-åtkomst-API
148	Java Accessibility Utilities (Utilidades de accesibilidad de Java)	Utility di Java Accessibility	Verktyg för Java-åtkomst
149	Java Development Kit (Kit de desarrollo de Java)	Java Development Kit	Java Development Kit
150	Java Foundation Classes (Clases básicas de Java)	Java Foundation Classes	Java Foundation Classes
151	JavaHelp	JavaHelp	JavaHelp
152	apariencia Java	aspetto Java	Java-känsla
153	aplicación JFC (Java Foundation Classes)	applicazione JFC	JFC-tillämpning
154	JPEG (Joint Photographic Experts Group)	JPEG (Joint Photographic Experts Group)	JPEG (Joint Photographic Experts Group)

TABLE 34   Word List for European Languages *(Continued)*

	English	French	German
155	**Justify** (item in Format menu)	**Justifié**	**Blocksatz**
156	keyboard activation	activation clavier	Tastaturaktivierung
157	keyboard focus	zone d'entrée clavier	Tastaturfokus
158	keyboard navigation	navigation clavier	Tastaturnavigation
159	keyboard operations	opérations clavier	Tastenbefehle
160	keyboard shortcuts	raccourcis clavier	Tastenkombinationen
161	labels	libellés	Bezeichnungen
162	layout managers	gestionnaires de disposition	Layout-Manager
163	leaf (in tree component)	noeud terminal (dans une arborescence)	Blatt (in Baumkomponente)
164	Left Margin (label in preferences dialog box)	Marge gauche (libellé dans la boîte de dialogue de préférences)	Linker Rand (Bezeichnung in Dialogfenster Einstellungen)
165	legal notices	notices légales	rechtlicher Hinweis
166	links	liens	Verknüpfungen
167	lists	listes	Listen
168	localization	localisation	Lokalisierung
169	**Log In** (button in login splash screen)	**Connexion**	**Anmelden**
170	login dialog boxes	boîtes de dialogue de connexion	Anmeldedialogfelder
171	Login Name text field	champ de texte Nom de connexion	Textfeld "Anmeldename"
172	login splash screens	écrans de connexion	Begrüßungsbildschirme
173	look and feel designs	apparences	Erscheinungsbild-Designs
174	major tick marks (in sliders)	marques de graduation principales (dans un curseur de sélection)	Hauptmarkierungen (in Schiebereglern)
175	Margins (checkbox in preferences dialog box)	Marges (libellé dans la boîte de dialogue de préférences)	Ränder (Kontrollkästchen im Dialogfenster Einstellungen)
176	Match Case (checkbox in find dialog box)	Respecter la casse (case à cocher dans la boîte de dialogue Rechercher)	Kontrollkästchen "Groß-/Kleinschreibung beachten"
177	menu bars	barre de menus	Menüleisten
178	menu items	options de menu	Menüelemente

TABLE 34 Word List for European Languages *(Continued)*

	Spanish	Italian	Swedish
155	**Justificar**	**Giustifica**	**Raka marginaler**
156	activación de teclado	attivazione della tastiera	aktiver ing med tangetbordet
157	orientación del teclado	immissione da tastiera	tangentbordsaktiverat
158	navegación por teclado	spostamento tramite tastiera	navigering med tangentbordet
159	operaciones del teclado	operazioni da tastiera	tangentbordsfunktioner, -arbete
160	teclas de método abreviado	tasti di scelta rapida	kortkommandon
161	etiquetas	etichette	etiketter
162	administradores de distribución	gestori di layout	layouthanterare
163	hoja (en componente de árbol)	foglia (riferito a un componente di una struttura ad albero)	löv
164	Margen izquierdo (etiqueta del cuadro de diálogo de preferencias)	Margine sinistro (etichetta nella finestra di dialogo delle preferenze)	Vänstermarginal
165	advertencias legales	note legali	jurdisk text
166	enlaces	collegamenti	länkar
167	listas	elenchi	listor
168	localización	localizzazione	lokal anpassning, översättning
169	**Iniciar sesión**	**Login**	**Logga in**
170	cuadros de diálogo de conexión	finestre di dialogo di login	dialogrutor för inloggning
171	campo de texto Nombre de inicio de sesión	campo di testo Nome di login	textfältet Användarnamn
172	pantalla de bienvenida	schermate iniziali di login	välkomstbild vid inloggning
173	diseños de apariencia	strutture di aspetto	design av utseende
174	marcas de comprobación principales (en los deslizadores)	segni di graduazione principali (nei cursori di scorrimento)	stora skalstreck
175	Márgenes (casilla de verificación del cuadro de diálogo de preferencias)	Margini (casella di selezione nella finestra di dialogo delle preferenze)	marginaler
176	Coincidir mayúsculas y minúsculas (casilla de verificación del cuadro de diálogo Buscar)	Maiuscole/minuscole (casella di selezione nella finestra di dialogo Trova)	matcha gemena/VERSALER
177	barras de menú	barre dei menu	menyrad
178	opciones de menú	voci di menu	menyalternativ

TABLE 34 Word List for European Languages *(Continued)*

	English	French	German
179	menu separators	séparateurs de menu	Menütrennlinien
180	menu titles	titres de menu	Menütitel
181	menus	menus	Menüs
182	message (in alert dialog box)	message (dans une boîte de dialogue d'alerte)	Meldung (in Dialogfenster Warnmeldung)
183	Microsoft Windows style look and feel	apparence de style Microsoft Windows	Erscheinungsbild im Microsoft Windows-Stil
184	middle mouse button	bouton central de la souris	mittlere Maustaste
185	MIME (Multipurpose Internet Mail Extensions)	MIME (abréviation de «Multipurpose Internet Mail Extensions»)	MIME (Multipurpose Internet Mail Extensions)
186	minimized internal windows	fenêtres internes réduites	minimierte interne Fenster
187	minimized windows	fenêtres réduites	minimierte Fenster
188	minor tick marks (in sliders)	marques de graduation secondaires (dans un curseur de sélection)	untergeordnete Markierungen (in Schiebereglern)
189	mnemonics	touches mnémotechniques	Mnemo-Technik
190	modal dialog boxes	boîtes de dialogue modales	modale Dialogfenster
191	model	modèle	Modell
192	modeless dialog boxes	boîtes de dialogue amodales	moduslose Dialogfenster
193	modifier keys	touches modificatrices	Zusatztaste
194	**Modify** (command button)	**Modifier**	**Ändern**
195	mouse button 1	bouton 1 de la souris	Maustaste 1
196	mouse button 2	bouton 2 de la souris	Maustaste 2
197	mouse buttons	boutons de souris	Maustasten
198	mouse devices	souris	Mausgeräte
199	mouse operations	opérations à la souris	Mausbefehle
200	mouse-over feedback	réaction au passage de la souris	Darstellungsänderung bei Berührung mit dem Maus-Cursor
201	move pointers	pointeurs de déplacement	Bewegungszeiger
202	multiple document interface (MDI)	interface MDI	Multiple Document Interface (MDI)
203	multiple selection	sélection multiple	Mehrfachauswahl

TABLE 34 Word List for European Languages *(Continued)*

	Spanish	Italian	Swedish
179	separadores de menú	separatori dei menu	menyavskiljare
180	títulos de menú	titoli dei menu	menyrubrik
181	menús	menu	menyer
182	mensaje (en cuadro de diálogo de alerta)	messaggio (in una finestra di avviso)	meddelande
183	apariencia de estilo Microsoft Windows	aspetto di stile Microsoft Windows	Microsoft Windows-känsla
184	botón central del ratón	pulsante centrale del mouse	mellersta musknappen
185	MIME (Multipurpose Internet Mail Extensions)	MIME (Multipurpose Internet Mail Extensions)	MIME (Multipurpose Internet Mail Extensions)
186	ventanas internas minimizadas	finestre interne ridotte ad icona	minimerade interna fönster
187	ventanas minimizadas	finestre ridotte ad icona	minimerade fönster, fönsterikon
188	marcas de comprobación secundarias (en deslizadores)	segni di graduazione secondari (nei cursori di scorrimento)	små skalstreck
189	mnemotecnia	(caratteri) mnemonici	memosymbol
190	cuadros de diálogo modales	finestre di dialogo modali	tillståndsberoende dialogrutor
191	modelo	modello	modell
192	cuadros de diálogo sin modo	finestre di dialogo non modali	tillståndsoberoende dialogrutor
193	teclas modificadoras	tasti modificatori	modifieringstangent
194	**Modificar**	**Modifica**	**Ändra**
195	botón 1 del ratón	pulsante 1 del mouse	musknapp 1
196	botón 2 del ratón	pulsante 2 del mouse	musknapp 2
197	botones del ratón	pulsanti del mouse	musknappar
198	dispositivos de ratón	dispositivi mouse	musenheter
199	operaciones de ratón	operazioni del mouse	mushantering, arbete med musen
200	información contextual del puntero	informazioni al passaggio del mouse	bekräftelse av markörposition
201	punteros de movimiento	puntatori di spostamento	förflyttningsmarkör
202	Interfaz de documentos múltiples (MDI)	MDI (Multiple Document Interface)	Multiple Document Interface (MDI)
203	selección múltiple	selezione multipla	flerval

TABLE 34   Word List for European Languages *(Continued)*

	English	French	German
204	native code	code natif	nativer Code
205	navigation	navigation	Navigation
206	nested split panes	sous-fenêtres divisées emboîtées	verschachtelte geteilte Fenster
207	**New** (item in File menu)	**Nouveau**	**Neu**
208	nodes (in tree components)	noeuds (dans une arborescence)	Knoten (in Baumkomponente)
209	noneditable combo boxes	boîtes de dialogue mixtes non modifiables	nichtbearbeitbare Kombinationsfelder
210	noneditable text fields	champs de texte non modifiables	nichtbearbeitbare Textfelder
211	nonfilling slider	curseur de sélection sans remplissage	nichtfüllende Schieberegler
212	**Normal** (item in Format menu)	**Normal**	**Normal**
213	notification dialog box	boîte de dialogue d'avertissement	Dialogfeld "Benachrichtigung"
214	**Object** (menu)	**Objet**	**Objekt**
215	**OK** (button)	**OK**	**OK**
216	padding (command buttons)	remplissage (boutons de commande)	Füllen (Befehlsschaltflächen)
217	**Page Setup** (item in File menu)	**Mise en page**	**Seite einrichten**
218	panels	panneaux	Bedienfelder
219	panes	sous-fenêtres	Teilfenster
220	**Paragraph** (item in Format menu)	**Paragraphe**	**Absatz**
221	password fields	champs de mot de passe	Paßwortfelder
222	**Paste** (item in Edit menu)	**Coller**	**Einfügen**
223	pixels	pixels	Pixel
224	plain text	texte ordinaire	Nur-Text
225	plain text area	zone de texte ordinaire	Nur-Text-Bereich
226	plain windows	fenêtres ordinaires	normale Fenster
227	platforms	plateformes	Plattformen
228	plug-in editor kit	kit d'édition de plug-ins	Plug-in-Editor-Kit
229	pluggable look and feel	apparence modulaire	leicht zu erfassendes Erscheinungsbild

TABLE 34 Word List for European Languages *(Continued)*

	Spanish	Italian	Swedish
204	código nativo	codice nativo	egen kod
205	navegación	navigazione	navigering
206	divisiones de panel anidadas	riquadri di divisione nidificati	kapslade delfönster
207	**Nuevo**	**Nuovo**	**Nytt**
208	nodos (en componentes de árbol)	nodi (riferito a componenti di una struttura ad albero)	noder
209	cuadros combinados no editables	caselle combinate non modificabili	icke redigerbar kombinaionsruta
210	campos de texto no editables	campi di testo non modificabili	icke redigerbara textfält
211	deslizador de no relleno	cursore senza riempimento	skjutreglage utan utfyllnad
212	**Normal**	**Normale**	**Normal**
213	cuadro de diálogo de notificación	finestra di dialogo di notifica	meddelanderuta
214	**Objeto**	**Oggetto**	**Objekt**
215	**Aceptar**	**OK**	**OK**
216	margen interior (botones de comando)	riempimento (pulsanti di comando)	utfyllning
217	**Configuración de página**	**Imposta pagina**	**Utskriftsformat**
218	paneles	pannelli	fönster med flikar
219	panel, división	riquadri	delfönster som kan förstoras eller förminskas
220	**Párrafo**	**Paragrafo**	**Stycke**
221	campos de contraseña	campi di immissione password	lösenordsfält
222	**Pegar**	**Incolla**	**Klistra in**
223	píxeles	pixel	pixel, bildpunkt
224	texto sin formato	testo normale	endast text
225	área de texto sin formato	area di testo normale	ruta med text
226	ventanas normales	finestre normali	vanliga fönster
227	plataformas	piattaforme	plattformar
228	módulo del kit de edición	kit dell'editor plug-in	insticksprogram för redigering
229	apariencia conectable	aspetto innestabile	inskicksmodul för utseende (känsla)

TABLE 34 Word List for European Languages *(Continued)*

	English	French	German
230	pointers	pointeurs	Zeiger
231	posted menus	menus postés	ständig sichtbare Menüs
232	posting menus	menus de postage	Menüs ständig sichtbar machen
233	**Preferences** (item in File menu)	**Préférences**	**Einstellungen**
234	preferences dialog boxes	boîte de dialogue de préférences	Dialogfelder "Einstellungen"
235	pressing a key	appuyer sur une touche	eine Taste drücken
236	preview panel (in a color chooser)	panneau de prévisualisation (dans un sélecteur de couleurs)	Vorschauteilfenster (in einer Farbauswahl)
237	primary colors	couleurs primaires	Grundfarben
238	primary windows	fenêtres principales	Basisfenster
239	**Print** (item in File menu)	**Imprimer**	**Drucken**
240	print dialog boxes	boîtes de dialogue d'impression	Dialogfelder "Drucken"
241	printer	imprimante	Drucker
242	product name	nom du produit	Produktbezeichnung
243	progress bars	barres de progression	Statusanzeige
244	progress dialog boxes	boîtes de dialogue de progression	Dialogfelder "Status"
245	progress feedback	réaction de progression	Status-Feedback
246	progress indication	indication de progression	Statusanzeige
247	Question alert boxes	boîtes d'alerte de question	Fragewarnhinweise
248	radio button group	groupe de boutons radio	Optionsfeldgruppe
249	radio button menu items	options de menu avec boutons radio	Optionsfeld-Menüelemente
250	radio buttons	boutons radio	Optionsfelder
251	**Redo** (item in Edit menu)	**Refaire**	**Wiederholen**
252	**Replace** (button in Warning alert box)	**Remplacer**	**Ersetzen**
253	**Reset** (button)	**Restaurer**	**Zurücksetzen**
254	resize pointers	pointeurs de redimensionnement	Größenänderungszeiger
255	resource bundles	ensembles de ressources	Ressourcenpaket
256	reverse video theme	thème vidéo inverse	umgekehrtes Videomotiv

TABLE 34   Word List for European Languages *(Continued)*

	Spanish	Italian	Swedish
230	punteros	puntatori	pekare, markörer
231	menús publicados	menu pubblicati	fasta menyer
232	publicar menús	pubblicazione dei menu	fästa menyer
233	**Preferencias**	**Preferenze**	**Inställningar**
234	cuadros de diálogo de preferencias	finestre di dialogo delle preferenze	dialogrutor för inställningar
235	pulsar una tecla	premere un tasto	trycka på en tangent
236	panel de vista previa (en selector de color)	pannello di anteprima (in un selettore del colore)	granskningsruta
237	colores primarios	colori primari	grundfärger
238	ventana principal	finestra primaria	huvudfönster
239	**Imprimir**	**Stampa**	**Skriv ut**
240	cuadros de diálogo de impresión	finestre di dialogo di stampa	dislogrutor för utskrift
241	impresora	stampante	skrivare
242	nombre de producto	nome del prodotto	produktnamn
243	barras de progreso	barre di avanzamento	förloppsindikator
244	cuadros de diálogo de progreso	finestre di dialogo di avanzamento	dialgrutor för status
245	información de progreso	informazioni sullo stato di avanzamento	statusruta
246	indicación de progreso	indicazione di avanzamento	statusmeddelande
247	cuadros de alerta de interrogación	finestre di avviso di richiesta	frågeruta
248	grupo de botones de radio	gruppo di pulsanti di scelta	(envals)knappgrupp
249	opciones de menú de botón de radio	voci di menu con pulsanti di scelta	knappalternativ
250	botones de radio	pulsanti di scelta	envalsknapp
251	**Rehacer**	**Ripeti**	**Gör om**
252	**Sustituir**	**Sostituisci**	**Ersätt**
253	**Restablecer**	**Reimposta**	**Återställ**
254	punteros de redimensión	puntatori di ridimensionamento	pekare som ändrar storleken
255	grupos de recursos	bundle di risorse	resursmängder
256	tema de vídeo inverso	tema di video inverso	skrivbordstemat omvänd video

TABLE 34   Word List for European Languages *(Continued)*

	English	French	German
257	RGB (tab for red, green, and blue values in a color chooser)	RGB (onglet de réglage des niveaux de rouge, vert et bleu dans un sélecteur de couleurs)	RGB (Register für Rot-, Grün- und Blauwerte in einer Farbauswahl)
258	Right Margin (label in preferences dialog box)	Marge droite (libellé dans la boîte de dialogue de préférences)	rechter Rand (Bezeichnung im Dialogfenster Einstellungen)
259	row (in tables)	ligne, rangée (d'un tableau)	Zeile (in Tabellen)
260	Ruler Units (label in preferences dialog box)	Graduations de la règle (libellé dans la boîte de dialogue de préférences)	Linealeinheiten (Bezeichnung im Dialogfenster Einstellungen)
261	**Save** (button or item in File menu)	**Enregistrer**	**Speichern**
262	**Save As** (item in File menu)	**Enregistrer sous**	**Speichern unter**
263	scale	mettre à l'échelle	skalieren
264	scroll	faire défiler	rollen
265	scroll arrows	flèches de défilement	Bildlaufpfeile
266	scroll box	curseur de défilement	Bildlauffeld
267	scroll channels	canaux de défilement	Bildlaufkanäle
268	scroll panes	sous-fenêtres de défilement	Bildlaufteilfenster
269	scrollbars	barres de défilement	Bildlaufleisten
270	**Search** (item in Help menu)	**Rechercher**	**Suchen**
271	secondary colors	couleurs secondaires	sekundäre Farben
272	secondary windows	fenêtres secondaires	untergeordnete Fenster
273	**Section** (item in Format menu)	**Section**	**Abschnitt**
274	select	sélectionner	auswählen
275	**Select** (button in notification dialog box)	**Sélectionner**	**Auswählen**
276	**Select All** (item in Edit menu)	**Sélectionner tout**	**Alles markieren**
277	selected items	éléments sélectionnés	markierte Elemente
278	selection	sélection	Auswahl
279	sentence capitalization	mise en majuscules de phrases	Großschreibung des Satzes
280	separators	séparateurs	Trennzeichen
281	Shift-clicking	Maj + clic	Klicken bei gedrückter Umschalttaste
282	Shift-Tab	Maj + Tab	STRG + Tab

TABLE 34 Word List for European Languages *(Continued)*

	Spanish	Italian	Swedish
257	RGB (pestaña de los valores rojo, verde y azul en el selector de color)	RGB (scheda per i valori di rosso, verde e blu in un selettore del colore)	RGB
258	Margen derecho (etiqueta del cuadro de diálogo de preferencias)	Margine destro (etichetta in una finestra di dialogo delle preferenze)	Högermarginal
259	fila (en tablas)	righe (nelle tabelle)	rader i tabeller
260	Unidades de la regla (etiqueta del cuadro de diálogo de preferencias)	Unità righello (etichetta nella finestra di dialogo delle preferenze)	linjalens gradering
261	**Guardar**	**Salva**	**Spara**
262	**Guardar como**	**Salva con nome**	**Spara som**
263	escalar	scalare	skala
264	desplazar	scorrere	bläddra, rulla
265	flechas de desplazamiento	frecce di scorrimento	rullningspilar
266	cuadro de desplazamiento	casella di scorrimento	bläddringsruta, rullningsruta
267	canales de desplazamiento	canali di scorrimento	bläddra bland kanaler
268	paneles de desplazamiento	riquadri di scorrimento	rullningsfönster
269	barras de desplazamiento	barre di scorrimento	rullningslist
270	**Búsqueda**	**Ricerca**	**Sök**
271	colores secundarios	colori secondari	sekundära färger
272	ventanas secundarias	finestre secondarie	sekundärfönster
273	**Sección**	**Sezione**	**Avsnitt**
274	seleccionar	selezionare	markera, välj(a)
275	**Seleccionar**	**Seleziona**	**Markera**
276	**Seleccionar todo**	**Seleziona tutto**	**Markera alla**
277	elementos seleccionados	voci selezionate	markerade objekt
278	selección	selezione	markerat, val
279	uso de mayúsculas en una frase	frase con iniziale maiuscola	gör mening versal
280	separadores	separatori	avskiljare
281	Mayús + clic	Maiusc + clic del mouse	Skift-klicka
282	Mayús + Tab	Maiusc + Tab	Skift-Tabb

TABLE 34   Word List for European Languages *(Continued)*

	English	French	German
283	Show (label in preferences dialog box)	Afficher (libellé dans la boîte de dialogue de préférences)	Anzeigen (Bezeichnung im Dialogfenster Einstellungen)
284	single-clicking	cliquer une fois	einmal klicken
285	**Size** (item in Format menu)	**Taille**	**Größe**
286	sliders	curseurs de sélection	Schieberegler
287	small type style	petits caractères	kleiner Schriftstil
288	sort order	ordre de tri	Sortierreihenfolge
289	Sound File (label in notification dialog box)	Fichier son (libellé dans la boîte de dialogue d'avertissement)	Sounddatei (Bezeichnung in Dialogfenster Benachrichtigung)
290	spacing	espacement	Abstand
291	splash screens	écrans de présentation	Eröffnungsbildschirme
292	split panes	sous-fenêtres divisées	geteilte Fenster
293	splitter bars	barres de division	Trennbalken
294	Start at Top (radio button in find dialog box)	Commencer en haut (bouton radio dans la boîte de dialogue Rechercher)	Abwärts (Optionsfeld im Dialogfenster Suchen)
295	Stationery (label in preferences dialog box)	Papier à lettres (libellé dans la boîte de dialogue de préférences)	Stationär (Bezeichnung im Dialogfenster Einstellungen)
296	**Stop** (button)	**Arrêter**	**abbrechen**
297	**Style** (item in Format menu)	**Style**	**Schriftstil**
298	styled text editor (styled text plug-in kit)	éditeur de texte stylisé (ensemble de plug-ins de style de texte)	Schriftart-Editor
299	submenus	sous-menus	Untermenüs
300	**Submit** (command button)	**Soumettre**	**Senden**
301	Swatches (tab in color choosers)	Echantillons (onglet dans un sélecteur de couleurs)	Muster (Register in Farbauswahl)
302	Swing class	classe Swing	Swing-Klasse
303	symbols	symboles	Symbole
304	system status animation	animation d'état du système	Systemstatusanimation
305	system type style	caractères de type système	Systemtypstil
306	tab traversal	parcours d'onglet	Registerdurchlauf
307	tabbed panes	sous-fenêtres à onglets	Teilfenster im Registerformat

TABLE 34   Word List for European Languages *(Continued)*

	Spanish	Italian	Swedish
283	Mostrar (etiqueta del cuadro de diálogo de preferencias)	Mostra (etichetta nella finestra di dialogo delle preferenze)	Visa
284	un solo clic	singolo clic del mouse	enkelklicka
285	**Tamaño**	**Dimensioni**	**Storlek**
286	deslizadores	cursori di scorrimento	reglage
287	estilo pequeño de fuente	stile a caratteri piccoli	liten stil
288	orden de clasificación	criterio di ordinamento	sorteringsordning
289	Archivo de sonido (etiqueta del cuadro de diálogo de notificación)	File sonori (etichetta nella finestra di dialogo di notifica)	Ljudfil
290	espaciar	spaziatura	avstånd
291	pantallas de bienvenida	schermate iniziali	välkomstskärm
292	paneles de división	riquadri di divisione	delade fönster, delfönster
293	barras de división	barre di divisione	delningslist
294	Iniciar en parte superior (botón de radio del cuadro de diálogo Buscar)	Cerca in basso (pulsante di scelta nella finestra di dialogo Trova)	radioknappen Sökriktning nedåt
295	Material de papelería (etiqueta del cuadro de diálogo de preferencias)	Elementi decorativi (etichetta nella finestra di dialogo delle preferenze)	Brevpapper
296	**Detener**	**Stop**	**Stopp**
297	**Estilo**	**Stile**	**Stil**
298	editor de texto con estilo (kit del complemento de estilos de texto)	editor di testo con stile (kit dei plug-in per testo con stile)	typografiprogram, typografiskt redigeringsprogram
299	submenús	menu secondari	undermeny
300	**Enviar**	**Inoltra**	**Skicka**
301	Muestras (pestaña en selectores de color)	Campioni (scheda nel selettore dei colori)	färgprov
302	clase Swing	classe Swing	Swing-klass
303	símbolos	simboli	symboler
304	animación del estado del sistema	animazione dello stato del sistema	animering av systemstatus
305	estilo de fuente del sistema	stile di caratteri del sistema	systemsteckensnitt
306	secuencias con la tecla Tab	spostamento tramite tasto Tab	tabbförflyttning
307	paneles con pestañas	riquadri a schede	fönster med flikar

TABLE 34   Word List for European Languages *(Continued)*

	English	French	German
308	tables	tables	Tabellen
309	text areas	zones de texte	Textbereiche
310	text fields	champs de texte	Textfelder
311	text pointers	pointeurs de texte	Textzeiger
312	theme mechanism	mécanisme de thème	Motivmechanismus
313	themes	thèmes	Motive
314	title bars (in windows)	barres de titre (dans une fenêtre)	Titelleisten (in Fenstern)
315	toggle buttons	boutons à bascule	Umschaltflächen
316	tool tips	info-bulles	Quickinfo
317	toolbar buttons	boutons de barre d'outils	Symbolleisten-Schaltflächen
318	toolbars	barres d'outils	Symbolleisten
319	trademark information	information sur les marques commerciales	Warenzeicheninformationen
320	tree components	composants d'une arborescence	Baumkomponenten
321	triple-clicking	triple-cliquer	dreimal klicken
322	turners (in tree components)	symbole +/- permettant de développer ou de réduire une arborescence	Symbol +/- zum Ein-/Ausblenden (in Baumstrukturkomponenten)
323	**Tutorial** (item in Help menu)	**Didacticiel**	**Lernprogramm**
324	unavailable items	options non disponibles	nichtverfügbare Elemente
325	**Underline** (item in Format menu)	**Souligner**	**Unterstreichen**
326	**Undo** (item in Edit menu)	**Défaire**	**Rückgängig**
327	usability testing	essai d'utilisation	Verwendbarkeitsprüfung
328	user interface elements	éléments d'interface utilisateur	Elemente der Benutzeroberfläche
329	user type style	caractères de type utilisateur	benutzerspezifisches Schriftformat
330	utility windows	fenêtres d'utilitaire	Dienstprogrammfenster
331	version numbers	numéros de version	Versionsnummern
332	vertical scrollbar	barre de défilement verticale	vertikale Bildlaufleiste
333	**View** (menu)	**Affichage**	**Ansicht**
334	visual design	conception visuelle	visueller Entwurf

TABLE 34   Word List for European Languages *(Continued)*

	Spanish	Italian	Swedish
308	tablas	tabelle	tabeller
309	áreas de texto	aree di testo	textområden
310	campos de texto	campi di testo	textfält, textrutor
311	punteros de texto	puntatori del testo	textmarkör
312	mecanismo de tema	meccanismo dei temi	tema-mekanism
313	temas	temi	skrivbordsteman
314	barras de título (en ventanas)	barre dei titoli (in windows)	namnlist
315	botones de conmutación	interruttori	växlingsknappar
316	información sobre herramientas	descrizione comandi	hjälpmeddelande
317	botones de barra de herramientas	pulsanti della barra degli strumenti	knappar i verktygsfält
318	barras de herramientas	barre degli strumenti	verktygsfält
319	información sobre marcas comerciales	informazioni sui marchi di fabbrica	information om varumärke
320	componentes de árbol	componenti di una struttura ad albero	trädkomponenter
321	hacer clic tres veces	triplo clic del mouse	trippelklicka
322	giradores (en componentes de árbol)	commutatori (riferito a componenti di una struttura ad albero)	nodpunkt
323	**Tutorial**	**Esercitazione**	**Självstudier**
324	elementos no disponibles	opzioni non disponibili	ej tillgängliga alternativ
325	**Subrayar**	**Sottolinea**	**Understruken**
326	**Deshacer**	**Annulla**	**Ångra**
327	prueba de uso	test d'uso	funktionstest
328	elementos de la interfaz de usuario	elementi dell'interfaccia utente	användargränssnittets delar
329	estilo de fuente del usuario	stile di carattere dell'utente	användarens typsnitt
330	ventanas de utilidades	finestre di utilità	verktygsfönster
331	números de versión	numeri di versione	versionsnummer
332	barra de desplazamiento vertical	barra di scorrimento verticale	vertikal rullningslist
333	**Ver**	**Visualizza**	**Visa**
334	diseño visual	progettazione visiva	grafisk layout

TABLE 34 Word List for European Languages *(Continued)*

	English	French	German
335	visual identifier	identificateur visuel	visueller Bezeichner
336	wait pointers	pointeurs d'attente	Wartezeiger
337	Warning alert boxes	boîtes d'alerte d'avertissement	Warnfelder
338	Whole Word (checkbox in find dialog box)	Mot entier (case à cocher dans la boîte de dialogue Rechercher)	Kontrollkästchen "Ganzes Wort"
339	window borders	bordures de fenêtre	Fensterrand
340	window controls	contrôles de fenêtre	Fenstersteuerelemente
341	window frame	cadre de fenêtre	Fensterrahmen
342	windows	fenêtres	Fenster
343	word order	ordre des mots	Wortstellung
344	word wrap	renvoi à la ligne	Wortumbruch
345	zoom buttons	boutons de zoom	Zoom-Schaltflächen
346	zooming panes	sous-fenêtres de zoom	Zoom-Bereiche

TABLE 34   Word List for European Languages *(Continued)*

	Spanish	Italian	Swedish
335	identificador visual	identificatore visivo	synlig identifierare
336	punteros de espera	puntatori di attesa	vänta-markör, timglas
337	cuadros de Advertencia	finestre di avviso Avvertenza	varningsruta
338	Palabras completas (casilla de verificación del cuadro de diálogo Buscar)	Parola intera (casella di selezione nella finestra di dialogo Trova)	Hela ord
339	bordes de ventana	bordi della finestra	fönsterkant, fönsterkontur
340	controles de ventana	controlli della finestra	fönsterreglage
341	marco de ventana	cornice della finestra	fönsterram
342	ventanas	finestre	fönster
343	orden de palabras	ordine delle parole	ordföljd
344	ajuste de línea	a capo automatico	radbrytning
345	botones de ampliación/reducción	pulsanti di ingrandimento/riduzione	zoom-knappar, knappar för att förstora eller förminska
346	paneles de ampliación/reducción	riquadri di ingrandimento/riduzione	zoom-rutor, delfönster som kan förstoras eller förminskas

Asian Languages

TABLE 35 Word List for Asian Languages

	English	Japanese	Simplified Chinese
1	**About** *{Application}* (item in Help menu)	[(アプリケーション名) について] ([ヘルプ] メニューの項目)	关于应用程序（"帮助"菜单中的项）
2	About boxes	[製品情報] ウィンドウ	关于框
3	Abstract Window Toolkit	Abstract Window Toolkit	摘要窗口工具箱
4	accessibility	ユーザ補助機能	可存取性
5	active components	アクティブコンポーネント	活动组件
6	active windows	アクティブウィンドウ	活动窗口
7	alert boxes	アラートボックス	报警框
8	**Align Center** (item in Format menu)	[中央揃え] ([書式] メニューの項目)	居中（"格式"菜单中的项）
9	**Align Left** (item in Format menu)	[左揃え] ([書式] メニューの項目)	左对齐（"格式"菜单中的项）
10	**Align Right** (item in Format menu)	[右揃え] ([書式] メニューの項目)	右对齐（"格式"菜单中的项）
11	alignment	配置	对齐
12	anchor point	アンカーポイント	锚点
13	animation	アニメーション	动画
14	applet	アプレット	小程序
15	application	アプリケーション	应用程序
16	**Apply** (button)	[適用] (ボタン)	应用（按钮）
17	arrow keys	矢印キー	箭头键
18	assistive technologies	ユーザ補助機能	辅助技术
19	background	バックグラウンド	背景
20	backing windows	バッキングウィンドウ	后备窗口
21	Beeps (label in notification dialog box)	[ビープ音] (通知ダイアログボックスのラベル)	蜂鸣（通知对话框中的标签）
22	bit depth	ビットの深さ	位色深度
23	**Bold** (item in Format menu)	[ボールド] ([書式] メニューの項目)	黑体（"格式"菜单中的项）
24	bold text	ボールドテキスト	黑体文字
25	borders	境界	边界
26	**Browse** (button)	[ブラウズ] (ボタン)	浏览（按钮）

TABLE 35　Word List for Asian Languages *(Continued)*

	English	Traditional Chinese	Korean
1	**About** *{Application}* (item in Help menu)	關於 {應用程式} (「輔助說明」功能表中的項目)	응용프로그램 정보 (도움말 메뉴의 항목)
2	About boxes	關於方塊	정보 상자
3	Abstract Window Toolkit	虛擬視窗工具組	추상 윈도우 툴킷
4	accessibility	輔助工具	액세스
5	active components	工作元件	활성 구성 요소
6	active windows	工作視窗	활성 창
7	alert boxes	警示方塊	경고 상자
8	**Align Center** (item in Format menu)	置中 (「格式」功能表中的項目)	가운데 정렬(서식 메뉴의 항목)
9	**Align Left** (item in Format menu)	**靠左對齊** (「格式」功能表中的項目)	**왼쪽 정렬** (서식 메뉴의 항목)
10	**Align Right** (item in Format menu)	**靠右對齊** (「格式」功能表中的項目)	**오른쪽 정렬**(서식 메뉴의 항목)
11	alignment	對齊	정렬
12	anchor point	控點	앵커 포인트
13	animation	動畫	애니메이션
14	applet	applet	애플릿
15	application	應用程式	응용프로그램
16	**Apply** (button)	**套用** (按鈕)	**적용** (버튼)
17	arrow keys	箭號鍵	화살표 키
18	assistive technologies	輔助技術	지원 기술
19	background	背景	백그라운드
20	backing windows	後備視窗	보조 창
21	Beeps (label in notification dialog box)	嗚聲 (通知對話方塊中的標籤)	경고음(통보 대화 상자의 레이블)
22	bit depth	位元深度	비트 깊이
23	**Bold** (item in Format menu)	粗體 (「格式」功能表中的項目)	굵은체 (서식 메뉴의 항목)
24	bold text	粗體文字	굵은체 텍스트
25	borders	邊線	경계
26	**Browse** (button)	**瀏覽** (按鈕)	**찾아보기** (버튼)

TABLE 35 Word List for Asian Languages *(Continued)*

	English	Japanese	Simplified Chinese
27	browser	ブラウザ	浏览器
28	button border	ボタン境界	按钮边界
29	button graphics	ボタングラフィックス	按钮图标
30	button text	ボタンテキスト	按钮文字
31	**Cancel** (button)	**[取消し]** (ボタン)	取消（按钮）
32	capitalization	大文字使用	大写
33	caution symbol	注意記号	小心标记
34	CDE style look and feel	CDE スタイルの Look & Feel	CDE 风格的界面外观
35	cells (in tables)	セル (テーブルで)	单元格（表中）
36	channels (in scrollbars)	チャネル (スクロールバーで)	通道（滚动条中）
37	checkbox menu items	チェックボックスメニュー項目	复选框菜单项
38	checkboxes	チェックボックス	复选框
39	choosers	チューザ	选择器
40	clicking	クリック	单击
41	client properties	クライアントプロパティ	客户属性
42	**Close** (button or item in File menu)	**[閉じる]** (ボタン), **[閉じる]** ([ファイル] メニューの項目)	关闭（按钮或 "文件" 菜单中的项）
43	close control	クローズコントロール	关闭控制
44	color choosers	カラーチューザ	颜色选择器
45	column (in tables)	列 (テーブルで)	列（表格中）
46	column header (in tables)	列ヘッダ (テーブルで)	列标题（表格中）
47	combo boxes	コンボボックス	组合框
48	command button row	コマンドボタン行	命令按钮行
49	command buttons	コマンドボタン	命令按钮
50	components	コンポーネント	组件
51	containers	コンテナ	容器
52	content panel (in a color chooser)	コンテンツパネル (カラーチューザで)	内容面板（颜色选择器中）
53	content panes	コンテンツ区画	内容窗格
54	**Contents** (item in Help menu)	**[目次]** ([ヘルプ] メニューの項目)	内容（"帮助" 菜单中的项）
55	contextual menus	コンテキストメニュー	上下文菜单

TABLE 35 Word List for Asian Languages *(Continued)*

	English	Traditional Chinese	Korean
27	browser	瀏覽器	브라우저
28	button border	按鈕邊線	버튼 경계
29	button graphics	按鈕圖形	버튼 그래픽
30	button text	按鈕文字	버튼 텍스트
31	**Cancel** (button)	取消 (按鈕)	**취소** (버튼)
32	capitalization	大寫	대문자 표시
33	caution symbol	小心符號	경고 기호
34	CDE style look and feel	CDE 樣式外視感覺	CDE 스타일 모양 및 색감
35	cells (in tables)	儲存格 (在表格中)	셀(표)
36	channels (in scrollbars)	通道 (在捲動軸中)	채널(스크롤 막대)
37	checkbox menu items	核取方塊功能表項目	확인란 메뉴 항목
38	checkboxes	核取方塊	확인란
39	choosers	選擇程式	선택기
40	clicking	按一下	누르기
41	client properties	用戶端屬性	클라이언트 등록 정보
42	**Close** (button or item in File menu)	關閉 (按鈕或「檔案」功能表中的項目)	닫기(파일 메뉴의 버튼 또는 항목)
43	close control	關閉控制	제어기 닫기
44	color choosers	色彩選擇器	색상 선택기
45	column (in tables)	行 (在表格中)	열(표)
46	column header (in tables)	行標頭 (在表格中)	열 머리글(표)
47	combo boxes	組合方塊	콤보 상자
48	command button row	指令按鈕列	명령 버튼 행
49	command buttons	指令按鈕	명령 버튼
50	components	元件	구성 요소
51	containers	儲存區	보관소
52	content panel (in a color chooser)	內容面板 (在色彩選擇器中)	내용 패널(색상 선택기)
53	content panes	內容窗格	내용 표시 영역
54	**Contents** (item in Help menu)	內容 (「輔助說明」功能表中的項目)	**목차**(도움말 메뉴의 항목)
55	contextual menus	上下文功能表	상황에 맞는 메뉴

TABLE 35   Word List for Asian Languages *(Continued)*

	English	Japanese	Simplified Chinese
56	**Continue** (button in Error alert box)	[継続] ボタン (エラーアラートボックスのボタン)	继续（错误报警框中的按钮）
57	control type style	コントロールタイプスタイル	控件字样
58	Control-clicking	Ctrl キー + クリック	按住 Ctrl 键并按一下
59	controls	コントロール	控件
60	Control-Tab	Ctrl キー + Tab キー	按住 Ctrl 键再按 Tab 键
61	**Copy** (item in Edit menu)	[コピー] ([編集] メニューの項目)	复制（"编辑"菜单中的项）
62	crosshair pointer	十字形ポインタ	十字指针
63	cross-platform color	クロスプラットフォームカラー	跨平台颜色
64	cross-platform delivery	クロスプラットフォーム配信	十字光标
65	currency formats	通貨書式	货币格式
66	**Cut** (item in Edit menu)	[カット] ([編集] メニューの項目)	剪切（"编辑"菜单中的项）
67	data structure	データ構造	数据结构
68	Date Format (label in preferences dialog box)	[日付書式] (設定の変更ダイアログボックスのラベル)	日期格式（首选项对话框中的标签）
69	default	デフォルト	默认
70	default command buttons	デフォルトコマンドボタン	默认命令按钮
71	Default Font (label in preferences dialog box)	[デフォルトフォント] (設定の変更ダイアログボックスのラベル)	默认字体（首选项对话框中的标签）
72	default Java look and feel theme	デフォルトの Java Look & Feel テーマ	默认 Java 界面外观主题
73	default pointer	デフォルトポインタ	默认光标
74	delay indication	遅延表示	延迟指示
75	destination feedback	宛先フィードバック	目标反馈
76	dialog boxes	ダイアログボックス	对话框
77	dimmed text	選択不可テキスト	暗淡的文字
78	disabilities	ディスアビリティ	禁用
79	disjoint selection	不連続選択	不相交选项
80	distribution	配布	分发
81	dithering	ディザリング	混色
82	dockable toolbars	ドッキングツールバー	可停放工具条

TABLE 35   Word List for Asian Languages *(Continued)*

	English	Traditional Chinese	Korean
56	**Continue** (button in Error alert box)	繼續 (錯誤警示方塊中的按鈕)	계속(오류 경고 상자의 버튼)
57	control type style	控制類型樣式	제어 유형 스타일
58	Control-clicking	按住 Ctrl 鍵並按一下	제어-누르기
59	controls	控制	제어기
60	Control-Tab	按住 Ctrl 鍵再按 Tab 鍵	제어-탭
61	**Copy** (item in Edit menu)	複製 (「編輯」功能表中的項目)	복사(편집 메뉴의 항목)
62	crosshair pointer	十字形指標	크로스헤어 포인터
63	cross-platform color	交叉平台色彩	크로스 플랫폼 색상
64	cross-platform delivery	交叉平台發送	크로스 플랫폼 배달
65	currency formats	貨幣格式	통화 형식
66	**Cut** (item in Edit menu)	剪下 (「編輯」功能表中的項目)	잘라내기(편집 메뉴의 항목)
67	data structure	資料結構	데이터 구조
68	Date Format (label in preferences dialog box)	日期格式 (個人喜好對話方塊中的標籤)	날짜 형식(환경 설정 대화 상자의 레이블)
69	default	預設	기본값
70	default command buttons	預設指令按鈕	기본 명령 버튼
71	Default Font (label in preferences dialog box)	預設字型 (個人喜好對話方塊中的標籤)	기본 글꼴(환경 설정 대화 상자의 레이블)
72	default Java look and feel theme	預設 Java 外視感覺主題	기본 Java 모양 및 색감 테마
73	default pointer	預設指標	기본 포인터
74	delay indication	延遲指示	지연 표시
75	destination feedback	目標回饋	대상 피드백
76	dialog boxes	對話方塊	대화 상자
77	dimmed text	無效文字	희미하게 표시된 텍스트
78	disabilities	無效	사용 불가
79	disjoint selection	非連接的選取	따로따로 떨어진 선택
80	distribution	分配	배포
81	dithering	漸層色	디더링
82	dockable toolbars	可停駐的工具列	도킹 가능한 도구 모음

TABLE 35   Word List for Asian Languages *(Continued)*

	English	Japanese	Simplified Chinese
83	**Document** (item in Format menu)	[ドキュメント] ([書式] メニューの項目)	文档（"格式"菜单中的项）
84	**Don't Save** (button in Warning alert boxes)	[保存しない] (警告アラートボックスのボタン)	不保存（警告报警框中的按钮）
85	double-clicking	ダブルクリック	双击
86	drag and drop	ドラッグ＆ドロップ	拖放
87	drag area	ドラッグ領域	拖动区
88	drag texture	ドラッグテクスチャ	拖动结构
89	dragging	ドラッグ	拖动
90	drop-down arrows	ドロップダウン矢印	下拉箭头
91	drop-down menus	ドロップダウンメニュー	下拉式菜单
92	**Edit** (menu)	[編集] メニュー	**编辑**（菜单）
93	editable combo boxes	編集可能コンボボックス	可编辑组合框
94	editable text fields	編集可能テキストフィールド	可编辑文本字段
95	editor panes	エディタ区画	编辑窗格
96	ellipsis marks	省略記号	省略号
97	Error alert boxes	エラーアラートボックス	错误警告框
98	error messages	エラーメッセージ	错误消息
99	exclusive choice (in toggle buttons)	排他的選択 (トグルボタンで)	唯一性的选项（在切换按钮中）
100	**Exit** (item in File menu)	[終了] ([ファイル] メニューの項目)	退出（"文件"菜单中的项）
101	extended selection	拡張選択	扩展选择
102	feedback	フィードバック	反馈
103	fields	フィールド	字段
104	**File** (menu)	[ファイル] メニュー	文件（菜单）
105	filling slider	フィリングスライダ	填充滑尺
106	**Find** (item in Edit menu)	[検索] ([編集] メニューの項目)	查找（"编辑"菜单中的项）
107	find dialog boxes	検索ダイアログボックス	查找对话框
108	**Find Next** (item in Edit menu)	[次を検索] ([編集] メニューの項目)	查找下一个（"编辑"菜单中的项）
109	Flashes (label in notification dialog box)	[点滅] (通知ダイアログボックスのラベル)	闪烁
110	flush 3D effects	フラッシュ 3D 効果	刷新 3D 效果

TABLE 35   Word List for Asian Languages *(Continued)*

	English	Traditional Chinese	Korean
83	**Document** (item in Format menu)	文件 (「格式」功能表中的項目)	문서 (서식 메뉴의 항목)
84	**Don't Save** (button in Warning alert boxes)	不要儲存 (警告警示方塊中的按鈕)	저장 안함(경고 상자의 버튼)
85	double-clicking	連按兩下	두 번 누르기
86	drag and drop	拖曳及放下	끌어 놓기
87	drag area	拖曳區	끌기 영역
88	drag texture	拖曳材質	텍스쳐 끌기
89	dragging	拖曳	끌기
90	drop-down arrows	下拉式箭頭	드롭다운 화살표
91	drop-down menus	下拉式功能表	드롭다운 메뉴
92	**Edit** (menu)	**編輯** (功能表)	**편집**(메뉴)
93	editable combo boxes	可編輯的組合方塊	편집 가능 콤보 상자
94	editable text fields	可編輯的文字欄位	편집 가능 텍스트 필드
95	editor panes	編輯程式窗格	편집기 표시 영역
96	ellipsis marks	省略標記	생략 기호 표시
97	Error alert boxes	錯誤警示方塊	오류 경고 상자
98	error messages	錯誤訊息	오류 메시지
99	exclusive choice (in toggle buttons)	專用選擇 (在切換按鈕中)	독점적 선택(토글 버튼)
100	**Exit** (item in File menu)	結束 (「檔案」功能表中的項目)	**종료**(파일 메뉴의 항목)
101	extended selection	延伸式選取	확장 선택
102	feedback	回饋	피드백
103	fields	欄位	필드
104	**File** (menu)	**檔案** (功能表)	**파일**(메뉴)
105	filling slider	填滿調整器	채우기 슬라이더
106	**Find** (item in Edit menu)	尋找 (「編輯」功能表中的項目)	**찾기**(편집 메뉴의 항목)
107	find dialog boxes	尋找對話方塊	찾기 대화 상자
108	**Find Next** (item in Edit menu)	**尋找下一個** (「編輯」功能表中的項目)	다음 **찾기**(편집 메뉴의 항목)
109	Flashes (label in notification dialog box)	閃爍 (通知對話方塊中的標籤)	플래시(통보 대화 상자의 레이블)
110	flush 3D effects	清除 3D 效應	3D 플러시 효과

TABLE 35   Word List for Asian Languages *(Continued)*

	English	Japanese	Simplified Chinese
111	**Font** (menu or item in Format menu)	[フォント] ([書式] メニューの項目), [フォント] メニュー	字体（"格式"菜单中的项），"字体"菜单
112	fonts	フォント	字体
113	**Format** (menu)	[書式] メニュー	**格式**（菜单）
114	formatted text panes	書式付きテキスト区画	格式化文本窗格
115	function keys	ファンクションキー	功能键
116	GIF (Graphics Interchange Format)	GIF (Graphics Interchange Format)	GIF（图形交换格式）
117	grids	グリッド	网格
118	hand pointers	手の形のポインタ	手形指针
119	headline capitalization	見出しの大文字使用	标题大写
120	**Help** (button or menu)	[ヘルプ] (ボタン), [ヘルプ] メニュー	帮助（按钮），"帮助"菜单
121	Hidden Text (checkbox in preferences dialog box)	[隠しテキスト] (設定の変更ダイアログボックスのチェックボックス)	隐藏文本（首选项对话框中的复选框）
122	highlighting	強調	高亮显示
123	horizontal scrollbar	水平スクロールバー	水平滚动条
124	hot spot	ホットスポット	热点
125	HSB (tab for hue, saturation, and brightness in color choosers)	HSB (カラーチューザでの色合い、彩度、明るさのタブ)	HSB（颜色选择器中色调、饱和度和亮度的标签页）
126	HTML editor kits	HTML エディタキット	HTML编辑工具箱
127	I-beam pointer	I-beam ポインタ	I-beam指针
128	icons	アイコン	图标
129	inactive components	アクティブでないコンポーネント	非活动组件
130	inactive menu items	アクティブでないメニュー項目	非活动菜单项
131	inactive windows	アクティブでないウィンドウ	无效窗口
132	independent choice (in toggle buttons)	他に依存しない選択 (トグルボタンで)	独立选项（开关按钮中）
133	**Index** (item in Help menu)	[索引] ([ヘルプ] メニューの項目)	索引（"帮助"菜单中的项）
134	indicators	インジケータ	指示器
135	Info alert box	情報アラートボックス	信息警告框
136	information symbol	情報記号	信息标记

TABLE 35 Word List for Asian Languages *(Continued)*

	English	Traditional Chinese	Korean
111	**Font** (menu or item in Format menu)	字型 (功能表或「格式」功能表中的項目)	글꼴(메뉴 또는 서식 메뉴의 항목)
112	fonts	字型	글꼴
113	**Format** (menu)	格式 (功能表)	서식(메뉴)
114	formatted text panes	格式化的文字窗格	서식이 지정된 텍스트 표시 영역
115	function keys	功能鍵	기능키
116	GIF (Graphics Interchange Format)	GIF (圖形交換格式)	GIF (Graphics Interchange Format)
117	grids	網點	격자
118	hand pointers	手形指標	손모양 포인터
119	headline capitalization	標題大寫	표제 대문자화
120	**Help** (button or menu)	**輔助說明** (按鈕或功能表)	도움말(버튼 또는 메뉴)
121	Hidden Text (checkbox in preferences dialog box)	隱藏文字 (個人喜好對話方塊中的核取方塊)	숨겨진 텍스트(환경 설정 대화 상자의 확인란)
122	highlighting	反白顯示	반전 표시
123	horizontal scrollbar	水平捲動軸	가로 스크롤 막대
124	hot spot	熱點	핫스폿
125	HSB (tab for hue, saturation, and brightness in color choosers)	HSB (色彩選擇器中色調、飽和度及亮度的標籤)	HSB(색 선택기의 색조, 채도, 밝기에 대한 탭)
126	HTML editor kits	HTML 編輯程式工具組	HTML 편집기 키트
127	I-beam pointer	工字形指標	I 빔 포인터
128	icons	圖示	아이콘
129	inactive components	非工作元件	비활성 구성 요소
130	inactive menu items	非工作功能表項目	비활성 메뉴 항목
131	inactive windows	非工作視窗	비활성 창
132	independent choice (in toggle buttons)	獨立選項 (在切換按鈕中)	독립 선택(토글 버튼)
133	**Index** (item in Help menu)	索引 (「輔助說明」功能表中的項目)	색인(도움말 메뉴의 항목)
134	indicators	指示器	표시기, 표시 기호
135	Info alert box	資訊警示方塊	정보 경고 상자
136	information symbol	資訊符號	정보 기호

TABLE 35   Word List for Asian Languages *(Continued)*

	English	Japanese	Simplified Chinese
137	initial keyboard focus	初期キーボードフォーカス	初始的键盘焦点
138	insertion point	挿入ポイント	插入点
139	installation screens	インストール画面	安装屏幕
140	internal utility windows	内部ユーティリティウィンドウ	内部功能窗
141	internal windows	内部ウィンドウ	内部窗口
142	internationalization	国際化	国际化
143	**Italic** (item in Format menu)	**[イタリック]** ([書式] メニューの項目)	斜体（"格式"菜单中的项）
144	italic text	イタリックテキスト	斜体文字
145	Java 2 SDK	Java 2 SDK	Java 2 SDK
146	Java 2D API	Java 2D API	Java 2D API
147	Java Accessibility API	Java Accessibility API	Java 可存取性 API
148	Java Accessibility Utilities	Java Accessibility ユーティリティ	Java 可存取性实用程序
149	Java Development Kit	Java Development Kit	Java 开发工具
150	Java Foundation Classes	Java Foundation Classes	Java 基类
151	JavaHelp	JavaHelp	JavaHelp
152	Java look and feel	Java Look & Feel	Java 界面外观
153	JFC application	JFC アプリケーション	JFC 应用程序
154	JPEG (Joint Photographic Experts Group)	JPEG (Joint Photographic Experts Group)	JPEG（联合图像专家组规范）
155	**Justify** (item in Format menu)	**[両端揃え]** ([書式] メニューの項目)	调整（"格式"菜单中的项）
156	keyboard activation	キーボードによる起動	键盘激活
157	keyboard focus	キーボードフォーカス	键盘焦点
158	keyboard navigation	キーボードナビゲーション	键盘导航
159	keyboard operations	キーボード操作	键盘操作
160	keyboard shortcuts	キーボードショートカット	快捷键
161	labels	ラベル	标签
162	layout managers	レイアウトマネージャ	布局管理器
163	leaf (in tree component)	リーフ (ツリーコンポーネントで)	叶（树组件）
164	Left Margin (label in preferences dialog box)	[左マージン] (設定の変更ダイアログ ボックスのラベル)	左边距（首选项对话框中的标签）

TABLE 35   Word List for Asian Languages *(Continued)*

	English	Traditional Chinese	Korean
137	initial keyboard focus	初始鍵盤焦點	초기 키보드 포커스
138	insertion point	插入點	삽입점
139	installation screens	安裝螢幕	설치 화면
140	internal utility windows	內部公用程式視窗	내부 유틸리티 창
141	internal windows	內部視窗	내부 창
142	internationalization	國際化	국제화
143	**Italic** (item in Format menu)	斜體 (「格式」功能表中的項目)	기울임꼴(서식 메뉴의 항목)
144	italic text	斜體文字	기울임꼴 텍스트
145	Java 2 SDK	Java 2 SDK	Java 2 SDK
146	Java 2D API	Java 2D API	Java 2D API
147	Java Accessibility API	Java 輔助工具 API	Java 액세스 API
148	Java Accessibility Utilities	Java 輔助工具公用程式	Java 액세스 유틸리티
149	Java Development Kit	Java 開發工具	Java 개발 키트
150	Java Foundation Classes	Java 基礎類別	Java 기반 클래스
151	JavaHelp	JavaHelp	JavaHelp
152	Java look and feel	Java 外視感覺	Java 모양 및 색감
153	JFC application	JFC 應用程式	JFC 응용프로그램
154	JPEG (Joint Photographic Experts Group)	JPEG (連接式攝影專家群組)	JPEG (Joint Photographic Experts Group)
155	**Justify** (item in Format menu)	對齊 (「格式」功能表中的項目)	맞춤(서식 메뉴의 항목)
156	keyboard activation	鍵盤啟動	키보드 활성화
157	keyboard focus	鍵盤焦點	키보드 포커스
158	keyboard navigation	鍵盤導航	키보드 이동
159	keyboard operations	鍵盤操作	키보드 작업
160	keyboard shortcuts	鍵盤捷徑	키보드 단축
161	labels	標籤	레이블
162	layout managers	佈局管理者	레이아웃 관리자
163	leaf (in tree component)	葉(在樹形元件中)	잎(트리 구성 요소에서)
164	Left Margin (label in preferences dialog box)	左邊界 (個人喜好對話方塊中的標籤)	왼쪽 여백(환경 설정 대화 상자의 레이블)

TABLE 35   Word List for Asian Languages *(Continued)*

	English	Japanese	Simplified Chinese
165	legal notices	著作権情報	合法通知
166	links	リンク	链接
167	lists	リスト	列表
168	localization	地域対応化	本地化
169	**Log In** (button in login splash screen)	**[ログイン]** (ログインスプラッシュ画面のボタン)	登录（登录闪现屏幕中的按钮）
170	login dialog boxes	ログインダイアログボックス	登录对话框
171	Login Name text field	[ログイン名] (テキストフィールド)	登录名文本字段
172	login splash screens	ログインスプラッシュ画面	登录闪现屏幕
173	look and feel designs	Look & Feel デザイン	界面外观设计
174	major tick marks (in sliders)	メジャーティックマーク (スライダで)	主刻度线（在滑尺上）
175	Margins (checkbox in preferences dialog box)	[マージン] (設定の変更ダイアログボックスのチェックボックス)	边距（首选项对话框中的复选框）
176	Match Case (checkbox in find dialog box)	[大文字と小文字を区別する] ([検索] ダイアログボックスのチェックボックス)	区分大小写（"查找"对话框中的复选框）
177	menu bars	メニューバー	菜单条
178	menu items	メニュー項目	菜单项
179	menu separators	メニューセパレータ	菜单分隔符
180	menu titles	メニュータイトル	菜单标题
181	menus	メニュー	菜单
182	message (in alert dialog box)	メッセージ (アラートダイアログボックスで)	消息（报警对话框中）
183	Microsoft Windows style look and feel	Microsoft Windows スタイルの Look & Feel	微软 Windows 风格的界面外观
184	middle mouse button	アジャストボタン	鼠标中键
185	MIME (Multipurpose Internet Mail Extensions)	MIME (Multipurpose Internet Mail Extensions)	MIME（通用 Internet 邮件扩展服务）
186	minimized internal windows	アイコン化された内部ウィンドウ	最小化内部窗口
187	minimized windows	アイコン化されたウィンドウ	最小化窗口
188	minor tick marks (in sliders)	マイナーティックマーク (スライダで)	次刻度线（在滑尺上）
189	mnemonics	ニーモニック	助记符
190	modal dialog boxes	モーダルダイアログボックス	样式对话框

TABLE 35   Word List for Asian Languages *(Continued)*

	English	Traditional Chinese	Korean
165	legal notices	法律啓事	법적 통지
166	links	連結	링크
167	lists	清單	목록
168	localization	本土化	지역화 기능
169	**Log In** (button in login splash screen)	登入 (登入閃現螢幕中的按鈕)	로그인(로그인 시작 화면의 버튼)
170	login dialog boxes	登入對話方塊	로그인 대화 상자
171	Login Name text field	登入名稱 (文字欄位)	로그인 이름(텍스트 필드)
172	login splash screens	登入閃現螢幕	로그인 시작 화면
173	look and feel designs	外視感覺設計	모양 및 색감 디자인
174	major tick marks (in sliders)	主要刻度標記 (在調整器中)	주눈금 표시(슬라이더)
175	Margins (checkbox in preferences dialog box)	邊界 (個人喜好對話方塊中的核取方塊)	여백(환경 설정 대화 상자의 확인란)
176	Match Case (checkbox in find dialog box)	大小寫須相符 (「尋找」對話方塊中的核取方塊)	대/소문자 구분(찾기 대화 상자의 확인란)
177	menu bars	功能表列	메뉴 표시줄
178	menu items	功能表項目	메뉴 항목
179	menu separators	功能表分隔符號	메뉴 구분자
180	menu titles	功能表標題	메뉴 제목
181	menus	功能表	메뉴
182	message (in alert dialog box)	訊息 (在警示對話方塊中)	메시지(경고 대화 상자)
183	Microsoft Windows style look and feel	Microsoft Windows 樣式外視感覺	Microsoft Windows 스타일 모양 및 색감
184	middle mouse button	滑鼠中間按鈕	중간 마우스 버튼
185	MIME (Multipurpose Internet Mail Extensions)	MIME (多用途網際網路郵件延伸)	MIME (Multipurpose Internet Mail Extensions)
186	minimized internal windows	最小化內部視窗	최소화된 내부 창
187	minimized windows	最小化視窗	최소화된 창
188	minor tick marks (in sliders)	次要刻度標記 (在調整器中)	부눈금 표시(슬라이더)
189	mnemonics	助憶符號	니모닉
190	modal dialog boxes	模態對話方塊	모달 대화 상자

TABLE 35 Word List for Asian Languages *(Continued)*

	English	Japanese	Simplified Chinese
191	model	モデル	模式
192	modeless dialog boxes	非モーダルダイアログボックス	无模式对话框
193	modifier keys	修飾キー	修改键
194	**Modify** (command button)	**[変更]** (コマンドボタン)	修改（命令按钮）
195	mouse button 1	マウスボタン 1	鼠标键 1
196	mouse button 2	マウスボタン 2	鼠标键 2
197	mouse buttons	マウスボタン	鼠标按钮
198	mouse devices	マウスデバイス	鼠标装置
199	mouse operations	マウス操作	鼠标操作
200	mouse-over feedback	マウスオーバーフィードバック	鼠标移动反馈
201	move pointers	移動ポインタ	移动指针
202	multiple document interface (MDI)	multiple document interface (MDI)	多文档界面（MDI）
203	multiple selection	複数選択	多重选择
204	native code	ネイティブコード	本机代码
205	navigation	ナビゲーション	浏览
206	nested split panes	入れ子の分割区画	嵌套分离窗格
207	**New** (item in File menu)	**[新規]** ([ファイル] メニューの項目)	新建（"文件"菜单中的项）
208	nodes (in tree components)	ノード (ツリーコンポーネントで)	节点（树组件）
209	noneditable combo boxes	編集不可コンボボックス	不可编辑的组合框
210	noneditable text fields	編集不可テキストフィールド	不可编辑的文本字段
211	nonfilling slider	非フィリングスライダ	不填充的滑尺
212	**Normal** (item in Format menu)	**[通常]** ([書式] メニューの項目)	普通（"格式"菜单中的项）
213	notification dialog box	通知ダイアログボックス	通知对话框
214	**Object** (menu)	**[オブジェクト]** メニュー	对象（菜单）
215	**OK** (button)	**[了解]** (ボタン)	确定（按钮）
216	padding (command buttons)	パディング (コマンドボタン)	填充（命令按钮）
217	**Page Setup** (item in File menu)	**[ページ設定]** ([ファイル] メニューの項目)	页面设置（"文件"菜单中的项）
218	panels	パネル	面板
219	panes	区画	窗格

TABLE 35 Word List for Asian Languages *(Continued)*

	English	Traditional Chinese	Korean
191	model	模型	모델
192	modeless dialog boxes	無模型的對話方塊	비정형 대화 상자
193	modifier keys	修飾按鍵	수정자 키
194	**Modify** (command button)	**修改** (指令按鈕)	**수정**(명령 버튼)
195	mouse button 1	滑鼠按鈕 1	마우스 버튼 1
196	mouse button 2	滑鼠按鈕 2	마우스 버튼 2
197	mouse buttons	滑鼠按鈕	마우스 버튼
198	mouse devices	滑鼠裝置	마우스 장치
199	mouse operations	滑鼠操作	마우스 동작
200	mouse-over feedback	滑鼠移動回饋	마우스를 위에 놓았을 때 피드백
201	move pointers	移動指標	이동 포인터
202	multiple document interface (MDI)	多重文件介面 (MDI)	다중 문서 인터페이스(MDI)
203	multiple selection	多重選取	복수 선택
204	native code	當地碼	원 코드
205	navigation	導航	이동
206	nested split panes	嵌套的分割窗格	중첩 분할 표시 영역
207	**New** (item in File menu)	**開新檔案** (「檔案」功能表中的項目)	새로 만들기(파일 메뉴의 항목)
208	nodes (in tree components)	節點 (在樹形元件中)	노드(트리 구성 요소에서)
209	noneditable combo boxes	非可編輯的組合方塊	편집 불가능 콤보 상자
210	noneditable text fields	非可編輯的文字欄位	편집 불가능 텍스트 필드
211	nonfilling slider	非填滿的調整器	채우지 않음 슬라이더
212	**Normal** (item in Format menu)	**一般** (「格式」功能表中的項目)	표준(서식 메뉴의 항목)
213	notification dialog box	通知對話方塊	알림 대화 상자
214	**Object** (menu)	**物件** (功能表)	객체(메뉴)
215	**OK** (button)	**確定** (按鈕)	**확인**(버튼)
216	padding (command buttons)	填補 (指令按鈕)	채워 넣기(명령 버튼)
217	**Page Setup** (item in File menu)	**版面設定** (「檔案功能表」中的項目)	페이지 **설정**(파일 메뉴의 항목)
218	panels	面板	패널
219	panes	窗格	표시 영역

TABLE 35   Word List for Asian Languages *(Continued)*

	English	Japanese	Simplified Chinese
220	**Paragraph** (item in Format menu)	[パラグラフ] ([書式] メニューの項目)	段落（"格式"菜单中的项）
221	password fields	パスワードフィールド	口令字段
222	**Paste** (item in Edit menu)	[ペースト] ([編集] メニューの項目)	粘贴（"编辑"菜单中的项）
223	pixels	ピクセル	象素
224	plain text	プレーンテキスト	无格式文本
225	plain text area	プレーンテキスト領域	无格式文本区
226	plain windows	プレーンウィンドウ	无格式窗口
227	platforms	プラットフォーム	平台
228	plug-in editor kit	プラグインエディタキット	插件编辑工具
229	pluggable look and feel	プラグイン可能な Look & Feel	可插式界面外观
230	pointers	ポインタ	指针
231	posted menus	固定表示状態メニュー	已发送的菜单
232	posting menus	固定表示メニュー	发送菜单
233	**Preferences** (item in File menu)	[設定の変更] ([ファイル] メニューの項目)	首选项（"文件"菜单中的项）
234	preferences dialog boxes	設定の変更ダイアログボックス	首选项对话框
235	pressing a key	キーの押下	按一个键
236	preview panel (in a color chooser)	プレビューパネル (カラーチューザで)	预览面板（在颜色选项中）
237	primary colors	原色	原色
238	primary windows	主ウィンドウ	主窗口
239	**Print** (item in File menu)	[印刷] ([ファイル] メニューの項目)	打印（"文件"菜单中的项）
240	print dialog boxes	印刷ダイアログボックス	打印对话框
241	printer	プリンタ	打印机
242	product name	製品名	产品名称
243	progress bars	進捗バー	进度条
244	progress dialog boxes	進捗ダイアログボックス	进度对话框
245	progress feedback	進捗フィードバック	进度反馈
246	progress indication	進捗表示	进度指示
247	Question alert boxes	質問アラートボックス	问题警告框
248	radio button group	ラジオボタングループ	单选按钮组

TABLE 35   Word List for Asian Languages *(Continued)*

	English	Traditional Chinese	Korean
220	**Paragraph** (item in Format menu)	段落(「格式」功能表中的項目)	단락(서식 메뉴의 항목)
221	password fields	密碼欄位	암호 필드
222	**Paste** (item in Edit menu)	貼上(「編輯」功能表中的項目)	붙여넣기(편집 메뉴의 항목)
223	pixels	像素	픽셀
224	plain text	一般文字	일반 텍스트
225	plain text area	一般文字區	일반 텍스트 영역
226	plain windows	一般視窗	일반 창
227	platforms	平台	플랫폼
228	plug-in editor kit	插入式編輯程式工具	플러그인 편집기 키트
229	pluggable look and feel	可插接式外視感覺	플러그 가능 모양 및 색감
230	pointers	指標	포인터
231	posted menus	已寄出功能表	게시된 메뉴
232	posting menus	寄送功能表	게시 메뉴
233	**Preferences** (item in File menu)	個人喜好(「檔案」功能表中的項目)	**환경 설정**(파일 메뉴의 항목)
234	preferences dialog boxes	個人喜好對話方塊	환경 설정 대화 상자
235	pressing a key	按下任一按鍵	키 누르기
236	preview panel (in a color chooser)	預覽面板(在色彩選擇器中)	미리 보기 표시 영역(색상 선택기)
237	primary colors	原色	원색
238	primary windows	主視窗	주 창
239	**Print** (item in File menu)	列印(「檔案」功能表中的項目)	인쇄(파일 메뉴의 항목)
240	print dialog boxes	列印對話方塊	인쇄 대화 상자
241	printer	印表機	프린터
242	product name	產品名稱	제품 이름
243	progress bars	進度列	진행 표시줄
244	progress dialog boxes	進度對話方塊	진행 대화 상자
245	progress feedback	進度回饋	진행 피드백
246	progress indication	進度指示	진행 표시
247	Question alert boxes	問題警示方塊	질의 경고 상자
248	radio button group	單選按鈕群組	라디오 버튼 그룹

TABLE 35   Word List for Asian Languages *(Continued)*

	English	**Japanese**	**Simplified Chinese**
249	radio button menu items	ラジオボタンメニュー項目	单选按钮菜单项
250	radio buttons	ラジオボタン	单选按钮
251	**Redo** (item in Edit menu)	**[再実行]** ([編集] メニューの項目)	重做（"编辑"菜单中的项）
252	**Replace** (button in Warning alert box)	**[選択]** (通知ダイアログボックスのボタン)	替换（按钮）
253	**Reset** (button)	**[リセット]** (ボタン)	重置（按钮）
254	resize pointers	サイズ変更ポインタ	调整指针大小
255	resource bundles	リソースバンドル	资源捆绑
256	reverse video theme	リバースビデオテーマ	反相视频显示
257	RGB (tab for red, green, and blue values in a color chooser)	RGB (カラーチューザでの赤、緑、青の値のタブ)	RGB（颜色选择器中红色、绿色和蓝色值的标签页）
258	Right Margin (label in preferences dialog box)	[右マージン] (設定の変更ダイアログボックスのラベル)	右边距（首选项对话框中的标签）
259	row (in tables)	行 (テーブルで)	行（在表格中）
260	Ruler Units (label in preferences dialog box)	[ルーラ単位] (設定の変更ダイアログボックスのラベル)	标尺单位（首选项对话框中的标签）
261	**Save** (button or item in File menu)	**[保存]** (ボタン), **[保存]** ([ファイル] メニューの項目)	保存（按钮或"文件"菜单中的项）
262	**Save As** (item in File menu)	**[別名保存]** ([ファイル] メニューの項目)	另存为（"文件"菜单中的项）
263	scale	スケール	缩放比例
264	scroll	スクロール	滚动
265	scroll arrows	スクロール矢印	滚动箭头
266	scroll box	スクロールボックス	滚动框
267	scroll channels	スクロールチャネル	滚动通道
268	scroll panes	スクロール区画	滚动窗格
269	scrollbars	スクロールバー	滚动条
270	**Search** (item in Help menu)	**[検索]** ([ヘルプ] メニューの項目)	搜索（"帮助"菜单中的项）
271	secondary colors	等和色 (2 つの原色を等分に混ぜた色)	辅色
272	secondary windows	副ウィンドウ	辅助窗口
273	**Section** (item in Format menu)	**[セクション]** ([書式] メニューの項目)	节（"格式"菜单中的项）
274	select	選択	选择

TABLE 35 Word List for Asian Languages *(Continued)*

	English	Traditional Chinese	Korean
249	radio button menu items	單選按鈕功能表項目	라디오 버튼 메뉴 항목
250	radio buttons	單選按鈕	라디오 버튼
251	**Redo** (item in Edit menu)	**重做**（「編輯」功能表中的項目）	다시 **실행**(편집 메뉴의 항목)
252	**Replace** (button in Warning alert box)	**取代**（按鈕）	바꾸기(버튼)
253	**Reset** (button)	**重設**（按鈕）	재설정(버튼)
254	resize pointers	調整指標大小	포인터 크기 조정
255	resource bundles	資源束	리소스 번들
256	reverse video theme	反白顯示主題	반전 영상 테마
257	RGB (tab for red, green, and blue values in a color chooser)	RGB（色彩選擇器中紅色、綠色及藍色值的標籤）	RGB(색상 선택기의 빨간색, 녹색 및 파란색 값에 대한 탭)
258	Right Margin (label in preferences dialog box)	右邊界（個人喜好對話方塊中的標籤）	오른쪽 여백(환경 설정 대화 상자의 레이블)
259	row (in tables)	列（在表中）	행(표)
260	Ruler Units (label in preferences dialog box)	尺規單位（個人喜好對話方塊中的標籤）	눈금자 단위(환경 설정 대화 상자의 레이블)
261	**Save** (button or item in File menu)	**儲存**（按鈕或「檔案」功能表中的項目）	저장(버튼 또는 파일 메뉴의 항목)
262	**Save As** (item in File menu)	**另存新檔**（「檔案」功能表中的項目）	다른 **이름**으로 저장(파일 메뉴의 항목)
263	scale	比例	크기 조정, 배율, 눈금
264	scroll	捲動	스크롤
265	scroll arrows	捲動箭頭	스크롤 화살표
266	scroll box	捲動方塊	스크롤 상자
267	scroll channels	捲動通道	스크롤 채널
268	scroll panes	捲動窗格	스크롤 표시 영역
269	scrollbars	捲動軸	스크롤 막대
270	**Search** (item in Help menu)	**搜尋**（「輔助說明」功能表中的項目）	검색(도움말 메뉴의 항목)
271	secondary colors	輔助色彩	보조 색상
272	secondary windows	輔助視窗	보조 창
273	**Section** (item in Format menu)	**區段**（「格式」功能表中的項目）	절(서식 메뉴의 항목)
274	select	選取	선택

TABLE 35   Word List for Asian Languages *(Continued)*

	English	Japanese	Simplified Chinese
275	**Select** (button in notification dialog box)	[選択] (通知ダイアログボックスのボタン)	选择（按钮）
276	**Select All** (item in Edit menu)	[すべてを選択] ([編集] メニュー の項目)	选择全部（"编辑"菜单中的项）
277	selected items	選択項目	选定项
278	selection	選択	选定
279	sentence capitalization	文単位の大文字使用	句子大写
280	separators	セパレータ	分隔符
281	Shift-clicking	Shift キー + クリック	按住 Shift 键并按一下
282	Shift-Tab	Shift キー + Tab キー	按住 Shift 键再按 Tab 键
283	Show (label in preferences dialog box)	[表示] (設定の変更ダイアログボックスのラベル)	显示（首选项对话框中的标签）
284	single-clicking	シングルクリック	单击
285	**Size** (item in Format menu)	[サイズ] ([書式] メニューの項目)	大小（"格式"菜单中的项）
286	sliders	スライダ	滑尺
287	small type style	スモールタイプスタイル	小写字样
288	sort order	ソート順序	排序顺序
289	Sound File (label in notification dialog box)	[サウンドファイル] (通知ダイアログボックスのラベル)	声音文件（通知对话框中的标记）
290	spacing	間隔	间距
291	splash screens	スプラッシュ画面	闪现屏幕
292	split panes	分割区画	分割窗格
293	splitter bars	分割バー	分割器条
294	Start at Top (radio button in find dialog box)	[先頭から開始] (検索ダイアログボックスのラジオボタン)	从顶端开始（查找对话框中的单选按钮）
295	Stationery (label in preferences dialog box)	[ステーショナリ] (設定の変更ダイアログボックスのラベル)	信纸（首选项对话框中的标签）
296	**Stop** (button)	[中止] (ボタン)	停止（按钮）
297	**Style** (item in Format menu)	[スタイル] ([書式] メニューの項目)	样式（"格式"菜单中的项）
298	styled text editor (styled text plug-in kit)	書式付きテキストエディタ (スタイルテキストプラグインキット)	样式文本编辑器（样式文本插件套件）
299	submenus	サブメニュー	子菜单

TABLE 35   Word List for Asian Languages *(Continued)*

	English	Traditional Chinese	Korean
275	**Select** (button in notification dialog box)	選取 (通知對話方塊中的按鈕)	선택 (통보 대화 상자의 버튼)
276	**Select All** (item in Edit menu)	選取全部 (「編輯」功能表中的項目)	모두 선택(편집 메뉴의 항목)
277	selected items	選取項目	선택한 항목
278	selection	選取	선택
279	sentence capitalization	句子大寫	문장 대문자화
280	separators	分隔符號	구분자
281	Shift-clicking	按住 Shift 鍵並按一下	Shift-누르기
282	Shift-Tab	按住 Shift 鍵再按 Tab 鍵	Shift-Tab
283	Show (label in preferences dialog box)	顯示 (個人喜好對話方塊中的標籤)	표시(환경 설정 대화 상자의 레이블)
284	single-clicking	單按一下	한 번 누르기
285	**Size** (item in Format menu)	大小 (「格式」功能表中的項目)	크기(서식 메뉴의 항목)
286	sliders	調整器	슬라이더
287	small type style	小型樣式	작은 유형 스타일
288	sort order	排序順序	정렬 순서
289	Sound File (label in notification dialog box)	聲音檔案 (在通知對話方塊中的標籤)	음성 파일(통보 대화 상자의 레이블)
290	spacing	間距	간격
291	splash screens	閃現螢幕	시작 화면
292	split panes	分割窗格	분할 표시 영역
293	splitter bars	分割器列	구분 표시줄
294	Start at Top (radio button in find dialog box)	由頂端開始 (尋找對話方塊中的單選按鈕)	처음부터 찾기(찾기 대화 상자의 라디오 버튼)
295	Stationery (label in preferences dialog box)	信籤 (個人喜好對話方塊中的標籤)	편지지(환경 설정 대화 상자의 레이블)
296	**Stop** (button)	停止 (按鈕)	정지(버튼)
297	**Style** (item in Format menu)	樣式 (「格式」功能表中的項目)	스타일(서식 메뉴의 항목)
298	styled text editor (styled text plug-in kit)	樣式化文字編輯程式 (樣式文字插入工具)	스타일 텍스트 편집기(스타일 텍스트 플러그인 킷)
299	submenus	子功能表	부속 메뉴

TABLE 35   Word List for Asian Languages *(Continued)*

	English	Japanese	Simplified Chinese
300	**Submit** (command button)	[送付] (コマンドボタン)	提交（命令按钮）
301	Swatches (tab in color choosers)	スウォッチ (カラーチューザのタブ)	色样（颜色选择器中的标签页）
302	Swing class	Swing クラス	Swing 类
303	symbols	シンボル	符号
304	system status animation	システム状態アニメーション	系统状态动画
305	system type style	システムタイプスタイル	系统字样
306	tab traversal	タブトラバーサル	制表符移动
307	tabbed panes	タブ付き区画	制表符窗格
308	tables	テーブル	表
309	text areas	テキスト領域	文本区
310	text fields	テキストフィールド	文本字段
311	text pointers	テキストポインタ	文本指针
312	theme mechanism	テーマメカニズム	主题机制
313	themes	テーマ	主题
314	title bars (in windows)	タイトルバー (ウィンドウで)	标题栏（窗口中）
315	toggle buttons	トグルボタン	切换按钮
316	tool tips	ツールヒント	工具提示
317	toolbar buttons	ツールバーボタン	工具栏按钮
318	toolbars	ツールバー	工具栏
319	trademark information	登録商標情報	商标信息
320	tree components	ツリーコンポーネント	树组件
321	triple-clicking	トリプルクリック	三击
322	turners (in tree components)	ターナ (ツリーコンポーネントで)	旋转器（树组件）
323	**Tutorial** (item in Help menu)	[チュートリアル] ([ヘルプ] メニューの項目)	**教程**（"帮助"菜单中的项）
324	unavailable items	選択不可の項目	不可用的选项
325	**Underline** (item in Format menu)	[下線] ([書式] メニューの項目)	下**划线**（"格式"菜单中的项）
326	**Undo** (item in Edit menu)	[元に戻す] ([編集] メニューの項目)	撤消（"编辑"菜单中的项）
327	usability testing	ユーザビリティテスト	可用性测试
328	user interface elements	ユーザインタフェース要素	用户界面组件

TABLE 35   Word List for Asian Languages *(Continued)*

	English	Traditional Chinese	Korean
300	**Submit** (command button)	提出（指令按鈕）	제출(명령 버튼)
301	Swatches (tab in color choosers)	色樣（色彩選擇器中的標籤）	견본(색 선택기의 탭)
302	Swing class	Swing 類別	스윙 클래스
303	symbols	符號	기호
304	system status animation	系統狀態動畫	시스템 상태 애니메이션
305	system type style	系統類型樣式	시스템 유형 스타일
306	tab traversal	標籤遍歷	탭 순회
307	tabbed panes	標籤式窗格	탭된 표시 영역
308	tables	表	테이블
309	text areas	文字區	텍스트 영역
310	text fields	文字欄位	텍스트 필드
311	text pointers	文字指標	텍스트 포인터
312	theme mechanism	主題機制	테마 기법
313	themes	主題	테마
314	title bars (in windows)	標題列（在視窗中）	제목 표시줄(창에 있음)
315	toggle buttons	切換按鈕	토글 버튼
316	tool tips	工具提示	도구 설명
317	toolbar buttons	工具列按鈕	도구 모음 버튼
318	toolbars	工具列	도구 모음
319	trademark information	商標資訊	상표권 정보
320	tree components	樹形元件	트리 구성 요소
321	triple-clicking	按三下	세 번 누르기
322	turners (in tree components)	旋轉器(在樹形元件中)	터너(트리 구성 요소에서)
323	**Tutorial** (item in Help menu)	指導（「輔助說明」功能表中的項目）	자습서(도움말 메뉴의 항목)
324	unavailable items	不供使用項目	사용할 수 없는 항목
325	**Underline** (item in Format menu)	底線（「格式」功能表中的項目）	밑줄(서식 메뉴의 항목)
326	**Undo** (item in Edit menu)	還原（「編輯」功能表中的項目）	실행 취소(편집 메뉴의 항목)
327	usability testing	可用性測試	가용성 테스트
328	user interface elements	使用者介面元素	사용자 인터페이스 요소

TABLE 35   Word List for Asian Languages *(Continued)*

	English	Japanese	Simplified Chinese
329	user type style	ユーザタイプスタイル	用户字样
330	utility windows	ユーティリティウィンドウ	实用程序窗口
331	version numbers	バージョン番号	版本号
332	vertical scrollbar	垂直スクロールバー	垂直滚动条
333	**View** (menu)	**[表示]** メニュー	**视图** （菜单）
334	visual design	視覚的デザイン	视件设计
335	visual identifier	製品を視覚的に識別する画像	视件标识符
336	wait pointers	待機ポインタ	等待指针
337	Warning alert boxes	警告アラートボックス	报警的警告框
338	Whole Word (checkbox in find dialog box)	[全文一致] ([検索] ダイアログボックスのチェックボックス)	全词匹配（"查找"对话框中的复选框）
339	window borders	ウィンドウ境界	窗口边框
340	window controls	ウィンドウコントロール	窗口控件
341	window frame	ウィンドウ枠	窗口框架
342	windows	ウィンドウ	窗口
343	word order	語順	词序
344	word wrap	折返し	文字换行
345	zoom buttons	ズームボタン	缩放按钮
346	zooming panes	ズーム区画	缩放窗格

TABLE 35   Word List for Asian Languages *(Continued)*

	English	Traditional Chinese	Korean
329	user type style	使用者類型樣式	사용자 유형 스타일
330	utility windows	公用程式視窗	유틸리티 창
331	version numbers	版本編號	버전 번호
332	vertical scrollbar	垂直捲動軸	세로 스크롤 막대
333	**View** (menu)	**檢視** (功能表)	보기(메뉴)
334	visual design	可視設計	영상 디자인
335	visual identifier	可視識別碼	영상 식별자
336	wait pointers	等待指標	대기 포인터
337	Warning alert boxes	警告警示方塊	경고 알림 상자
338	Whole Word (checkbox in find dialog box)	全字拼寫相符(「尋找」對話方塊中的核取方塊)	단어 단위로(찾기 대화 상자의 확인란)
339	window borders	視窗邊線	창 경계
340	window controls	視窗控制	창 제어기
341	window frame	視窗框架	창 프레임
342	windows	視窗	창
343	word order	文字次序	단어 순서
344	word wrap	文字自動換行	단어별 줄 바꾸기
345	zoom buttons	縮放按鈕	확대/축소 버튼
346	zooming panes	縮放窗格	확대/축소 표시 영역

D: SWITCHING LOOK AND FEEL DESIGNS

As a developer, you might want to provide users with the ability to switch the appearance of components within applications. This appendix contains some information about the pitfalls of letting users change the look and feel, along with guidelines on how to present the choice to users when necessary. The ability to switch look and feel designs is intended for use as a design-time feature rather than a runtime feature.

Pitfalls of User-Controlled Switching

The Swing components and the pluggable look and feel mechanism enable users to select the look and feel of an application. This choice is misleading, however, since a significant portion of the feel of an application is its general design, layout, and terminology.

It is usually unwise to give end users the ability to swap look and feel designs while working in your application. Switching look and feel designs in this way primarily swaps the appearance of the components. The layout and vocabulary used are programmed in and do not change. For instance, swapping look and feel designs does not change the titles of the menus.

The JFC has no special provisions that enable users to select a look and feel on the fly. The look and feel switching seen in many demos shows some of the power of the JFC, but on-the-fly look and feel switching was not a core design goal. As a result, there is no guarantee that user interfaces designed properly in one look and feel can migrate cleanly to another look and feel.

Successful user-controlled switching requires that the infrastructure behind the components have an understanding of each platform's design, layout, and nomenclature. In practice, there is more to a Microsoft Windows, Mac OS, or CDE application than the appearance and behavior of individual components.

☕ Do not enable user-controlled look and feel switching in your application without careful consideration.

The following figure illustrates a file chooser built in the CDE style, using Swing components.

FIGURE 201 CDE File Chooser

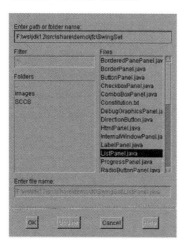

The next figure shows what a component-level switch from the CDE to the
Macintosh look and feel might look like.

FIGURE 202 Macintosh File Chooser (Simple Look and Feel Switch)

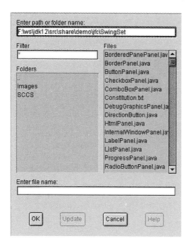

The component-level look and feel switch has not created a Macintosh file
chooser. A higher level of understanding of the design principles for the
Macintosh platform would be needed for this transformation to occur
correctly. The following figure shows what a correct transformation to the
Macintosh file chooser might look like.

FIGURE 203 Macintosh File Chooser (Following Macintosh Style)

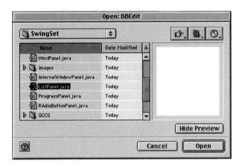

While the JFC does not provide a general solution to complete user-controlled look and feel switching, a specific application could ensure the correct layout and nomenclature for each look and feel that it supports. However, this would likely entail a significant amount of work.

If you are developing an application with more than a single target platform, consider using a cross-platform look and feel design, such as the Java look and feel.

Guidelines for Switching Look and Feel Designs   If you

absolutely must switch look and feel designs, follow these guidelines.

How to Present the Choice

☕ Place the choice of look and feel designs inside your application's preferences dialog box.

☕ List your application's default look and feel first. If the default is the Java look and feel, it should be followed by the look and feel of the platform your application is most likely to run on. Make these choices radio button menu items because only one main look and feel can be active at any time.

Nomenclature

☕ Always use "Java look and feel," not "Java" or "Metal." (Metal is the package name for the Java look and feel.)

GLOSSARY

Abstract Window Toolkit See **AWT**.

accessibility The degree to which software can be used comfortably by a wide variety of people, including those who require assistive technologies or those who use the keyboard instead of a pointing device. An accessible JFC application employs the Java Accessibility API and provides keyboard operations for all actions that can be carried out by use of the mouse. See also **assistive technology**, **Java Accessibility API**, **Java Accessibility Utilities**, **keyboard operations**.

activation Starting the operation of a component. See also **available**, **choose**, **navigation**, **select**.

alert box A secondary window used by an application to convey a message or warning or to gather a small amount of information from the user. Four standard alert boxes (Info, Warning, Error, and Question) are supplied for JFC applications. Alert boxes are created using the `JOptionPane` component. See also **dialog box**.

anti-aliasing A change in the appearance of the border of an application graphic such as an icon, so that it looks smoother at screen resolution and in relationship to a specific color.

applet A program, written in the Java language, that a user can interact with in a web browser. See also **application**, **browser**.

application A program that combines all the functions necessary for a user to accomplish a particular set of tasks (for instance, word processing or inventory tracking). Unless stated otherwise, this book uses "application" to refer to both applets and standalone applications. See also **applet**.

assistive technology Hardware or software that helps people with disabilities use a computer (or provides alternative means of use to all users). Examples include pointing devices other than the mouse, audio or text-only browsers, and screen readers that translate the contents of the screen into Braille, voice output, or audible cues. See also **accessibility**.

available   Able to be interacted with. When a component is unavailable, it is dimmed and is unable to receive keyboard focus.

AWT   (Abstract Window Toolkit) The class library that provides the standard API for building GUIs for Java programs. The Abstract Window Toolkit (AWT) includes imaging tools, data transfer classes, GUI components, containers for GUI components, an event system for handling user and system events among parts of the AWT, and layout managers for managing the size and position of GUI components in platform-independent designs. (The GUI components in the AWT are implemented as native-platform versions of the components, and they have largely been supplanted by the Swing components.) See also **JFC**, **Swing classes**.

backing window   A container, a sort of "virtual desktop," for an MDI application. Backing windows are created using the JDesktopPane component. See also **internal window**, **MDI**.

badge   A graphic added to existing toolbar buttons that indicates a change in the action of the button—for instance, the display of a menu, the creation of a new object, the addition of an object to a collection, or the review or editing of settings and properties.

bean   A reusable software component written to the JavaBeans specification. See also **JavaBeans**.

bit depth   The amount of information (in bits) used to represent a pixel. A bit depth of 8 supports up to 256 colors; a bit depth of 24 supports up to 16,777,216 colors.

bookmark   A URL (uniform resource locator) that has been added to a list of saved links. When users view a particular web site and want to return to it subsequently, they can create a bookmark for it.

browser   An application that enables users to view, navigate through, and interact with HTML documents and applets. Also called a "web browser." See also **applet**.

button   A collective term for the various controls whose on-screen appearance typically simulates a push button or a radio button. The user clicks buttons to specify commands or set options. See also **checkbox**, **command button**, **radio button**, **toggle button**, **toolbar button**.

checkbox	A control, consisting of a graphic and associated text, that a user clicks to turn an option on or off. A check mark in the checkbox graphic indicates that the option is turned on. Checkboxes are created using the `JCheckBox` component. See also **radio button**.
checkbox menu item	A menu item that appears with a checkbox next to it to represent an on or off setting. A check mark in the checkbox graphic indicates that the menu item is turned on. Checkbox menu items are created using the `JCheckBoxMenuItem` component. See also **checkbox**, **menu item**.
choose	(1) In human interface design, refers narrowly to turning on a value in a component that offers a set of possible values, such as a combo box or a list box.
	(2) In technical documentation, refers generally to the action of clicking a menu title or menu item. See also **activation**, **select**.
click	To press and release a mouse button. Clicking selects or activates the object beneath the button.
client	In the client-server model of communications, a process that requests the resources of a remote server, such as computation and storage space. See also **server**.
color chooser	A component that enables a user to select a color. Color choosers are created using the `JColorChooser` component. See also **HSB**, **RGB**, **utility window**.
combo box	A component with a drop-down arrow that the user clicks to display a list of options. Noneditable combo boxes have a list from which the user can choose one item. Editable combo boxes offer a text field as well as a list of options. The user can make a choice by typing a value in the text field or by choosing an item from the list. Combo boxes are created using the `JComboBox` component.
command button	A button with a rectangular border that contains text, a graphic, or both. A user clicks a command button to specify a command to initiate an action. Command buttons are created using the `JButton` component. See also **button**, **toggle button**, **toolbar button**.
component	A subclass of `java.awt.component` or, by extension, the interface element implemented by that subclass. See also **control**, **object**, **Swing classes**.

container
A component (such as an applet, window, pane, or internal window) that holds other components.

contextual menu
A menu that is displayed when a user presses mouse button 2 while the pointer is over an object or area associated with that menu. A contextual menu offers only menu items that are applicable to the object or region at the location of the pointer. Contextual menus are created using the `JPopupMenu` component. See also **menu**.

control
An interface element that a user can manipulate to perform an action, choose an option, or set a value. Examples include buttons, sliders, list boxes, and combo boxes. See also **component**, **object**.

CORBA
(Common Object Request Broker Architecture) An architecture for the creation, exchange, and management of distributed program objects in a network. CORBA enables programs on different platforms to communicate in a distributed environment.

cross-platform
Pertaining to heterogeneous computing environments. For example, a cross-platform application is one that has a single code base for multiple operating systems.

cursor
See **pointer**.

default command button
The command button that the application activates if a user presses Enter or Return. Default buttons in Java look and feel applications have a heavier border than other command buttons. See also **command button**.

deployment
The process of installing software into an operational environment.

designer
A professional who specifies the way that users will interact with an application, chooses the interface components, and lays them out in a set of views. The designer might or might not be the same person as the developer who writes the application code.

dialog box	A secondary window displayed by an application to gather information from users. Examples of dialog boxes include windows that set properties of objects, set parameters for commands, and set preferences for use of the application. Dialog boxes can also present information, such as displaying a progress bar. A dialog box can contain panes, lists, buttons, and other components. Dialog boxes are created using the `JDialog` component. See also **alert box**, **color chooser**, **internal utility window**, **secondary window**, **utility window**.
dithering	Simulating unavailable colors in a displayed graphic by using a pattern of two or more available colors.
drag	To move the mouse while holding down a mouse button. See also **drag and drop**.
drag and drop	To drag an interface element to a new location in order to move, copy, or link it. See also **drag**.
drop-down arrow	The triangular indicator that a user clicks to view more options than are visible on screen—such as the list attached to a combo box or the menu provided by some toolbar buttons. See also **badge**.
drop-down menu	A menu that is displayed when a user activates a menu title in the menu bar or toolbar. Drop-down menus are created using the `JMenu` component. See also **menu**, **menu bar**.
EAR	(Enterprise Archive) A file format used for deploying a J2EE application. An `.ear` (Enterprise Archive) file consists of one or more J2EE modules and a deployment descriptor. Within the `.ear` file, components are grouped into separate module types—JSP pages, servlets, and HTML pages are grouped into web archive files (`.war` files) while enterprise beans are grouped into EJB modules (EJB `.jar` files). See also **EJB**, **J2EE application**, **JSP**, **WAR**.
editable combo box	See **combo box**.
editor pane	A text component that supports a variety of plug-in editor kits. The JFC includes editor kits that can display plain, styled, HTML, and RTF data. Editor panes are created using the `JEditorPane` component. See also **plug-in editor kit**.

EJB   (Enterprise JavaBeans) A component architecture for development and deployment of object-oriented, distributed, enterprise-level applications. Applications written using the Enterprise JavaBeans architecture are scalable, transactional, multiuser, and secure. See also **JavaBeans**.

export   To save an object or data in a format other than the application's native format. See also **import**.

flush 3D style   In the Java look and feel, the effect created by rendering on-screen graphics whose surfaces appear to be in the same plane as the surrounding canvas and whose border has a bevel.

focus   See **keyboard focus**.

GIF   (Graphics Interchange Format) An 8-bit graphics format developed by CompuServe and commonly used on the World Wide Web. GIF files are limited to 256 colors, and they compress without loss of information. The GIF format is typically used for graphics in the Java look and feel. See also **bit depth**, **JPEG**.

host   A computer system that is accessed by one or more computers and workstations at remote locations.

HSB   For "hue, saturation, brightness." In computer graphics, a color model in which hue refers to a color's light frequency, saturation is the amount or strength of the hue (its purity), and brightness is the amount of black in the color (its lightness or darkness). See also **RGB**.

HTTP   (Hypertext Transfer Protocol) An application protocol that governs the exchange of files (including text, images, sound, and video) on the World Wide Web. See also **HTTPS**.

HTTPS   (Secure Hypertext Transfer Protocol) A web protocol that governs encryption and decryption (including user page requests and pages sent back by web servers). Developed by Netscape, HTTPS is nonproprietary. See also **HTTP**.

icon   An on-screen graphic representing an interface element that a user can select or manipulate—for example, an application, document, or disk.

IIOP   (Internet Inter-ORB Protocol) A protocol used for communication between CORBA common object request brokers. See also **CORBA**.

import   To bring an object or data file (for instance, a document created in another application, a text file, or a graphics file) into an application. See also **export**.

input focus   See **keyboard focus**.

insertion point   The place, usually indicated by a blinking bar, where typed text or a dragged or pasted selection will appear. See also **pointer**.

internal window   A window used in MDI applications that a user cannot drag outside of the backing window. In an MDI application that uses the Java look and feel, internal windows have a window border, title bar, and standard window controls with the Java look and feel. Internal windows correspond to a non-MDI application's primary windows. Internal windows are created using the `JInternalFrame` component. See also **backing window**, **MDI**, **primary window**.

internal utility window   In an MDI application with the Java look and feel, a modeless window that typically displays a collection of tools, colors, or patterns. Internal utility windows float on top of document (internal) windows. User choices made in an internal utility window affect whichever internal window is active. Internal utility windows are created using the `JInternalFrame` component. See also **internal window**, **utility window**.

internationalization The process of preparing software so that it is suitable for the global marketplace, taking into account wide variations in regions, languages, and cultures. Internationalization usually requires the separation of component text from code to ease the process of translation. See also **localization**, **resource bundle**.

J2EE   (Java 2 Platform, Enterprise Edition) The edition of the Java 2 platform that combines a number of technologies (such as enterprise beans, JSP pages, CORBA, and XML) in one architecture with a comprehensive application programming model and compatibility test suite for building enterprise-class server-side applications. See also **CORBA**, **EJB**, **JSP**.

J2EE application   An application that consists of J2EE components (application clients, applets, HTML pages, JSP pages, servlets, and enterprise beans) that run on the J2EE platform. J2EE applications are typically designed for distribution across multiple computing tiers. For deployment, a J2EE application is packaged in an `.ear` (Enterprise Archive) file. See also **EAR**, **J2EE**.

J2EE application client	A first-tier client program that executes in its own Java virtual machine but might access J2EE components in the web or business tier.
J2EE server	The collection of runtime services provided by the J2EE platform. These include HTTP, HTTPS, JTA, RMI-IIOP, Java IDL, JDBC, JMS, JNDI, JavaMail, and JAF. Although J2EE servers usually come packaged with web and EJB containers, they are not required to. For example, an OS vendor could supply the runtime services while a separate vendor supplied the J2EE containers.
J2SE	(Java 2 Platform, Standard Edition) The standard edition of the essential Java 2 platform, which includes tools, runtime services, and APIs for developers who are writing, deploying, and running applets and applications in the Java programming language. See also **Java 2 SDK**.
JAF	(JavaBeans Activation Framework) A standard extension to the J2SE and J2EE platforms. JAF enables developers to use standard services to determine the type of an arbitrary piece of data, gain access to and discover available operations, and instantiate the appropriate bean to perform those operations. See also **JavaBeans**.
JAR	(Java Archive) A platform-independent file format that bundles classes, images, and other files into one compressed file, speeding download time.
Java 2D API	A programming interface (part of the JFC in the Java 2 SDK) that provides an advanced two-dimensional imaging model for complex shapes, text, and images. Features include enhanced font and color support and a single, comprehensive rendering model. See also **JFC**.
Java 2 Platform, Enterprise Edition	See **J2EE**.
Java 2 Platform, Standard Edition	See **J2SE**.
Java 2 SDK	The software development kit that developers need to build applications for the Java 2 Platform, Standard Edition, v. 1.3, and the Java 2 Platform, Enterprise Edition. See also **JDK**, **J2EE**, **J2SE**.

Java Accessibility API   A programming interface (part of the JFC) that enables assistive technologies to interact and communicate with JFC components. A Java application that fully supports the Java Accessibility API is compatible with such technologies as screen readers and screen magnifiers. See also **accessibility, assistive technology, Java Accessibility Utilities, JFC.**

Java Accessibility Utilities   A set of classes (provided in the Java 2 SDK) for use by the vendors who create assistive technologies or automated tool tests. They enable assistive technologies to locate and query user interface objects inside a Java application. See also **accessibility, assistive technology, Java Accessibility API, JFC.**

JavaBeans   An architecture that defines a portable, platform-independent, reusable component model. Beans are the basic unit in this model. You can deploy beans in a network on any major operating system. See also **EJB.**

JavaBeans Activation Framework   See **JAF.**

Java Development Kit   See **JDK.**

Java Foundation Classes   See **JFC.**

Java IDL   An interface definition language that provides CORBA interoperability and connectivity capabilities for the J2EE platform. See also **CORBA, J2EE.**

Java look and feel   The default appearance and behavior for JFC applications, designed for cross-platform use. The Java look and feel works in the same way on any platform that supports the JFC. See also **JFC, pluggable look and feel architecture.**

JavaMail   An API for sending and receiving email.

JavaServer Pages   See **JSP.**

JDBC   (Java Database Connectivity) An industry standard for database-independent connectivity between the Java platform and a wide range of databases. The JDBC interface provides a call-level API for SQL-based database access.

JDK	(Java Development Kit) Software that includes the APIs and tools that developers need to build applications for those versions of the Java platform that preceded the Java 2 platform. See also **Java 2 SDK**.
JFC	(Java Foundation Classes) A part of the Java 2 platform that includes the Swing classes, pluggable look and feel designs, and the Java Accessibility API. The JFC also includes the Java 2D API, drag and drop, and other enhancements. See also **AWT**, **pluggable look and feel architecture**, **Swing classes**.
JFC application	An application built with the JFC. See also **JFC**.
JMS	(Java Message Service) An API for enterprise messaging systems.
JNDI	(Java Naming and Directory Interface) An interface to multiple naming and directory services. As part of the Java Enterprise API set, JNDI enables seamless connectivity to heterogeneous enterprise naming and directory services. Developers can build powerful and portable directory-enabled Java applications using this industry-standard interface.
JPEG	A graphics format developed by the Joint Photographic Experts Group. The JPEG format is frequently used for photographs and other complex images that benefit from a larger color palette than a GIF image can provide. JPEG compression is "lossy"; decompressed images are not identical to uncompressed images. See also **GIF**.
JSP	(JavaServer Pages) An extensible web technology that uses template data, custom elements, scripting languages, and server-side Java objects to return dynamic content to a client. Typically, the template data consists of HTML or XML elements, and, in many cases, the client is a web browser. JSP technology is an extension of servlet technology. It facilitates the addition of dynamic data to an otherwise static web page. See also **servlets**.
JTA	(Java Transaction API) An API that enables applications and J2EE servers to access transactions.
keyboard focus	The active window or component where the user's next keystrokes will take effect. Sometimes called the "input focus." See **navigation**, **select**.
keyboard operations	A collective term for keyboard shortcuts, mnemonics, and other forms of navigation and activation that utilize the keyboard instead of the mouse. See also **keyboard shortcut**, **mnemonic**.

keyboard shortcut   A keystroke combination (usually a modifier key and a character key, like Control-C) that activates a menu item from the keyboard even if the relevant menu is not currently displayed. See also **keyboard operations**, **mnemonic**.

label   Static text that appears in the interface. For example, a label might identify a group of checkboxes. (The text that accompanies each checkbox within the group, however, is specified in the individual checkbox component and is therefore not considered a label.) Labels are created using the JLabel component.

layout manager   Software that assists the designer in determining the size and position of components within a container. Each container type has a default layout manager. See also **AWT**.

list box   A set of choices from which a user can choose one or more items. Items in a list can be text, graphics, or both. List boxes can be used as an alternative to radio buttons and checkboxes. The choices that users make last as long as the list is displayed. List boxes are created using the JList component. See also **combo box**, **selectable list**.

list components   A collective term for the two components that provide a one-column arrangement of data. See also **list box**, **selectable list**.

localization   The process of customizing software for a particular locale. Localization usually involves translation and often requires changes to colors, fonts, keyboard usage, number formats, and date and time formats. See also **internationalization**, **resource bundle**.

look and feel   The appearance and behavior of a complete set of GUI components. See also **Java look and feel**.

MDI   (multiple document interface) An interface style that confines all of an application's internal windows inside a backing window. See also **backing window**, **internal window**, **internal utility window**.

menu   A list of choices (menu items) logically grouped and displayed by an application so that a user need not memorize all available commands or options. Menus in the Java look and feel are "sticky"—that is, they remain posted on screen after the user clicks the menu title. Menus are created using the JMenu component. See also **contextual menu**, **drop-down menu**, **menu bar**, **menu item**, **submenu**.

menu bar	The horizontal strip at the top of a window that contains the titles of the application's drop-down menus. Menu bars are created using the `JMenuBar` component. See also **drop-down menu**.
menu item	A choice in a menu. Menu items (text or graphics) are typically commands or other options that a user can select. Menu items are created using the `JMenuItem` component. See also **checkbox menu item**, **radio button menu item**.
menu separator	See **separator**.
middle mouse button	The central button on a three-button mouse (typically used in UNIX environments). The Java look and feel does not utilize the middle mouse button. See also **mouse button 2**.
MIME	(Multipurpose Internet Mail Extensions) An Internet standard for sending and receiving non-ASCII email attachments (including video, audio, and graphics). Web browsers also use MIME types to assign applications that interpret and display files that are not formatted in HTML.
minimized internal window	A reduced representation of an internal window in an MDI application. Minimized internal windows look like horizontally oriented tags that appear at the lower-left corner of the backing window. The user can drag minimized internal windows to rearrange them. See also **MDI**.
mnemonic	An underlined alphanumeric character, typically in a menu title, menu item, or the text of a button or component. A mnemonic shows the user which key to press (in conjunction with the Alt key) to activate a command or navigate to a component. See also **keyboard operations**, **keyboard shortcut**.
modal dialog box	In a JFC application, a dialog box that prevents the user's interaction with other windows in the current application. Modal dialog boxes are created using the `JDialog` component. See also **dialog box**, **modeless dialog box**.
modeless dialog box	In a JFC application, a dialog box whose presence does not prevent the user from interacting with other windows in the current application. Modeless dialog boxes are created using the `JDialog` component. See also **dialog box**, **modal dialog box**.
modifier key	A key (for example, the Control or the Shift key) that does not produce an alphanumeric character but rather modifies the meaning of other keys.

mouse button 1   The primary button on a mouse (the only button, for Macintosh users). By default, mouse button 1 is the leftmost button, though users might switch the button settings so that the rightmost button becomes mouse button 1. See also **middle mouse button**, **mouse button 2**.

mouse button 2   On a two-button or three-button mouse, the button that is used to display contextual menus. By default, mouse button 2 is the rightmost button on the mouse, though users might switch the settings so that the leftmost button becomes mouse button 2. On mouse devices with only one button, users get the effect of mouse button 2 by holding down the Control key when pressing mouse button 1. See also **contextual menu**, **middle mouse button**, **mouse button 1**.

mouse-over feedback   A change in the visual appearance of an interface element that occurs when the user moves the pointer over it—for example, the display of a button border when the pointer moves over a toolbar button.

movie   A full-motion video with sound that is formatted for inclusion in an application.

multiple document interface   See **MDI**.

native code   Code that refers to the methods of a specific operating system or is compiled for a specific processor.

navigation   The movement of input focus from one user interface component to another via the mouse or the keyboard. Navigation by itself doesn't result in activation of a component or selection of an object. See also **activation**, **keyboard focus**, **select**.

noneditable combo box   See **combo box**.

object   (1) In user interfaces, a logical entity that an application presents in an interface and that users manipulate—for instance, a document, chapter, or paragraph in a word-processing application, or a mail server, mailbox, or mail message in a mail program.

(2) In programming, the principal building block of object-oriented applications. Each object is a programming unit consisting of data (instance variables) and functions (instance classes). A component is a particular type of object. See **component**.

padding   The empty space between the text and the border of command buttons. (Padding is also used to denote the spaces between the contents of table cells and cell borders.)

pane   A collective term for scroll panes, split panes, and tabbed panes.

panel   A container for organizing the contents of a window, dialog box, or applet. Panels are created using the JPanel component. See also **tabbed pane**.

password field   A special text field in which the user types a password. The field displays a masking character for each typed character. Password fields are created using the JPasswordField component.

plain window   An unadorned window with no title bar or window controls, typically used for splash screens. Plain windows are created using the JWindow component. See also **primary window**, **window controls**.

pluggable look and feel architecture   An architecture that separates the implementation of interface elements from their presentation, enabling an application to dynamically choose how its interface elements interact with users. When a pluggable look and feel is used for an application, the designer can select from several look and feel designs.

plug-in editor kit   An editor that can be used by the editor pane. The JFC supplies plug-in editor kits for plain, styled, RTF, and HTML data.

pointer   A small graphic that moves around the screen as the user manipulates the mouse (or another pointing device). Depending on its location and the active application, the pointer can assume various shapes, such as an arrowhead, crosshair, or clock. By moving the pointer and pressing mouse buttons, a user can select objects, set the insertion point, and activate windows. Sometimes called the "cursor." See also **insertion point**.

primary window   A top-level window of an application, where the principal interaction with the user occurs. The title bar and borders of primary windows always retain the look and feel of the user's native platform. Primary windows are created using the JFrame component. See also **dialog box**, **secondary window**.

progress bar   An interface element that indicates one or more operations are in progress and shows the user what proportion of the operations has been completed. Progress bars are created using the `JProgressBar` component. See also **control, slider.**

radio button   A button that a user clicks to set an option. Unlike checkboxes, radio buttons are mutually exclusive—choosing one radio button turns off all other radio buttons in the group. Radio buttons are created using the `JRadioButton` component. See also **checkbox.**

radio button menu item   A menu item that appears with a radio button next to it. Separators indicate which radio button menu items are in a group. Choosing one radio button menu item turns off all others in that group. Radio button menu items are created using the `JRadioButtonMenuItem` component.

resource bundle   The place where an application retrieves its locale-specific data (isolated from source code). See **internationalization, localization.**

RGB   For "red, green, blue." In computer graphics, a color model that represents colors as amounts of red, green, and blue. See also **HSB.**

RMI   (Remote Method Invocation) A distributed object model for Java programs in which the methods of remote objects written in the Java programming language can be called from other virtual machines, possibly on different hosts.

scroll arrow   In a scrollbar, one of the arrows that a user can click to move through displayed information in the corresponding direction (up or down in a vertical scrollbar, left or right in a horizontal scrollbar). See also **scrollbar.**

scroll box   A box that a user can drag in the channel of a scrollbar to cause scrolling in the corresponding direction. The scroll box's position in the scrollbar indicates the user's location in the list, window, or pane. In the Java look and feel, the scroll box's size indicates what proportion of the total information is currently visible on screen. A large scroll box, for example, indicates that the user can peruse the contents with just a few clicks in the scrollbar. See also **scrollbar.**

scroll pane   A container that provides scrolling with optional vertical and horizontal scrollbars. Scroll panes are created using the `JScrollPane` component. See also **scrollbar.**

scrollbar

A component that enables a user to control what portion of a document or list (or similar information) is visible on screen. A scrollbar consists of a vertical or horizontal channel, a scroll box that moves through the channel of the scrollbar, and two scroll arrows. Scrollbars are created using the `JScrollBar` component. See also **scroll arrow**, **scroll box**, **scroll pane**.

secondary window

A modal or modeless window created from and dependent upon a primary window. Secondary windows set options or supply additional details about actions and objects in the primary window. Secondary windows are dismissed when their associated primary window is dismissed. Secondary windows are created using either the `JDialog` component (for dialog boxes and utility windows) or the `JOptionPane` component (for alert boxes). See also **alert box**, **dialog box**, **primary window**.

selectable list

A one-column arrangement of data in which the items that users select from the list are designated for a subsequent action. Command buttons can operate on this selection. When another selection is made, any previous selection in the selectable list is deselected. Selectable lists are created using the `JList` component. See also **list box**.

select

(1) In human interface design, refers narrowly to designating one or more objects, typically for a subsequent action. UI components are *activated* while user objects are *selected*.

(2) In technical documentation, refers generally to the action of clicking list items, checkboxes, radio buttons, and so forth. See also **activation**, **choose**, **navigation**.

separator

A line graphic that is used to divide menu items into logical groupings. Separators are created using the `JSeparator` component.

server

A network device that manages resources and supplies services to a client. See also **client**.

servlets

Server-side programs that give Java technology-enabled servers additional features. Servlets provide web developers with a simple, consistent mechanism for extending the features of a web server and for gaining access to existing business systems. See also **JSP**.

slider

A control that enables the user to set a value in a range—for example, the RGB values for a color. Sliders are created using the `JSlider` component.

splash screen	A plain window that appears briefly in the time between the launch of a program and the appearance of its main application window.
split pane	A container that enables the user to adjust the relative size of two adjacent panes. Split panes are created using the JSplitPane component.
submenu	A menu that is displayed when a user chooses an associated menu item in a higher-level menu. (Such menu items are identified by a rightward-facing triangle.) Submenus are created using the JMenu component.
Swing classes	A set of GUI components, featuring a pluggable look and feel, that are included in the JFC. The Swing classes implement the Java Accessibility API and supply code for interface elements such as windows, dialog boxes and choosers, panels and panes, menus, controls, text components, tables, lists, and tree components. See also **AWT**, **JFC**, **pluggable look and feel architecture**.
tabbed pane	A container that enables the user to switch between several components (usually JPanel components) that appear to share the same space on screen. The user can view a particular panel by clicking its tab. Tabbed panes are created using the JTabbedPane component.
table	A two-dimensional arrangement of data in rows and columns. Tables are created using the JTable component.
text area	A multiline region for displaying (and sometimes editing) text. Text in such areas is restricted to a single font, size, and style. Text areas are created using the JTextArea component. See also **editor pane**.
text field	An area that displays a single line of text. In a noneditable text field, a user can copy, but not change, the text. In an editable text field, a user can type new text or edit the existing text. Text fields are created using the JTextField component. See also **password field**.
theme mechanism	A feature that enables a designer to specify alternative colors and fonts across an entire Java look and feel application. See also **Java look and feel**.
time-based media	Information that is time sensitive, including spoken audio, music, animation, and video.

title bar   The strip at the top of a window that contains its title and window controls. See also **window controls**.

toggle button   A button that alternates between two states. For example, a user might click one toggle button in a toolbar to turn italics on and off. A single toggle button has checkbox behavior; a programmatically grouped set of toggle buttons can be given the mutually exclusive behavior of radio buttons. Toggle buttons are created using the JToggleButton component. See also **checkbox**, **radio button**, **toolbar button**.

tool tip   A short text string that appears on screen to describe the interface element beneath the pointer.

toolbar   A collection of frequently used commands or options. Toolbars typically contain buttons, but other components (such as text fields and combo boxes) can be placed in toolbars as well. Toolbars are created using the JToolBar component. See also **toolbar button**.

toolbar button   A button that appears in a toolbar, typically a command or toggle button. A toolbar button can also display a menu. Toolbar buttons are created using the JButton or JToggleButton component. See also **command button**, **toggle button**.

top-level container   The highest-level container for a Java application. The top-level containers are JWindow, JFrame, and JDialog.

tree component   A representation of hierarchical data (for example, directory and file names) as a graphical outline. Clicking expands or collapses elements of the outline. Tree components are created using the JTree component.

turner   A graphic used in the tree component. The user clicks a turner to expand or collapse a container in the hierarchy.

unavailable   Not applicable in the current system state. When a component is unavailable, it appears dimmed and is skipped by keyboard navigation.

utility window   A modeless window that typically displays a collection of tools, colors, fonts, or patterns. Unlike internal utility windows, utility windows do not float. User choices made in a utility window affect whichever primary window is active. A utility window is not dismissed when a primary window is dismissed. Utility windows are created using the JDialog component. See also **internal utility window**, **secondary window**.

WAR

(Web Archive) A file format used for files that contain the web content of a J2EE application. See **J2EE application, web component.**

web browser

See **browser.**

web component

An executable file (for instance, a servlet or JSP page) that is contained in a WAR (Web Archive) file. See also **WAR.**

window

A user interface element that organizes and contains the information that users see in an application. See also **dialog box, internal utility window, plain window, primary window, secondary window, utility window.**

window controls

Controls that affect the state of a window (for example, the Maximize button in Microsoft Windows title bars).

INDEX

Colophon

LEAD WRITER
Patria Brown

LEAD HUMAN INTERFACE DESIGNER
Teresa Roberts

MANAGING EDITOR
Sue Factor

GRAPHIC DESIGNER AND COVER ART
Bruce Lee

PRODUCTION EDITOR
Bob Silva

MANAGEMENT TEAM
Kartik Mithal, Teresa Roberts, Lynn Weaver

GUIDELINE CONTRIBUTORS
Michael Albers, David-John Burrowes, Jeff Dunn, Don Gentner,
Robin Jeffries, Bruce Lee, Teresa Roberts, Harry Vertelney

CODE SAMPLE CONTRIBUTORS
Jeff Dunn and Peter Zavadsky

CD-ROM WRITER
Jason Duran

Special thanks to Don Gentner for his work on the first edition and
for considerable contributions to the second edition before his
retirement.

Grateful acknowledgments to Susanne Andersson, Marney Beard,
Jim Dibble, Jeff Dunn, Earl Johnson, Dave Mendenhall, Mike
Mohageg, Lynn Monsanto, Jennifer Ofiana, Raj Premkumar,
Moazam Raja, Luke Shi, Young Song, Terri Walton, and the SOLVE
team.

This book was written on Sun Microsystems workstations using
Adobe® FrameMaker software. PostScript files were digitally
imposed and then printed computer-to-plate on a Creo iMPAct
system. Line art was created using Adobe Illustrator. Screen shots
were edited in Adobe Photoshop.

Text type is SunSans and bullets are ITC Zapf Dingbats. Courier is
used for computer voice.

About the Companion CD-ROM

To view the contents of the CD-ROM, insert it into your CD-ROM drive. Then navigate to and open the file `index.html`.

The CD-ROM contains the following items:

- **Sample code.** Code examples that correspond to JFC windows, menus, dialog boxes, basic controls, text components, and table and tree views as described in the book. This code provides a starting place for you to design and develop some of the fundamental elements of Java look and feel applications.

- **Graphics.** A large collection of toolbar button and menu item graphics designed specifically for use in Java look and feel applications. The repository includes graphics for navigation, tables, text, media, and development tools.

- **Localized words.** Words and phrases encountered in using or developing standard Java applications with the Java look and feel. Tables provide translations for interface elements and concepts in French, German, Spanish, Italian, Swedish, Japanese, Simplified Chinese, Traditional Chinese, and Korean.

- **Accessibility.** Java Accessibility Helper, a Java utility class that aids in the assessment of how well an application helps people with disabilities.

- **Book.** The full text of the *Java Look and Feel Design Guidelines*, second edition, in HTML format.